STUDIES IN ARCHITECTURE

EDITED BY ANTHONY BLUNT AND RUDOLF WITTKOWER

VOLUME V

MICHELANGELO CATALOGUE

JAMES S. ACKERMAN

THE ARCHITECTURE OF
MICHELANGELO

JAMES S. ACKERMAN

FORMERLY PROFESSOR OF ARCHITECTURE AND ART

UNIVERSITY OF CALIFORNIA

CATALOGUE

1961

A. ZWEMMER LTD

LONDON

TO MY PARENTS

© 1961

A. ZWEMMER LTD, 76–80 CHARING CROSS ROAD, LONDON WC2

MADE AND PRINTED IN GREAT BRITAIN

BLOCKS ETCHED BY W. F. SEDGWICK LTD, LONDON SE1

TEXT AND ILLUSTRATIONS

PRINTED BY PERCY LUND, HUMPHRIES AND CO LTD, BRADFORD

BOUND BY KEY AND WHITING, LONDON N1

Contents

Rome, Castel Sant' Angelo,
Exterior of the Chapel of Leo X, 1514

The chapel of Leo X in Castel Sant' Angelo (Pl. 2a) is on the north-east end of the Cortile delle Palle overlooking the Tiber. It was built under the direction of Antonio da Sangallo the younger, as we know from an estimate of 10 November 1514, for laying the foundation and raising a door. At this time the entire fortress was remodelled as an emergency papal residence (K. Frey 1910, p. 34, doc. 19). The chapel is dedicated to the Medici patron saints, Cosmas and Damian; the Medici arms appear on the interior, and symbols of Leo's patronage on the exterior (lion heads; the ring with three feathers; both appear on the borders of Raphael's tapestries of 1515–1516 for the Sistine chapel). The interior also contains the arms of Raffaello Petrucci, Bishop of Grosseto, who was Castellan of the fortress from 1513 to 1517 (M. Borgatti 1931, p. 280).

The marble front facing the court (not a façade in the usual sense, since it covers the right wall rather than the entrance) could have been added later in Leo's pontificate but both its style and the fact that Michelangelo left Rome in 1516 recommend a date contemporary with the interior. The attribution to Michelangelo first appears in the sketchbook of *ca.* 1535–1540 by Aristotile and Giovanni Battista da Sangallo in Lille (Pl. 2b; Musée des Beaux-Arts, No. 733; first cited by Geymüller 1904, p. 38, with an obsolete accession number retained by later authors). Battista's inscription reads "queste in chastello diroma di mano di Michelagnolo di traverti (no)". This drawing probably was the basis for another, also with an attribution to Michelangelo, in the sketchbook compiled around 1580 by Oreste Vannocci Biringucci (Siena, Bibl. Comunale, S. IV. I., fol. 12v), and it appears again in a collection of the same period by an anonymous Florentine (Uffizi, *Arch.* 4686; "Finestre e porte", No. 92, attributed to Giorgio Vasari the Younger).

There are important differences between the façade illustrated here and Battista's drawing (compare Pl. 2a, 2b). In the latter the upper windows (inscribed "invetriate") are roundels and the lower ones have broad frames; the base of the central bay flares outward to make a basin-like bench, and there are no lion masks above the lateral niches. Certain of these deficiencies have been eliminated by a modern restoration recorded by Borgatti (p. 282 and accompanying Fig.), based on the Uffizi drawing. Whether the glazed roundels indicated in the drawings were planned or built by Michelangelo is uncertain, since they are ill suited to the proportions of the surviving structure. No original drawing by Michelangelo has been published (though Tolnay informs me that he has discovered one); the sketch associated with the chapel by Schiavo (1953, p. 154, Fig. 38) was made in 1524 and is related to the Laurentian library (see No. III, 5 on p. 40 below), and Uffizi, *Figur.* 18724 (Ferri-Jacobsen 1905, Pl. xix; D. 511, Fig. 236) is at best a shop sketch for an unidentified purpose.

There is no reason to question the attribution to Michelangelo: the design fits comfortably into the style of the documented works of the period. Sangallo, the executor, was at this time a carpenter on the payroll of Castel Sant' Angelo, and became a *bona fide* architect only in 1516. The choice of marble is characteristic; it is the material of all the early architectural works – the Julius and Medici tombs and the façade of San Lorenzo – and it is treated in the linear, almost dry fashion that distinguishes those projects from contemporary Roman architecture. The overall form, with its pedimented, projecting central bay, emerges again in the last of the San Lorenzo drawings (Pl. 5a) where there are also lateral niches of the same proportions, similarly topped by tablets. The large central bracket is a simplified version of those on the Julius tomb, and appears again in the Laurentian library. Tolnay has suggested to me that the design of the apertures was inspired by Roman Quattrocento windows, with their cross-shaped mullions. A sheet of drawings for an unidentified altar, which seems to be contemporary to the San Lorenzo studies, is the closest of all in design (Oxford, Christ Church, No. DD24v. Dussler, 638, and Tolnay 1948, p. 209, Pl. 123, question the attribution).

The similarity of the Leo X chapel to tomb designs is not surprising; given its small scale and its function as a relief to be applied to a pre-existing wall in an enclosed space. Probably we would not detect in it the symptoms of architectural genius if we were deprived of the knowledge of Michelangelo's later buildings. Yet the façade is a work of notable individuality: no other architect of the period would have displaced major openings to one side in order to put a support on the central axis. Its success, however, is not due to eccentricity, but to the achievement of monumentality without mass: grandeur is suggested by the subtle arrangement of delicate members.

Our impression of the façade is not aided by the overscaled statue niches which Antonio da Sangallo the Younger must have designed as a revenge on Michelangelo (added after 1534 as indicated by the Farnese *giglio*; drawings for a similar niche, Uffizi *Arch*. 846, 1223v).

Florence, Façade of San Lorenzo, 1515–1520

I HISTORY

The construction of San Lorenzo in Florence had been supported as a family project of the Medici since the foundation of the Renaissance church on designs by Filippo Brunelleschi in 1420/1421. The interior was finished only under Piero de' Medici (†1469) and the exterior blind arcades at the end of the fifteenth century (Paatz 1952, II, pp. 465 ff.) But the rough masonry of the façade (Pl. 15) remained exposed on both the interior and exterior in 1513, when the Medici gained their greatest distinction with the election of Cardinal de' Medici to the pontificate as Leo X.

The genesis of the San Lorenzo façade design is particularly obscure because contemporary sources give us conflicting evidence. Vasari (VII, 188) and Condivi (Ch. XXXIV) agree that Leo X ordered Michelangelo to take charge of the project although he was unwilling, and wanted to finish the tomb of Julius II. Vasari then offers three versions of the initial proceedings. In one (VII, 496), the Pope decides on the façade during his visit to Florence (late 1515; cf. Paatz, pp. 467, 527). He sends for Michelangelo and Raphael in Rome (this part of the story is confirmed by a letter of Baccio Bandinelli of 1547 [V. Golzio, *Raffaello*, Vatican City, 1936, p. 36]), and meanwhile asks Jacopo Sansovino, who is in Florence, to do a drawing and subsequently a model to be executed by Baccio d'Agnolo. Michelangelo also makes a model, and accompanies Sansovino to Pietrasanta to find marble. The Pope having by now left Florence, they return separately to Rome with their models. Michelangelo's is accepted, and Sansovino, who expected at least a share in the sculpture, is dismissed because Michelangelo wants to work alone. The story is partly confirmed by a vituperative letter from Sansovino to Michelangelo of June 1517, claiming "sapiate chel papa mi promesse le storie [i.e., reliefs] e Jacopo [Salviati] ancora . . ." (Gotti 1875, I, p. 136).

In a more complete account (VII, 188), several artists want to share in the work, apparently after Michelangelo is put in charge. Consequently, "for the architecture many artists competed in Rome before the Pope; drawings were made by Baccio d'Agnolo, Antonio da Sangallo, Andrea and Jacopo Sansovino, and the elegant Raphael who, when the Pope came, was then taken to Florence for this purpose. So Michelangelo decided to make a model, not wishing in this job to have anyone but himself in charge of or guiding the architecture. But because of this unwillingness to accept aid neither he nor the others achieved anything, and those masters returned to their accustomed activities in disgust, while Michelangelo, going to Carrara with a 1000-scudi commission . . ."

Vasari's third version occurs in the Life of Leonardo (IV, 47): "Era sdegno grandissimo fra Michelagnolo Buonarroti e lui: per il che partì di Fiorenza Michelagnolo per la concorrenza, con la scusa del duca Giuliano, essendo chiamato dal papa per la facciata di San Lorenzo. Leonardo intendendo ciò, partì ed andò in Francia, dove il re avendo avuto opere sue . . ." The "concorrenza", which has been mistaken by translators for the

San Lorenzo competition, should be read as the "rivalry" between the two great Florentines, as suggested to me by Carlo Pedretti, who has evidence of a visit by Leonardo to Florence in 1515, and even of an architectural commission from the Medici relating to the area around San Lorenzo, if not to the church itself. But this does not solve the conundrum of Vasari's passage; Michelangelo was indeed called by the Pope, but why, then, should he have needed permission from Leo's puppet Giuliano (died March, 1516)? And further, why should Leonardo, whose permanent residence was now in Rome, leave Italy (in the autumn of 1516) to get away from Michelangelo, who was in Florence?

The report of the Pope's command and of Michelangelo's unwillingness is convincing because Leo could not have wanted the greatest Florentine artist to be monopolized by his predecessor's heirs, the Rovere, while Michelangelo surely wanted freedom to complete the tomb. But this evidence must be reconciled with correspondence that reveals Michelangelo, in partnership with Baccio d'Agnolo, actually intriguing to get the commission through Buoninsegni, the secretary of Cardinal Giulio de' Medici (*Briefe*, pp. 35, 47). No doubt Vasari's confusion is partly due to the fact that Michelangelo later found it comforting to forget his own responsibility for what proved to be an appalling waste of time, and hid the intrigue from his biographers and friends (*Lettere*, p. 414).

The intrigue and the association with Baccio, which took place in the autumn of 1516, nearly a year after the original activity, make sense only if Michelangelo was already involved in the project and wanted to make sure he would not have to collaborate with anybody whom he could not dominate (Baccio was the most insignificant of the competitors). Vasari, in identifying the competition as architectural, suggests that the original plan was to assign the sculpture to Michelangelo and the architecture to someone else. In neither of Vasari's versions was Michelangelo's model made by papal order; architects at the Vatican could easily have persuaded the Pope not to let the inexperienced Michelangelo begin his architectural career on such an important building. Perhaps an additional reason for his unholy alliance with Baccio was to silence such criticism.

It is hard to confirm Vasari's report about the competition. The best supporting evidence is a group of six drawings in the Uffizi (*Arch*. 276–281) identified as Giuliano da Sangallo's studies for the façade (Geymüller 1904, V, Pls. 1, 2; G. Marchini, *Giuliano da Sangallo*, Florence, 1942, pp. 100–101). Giuliano was not mentioned by Vasari, but these drawings which, paradoxically, belonged to Vasari's collection, prove his participation. Richard Pommer has demonstrated ("Drawings for the Façade of San Lorenzo by Giuliano da Sangallo . . .", unpublished thesis for New York University, 1957) that No. 281 and the study for it, No. 276, were designed for San Lorenzo (Medici Arms and inscriptions; statue of San Lorenzo; dated 1516; etc.), as was No. 280, a different and probably earlier version with high campanili flanking the façade. But Nos. 277 (Pl. 3a) and 278 were apparently made under Julius II, possibly for the Basilica of Santa Maria di Loreto, and exhibited to Leo X as samples, with the offending arms and iconography blocked out. No. 279 is not a religious structure; it may have been drawn a decade earlier for the Palazzo dei Penitenzieri in Rome. Another sign of Giuliano's interest in San Lorenzo is the plan of the entire church in his Siena notebook (R. Falb, *Il taccuino senese di G.S.G.*, Siena, 1899, fol. 21v; Pommer, pp. 81 ff.), in which a five-domed portico is proposed along the façade, as well as domes throughout the church. Of two other drawings associated with the competition, the one in the Biblioteca Nazionale (MS. II, i, 429; Pommer, p. 109, Fig. 170) is entirely unrelated, but Uffizi 2048A (*ibid.*, pp. 107–108, Fig. 16) could be one of the competition designs. Pommer correctly abandons an earlier ascription to Giuliano; Jacopo Sansovino would be a likely substitute, but since we hardly know his drawing style, and since the sketch is possibly influenced by Michelangelo's later projects, the identification remains a problem.

Giuliano died in October 1516, just as Michelangelo bid for the commission. Were it not for Vasari's garbled story we would assume that Giuliano won the initial competition and that his death explains Michelangelo's intervention, but this leaves in obscurity Michelangelo's role in 1515–1516. Without further information there is little hope of clarifying the history of the competition (see summary in Paatz 1952, pp. 527 ff.)

The correspondence between Michelangelo and Domenico Buoninsegni at the Papal court – together with the account-books – makes it easier to follow the chronology of the design once Michelangelo and Baccio are chosen. As the material is excellently summarized by Tolnay, who first published a number of the letters (1934, pp. 25 ff.; see also 1948, pp. 3–7) and by Paatz (*loc. cit.*), I outline it briefly here.

A. THE GAINING OF THE COMMISSION: OCTOBER–NOVEMBER 1516

The Pope agrees early in October to allow Michelangelo and Baccio to do the façade, and Buoninsegni asks that both come to Rome to settle the matter, or at least that Michelangelo go from Carrara to Florence to confer with Baccio. But Michelangelo stalls, saying that Baccio may speak for him (*Briefe*, pp. 35–36, 39–40, 47–48; Tolnay 1934, doc. 1).

B. ACCEPTANCE OF A DESIGN: DECEMBER 1516

Michelangelo writes that he suspects Baccio d'Agnolo of duplicity; intrigues are still going on, for Nanni di Baccio Bigio tries at court to get a share of the work. Perhaps this impels Michelangelo to Rome on 1 or 5 December, by his own records (*Lettere*, 414, 564, 567; *Aufzeichnungen*, pp. 41–49, 53) or after 11 December, by Buoninsegni's testimony (Tolnay 1934, doc. 2). Permission already has been given to drop Baccio if necessary. In Rome his sketch is accepted by the Pope and he returns to Florence before 22 December to have a model made (*Briefe*, pp. 66–67; Tolnay, doc. 3).

C. THE FIRST MODEL: JANUARY–MARCH 1517

Michelangelo leaves his drawing with Baccio, who is to make the model, and departs for Carrara on 31 December. He returns in January and again in February to check on Baccio and disapproves of changes made in the original design, demanding at the end of January that the model be remade (Tolnay, doc. 4). The Pope and Cardinal back up Michelangelo in his attempt to subdue Baccio, but when the model is completed on 7 March, Michelangelo rejects it as "una cosa da fanciulli", and says he shall make a clay one himself (*Briefe*, pp. 55, 61, 63; *Lettere*, pp. 133, 381, 565 ff.; Tolnay 1934, docs. 4–7).

D. THE CLAY MODEL: MARCH–MAY 1517

Together with an assistant called "La Grassa", Michelangelo starts a clay model in March which is finished by 2 May. It is misshapen "like pastry" and he fails to fulfil a promise to send it to Rome, so the Pope asks for a wooden model. We assume that the clay model represents a new design because Michelangelo, who has now been put in sole charge of the project, raises the estimate of cost from the 25,000 scudi agreed upon at the start, to 35,000 scudi. He says that he intends to make the new façade "the crown of all the architecture and sculpture of Italy" (*Briefe*, p. 68; *Lettere*, pp. 133, 381, 383–384, 567; Tolnay 1934, docs. 7–9).

E. THE SECOND WOOD MODEL: AUTUMN 1517

Michelangelo goes to Florence on 31 August to have a wood model with 24 wax figures executed by Pietro Urbano, but both fall sick and the work is completed only shortly before 22 December, when Urbano takes it to Rome. Payment is made for the first (Baccio) and second model at this time, and Michelangelo is called to Rome to sign a contract dated 19 January 1518, for the execution of a façade based on the new model (*Briefe*, pp. 71, 86, 88; *Lettere*, pp. 414, 565–572, 671; *Aufzeichnungen*, pp. 46, 49, 53).

F. THE FOUNDATIONS: DECEMBER 1516–DECEMBER 1517

The existing foundations for the façade are inspected and found too weak for the new construction at the end of 1516. Michelangelo plans new ones in January, but his absence from Florence delays progress on them until July. They are completed in December (*Briefe*, pp. 54–55, 68, 74–75; *Lettere*, pp. 565, 571–572; Tolnay 1934, docs. 4, 7, 8, 9; *Aufzeichnungen*, pp. 41, 45).

G. PROBLEMS AT CARRARA: DECEMBER 1516–AUTUMN 1519

During the entire period of the designing of San Lorenzo, Michelangelo is living in the Carrara area to supervise quarrying, and he remains there until 1519. From the beginning of the project, the Pope insists on excavations in Pietrasanta and Seravezza, which are in Florentine territory, rather than in Carrara. This means that Michelangelo has to change his base of operations in 1517, to build a difficult road into the mountains, and to train crews with whom he has not worked. As a crowning indignity, the Cardinal permits the Cathedral *Opera* to raid the veins opened by Michelangelo. The waste of three years in these purely mechanical activities is one of the tragedies of Michelangelo's career. His bitterness is conveyed in a letter of 1520 to an unknown recipient (*Lettere*, pp. 414 ff.; *Aufzeichnungen*, pp. 53 ff.) The period is well documented in letters and *Ricordi* (*Lettere*, pp. 564 ff.; summary in Tolnay 1948, pp. 3–7).

H. TERMINATION OF THE CONTRACT: MARCH 1520

Sometime after his arrival in Florence on 13 February 1520, Cardinal Giulio, who wants some of the newly quarried marble for the Cathedral, demands a reckoning from Michelangelo of his expenses at Carrara. Michelangelo, in an enraged letter to Rome, asks that the Pope issue a Breve absolving him of any debt arising from disbursements for quarrying (*Lettere*, pp. 415–416; *Aufzeichnungen*, pp. 53 ff.) On 10 March he is released from his responsibilities in procuring marble and the Pope declares the financial accounts balanced. Michelangelo claims in his notebook (*Lettere*, p. 581) that the purpose was "forse per fare più presto la sopra detta facciata". Though it is not the purpose of this agreement to cancel the project, little more is done for the façade. Columns are mentioned in the correspondence of December 1520 (Tolnay 1948, pp. 225–226), and action is sporadically considered in the next few years (*Aufzeichnungen*, pp. 64–65; *Lettere*, p. 421; see the remarks on the façade interior, p. 32). I can offer no good reason for the abandonment of the façade. If, as Tolnay proposed (1948, p. 7), the funds were used up on military operations, it would not have been possible to start the equally costly Medici chapel at the same time.

II THE DESIGN: SOURCES

Ample sources are preserved for reconstructing the façade and for tracing the development of the design: the original drawings, sketches of the marble members cut at Carrara, many copies of lost drawings or models, and a wooden model traditionally ascribed to Michelangelo. We get from these an idea of the stages through which the conception passed; our problem is to arrange the stages in a convincing chronological order and to discover what Michelangelo's final design was like. Contemporary identifications of a first and a last design simplify the solution: three drawings copied from Michelangelo are inscribed "primo disegno . . . per la facciata di San Lorenzo", while the definitive project is partly described in a contract of January 1518. But this evidence is insufficient, and modern writers have differed widely in interpreting it, particularly in its bearing on the date and authorship of the wooden model preserved in the Casa Buonarroti. However, a wealth of new evidence on the definitive design was recently made available by Tolnay (1954, pp. 155–156; Pls. 145–157, 171, 176 ff.), with the publication of Michelangelo's sketches from the Archivio Buonarroti and elsewhere of the separate blocks cut for the façade, chiefly during 1518–1519. The blocks are so precisely measured and so carefully drawn that they may be pieced together like a Chinese puzzle to reconstruct almost the entire façade. This is convincing evidence of the final design, since changes would not have been made once the blocks were cut. I use this material with particular gratitude to Tolnay, since he generously made it available before having had the opportunity to publish his evaluation of it.

1. THE "FIRST DESIGN" (Pl. 3b)

None of Michelangelo's drawings can be associated with the project that Battista da Sangallo reproduced in his sketchbook as the "primo disegno" (Lille, Musée des Beaux-Arts, No. 790; Geymüller 1904, VIII, Fig. 3), but it appears in several other copies: by Aristotile da Sangallo, who also refers to the "primo disegno" (Cambridge, Rugby School, *Jhb. d. preuss. Kunstslg.*, IX, 1888, pp. 134–135; and a second in Munich, Kupferstichkabinett, Geymüller, Fig. 2); by Oreste Vannocci, who used the Lille Sketchbook as a source (Siena, Bibl. Communale, S. IV. 1, fol. 145, unpublished); by Dosio (Modena,

Bibl. Estense, Campori 1755, fol. 73; Luporini 1957, Fig. 6); and probably the best known of the group (Pl. 3b) by an artist who appears from both his figural and architectural style to be a Mannerist of the mid- or late Cinquecento (Casa Buonarroti, Tolnay 1934, Fig. 14; Geymüller 1904, VII, Pl. 1).

The characteristic feature of this design is the giant Order of four columns on high pedestals at the centre of the façade flanking the main portal. The side portals are recessed and the outermost bays become almost isolated two-tiered tabernacles crowned by curved gables. The upper level of the façade, which is only as wide as the central nave, is a kind of temple-front with a pediment; in most copies it has a large round window in the centre. This whole group may have evolved from a three-story project such as Uffizi, *Arch.* 1293 (Geymüller, Fig. 1) but the relationship of this to Michelangelo has not been proved.

2. THE SECOND DESIGN (Pls. 3c, 3d, 4a)

A group of three related Michelangelo drawings combine the "primo disegno" motifs with a three-story elevation. In Pl. 3c (Casa Buonarroti, No. 91; D.123, F.96a), the three-story system introduces a high attic or mezzanine between two orders of columns or pilasters; the top story resembles that of the preceding group, but the outer tabernacles and colossal Order are absent. As this drawing is the only one in either group without tabernacles at the sides, it might precede the "primo disegno", but since it is better adapted to the ten figures requested by the Pope early in 1517, I prefer to leave it in the second group (as Thode 1908, II, pp. 92–93; Paatz 1952, II, p. 531). Pl. 3d (Casa Buonarroti; No. 44, D.86, F.29) is a rapid sketch that appears to have begun as a three-story design like Pl. 3c, but the curved-top tabernacles of the "primo disegno" enter as *pentimenti*. These tend to increase the height of the mezzanine and to squeeze the upper story, so the latter is raised in two stages in hasty strokes. Perhaps the rapid sketch at the lower right of this sheet indicates that the central portion of the lower story, which now has a pediment, too, was to project forward as a Pantheon-like porch. In Pl. 4a (Casa Buonarroti, No. 47; D.89, F.96b), these studies mature into a convincing project that retains something of the three-story system and something of the flanking tabernacles, now brought into a tight equilibrium in which neither horizontals nor verticals dominate.

3. THE FIRST AND SECOND DESIGNS: CHRONOLOGY

On 2 February 1517, Michelangelo was instructed on the iconography of the ten façade figures: four standing on the lower level, four seated above, and two standing on the upper order (Tolnay 1934, doc. 4). This means that the sketches with ten statue bays on three levels – in other words, those for the second design (Pls. 3c–d, 4a) – were made late in 1516 or early in 1517 (Tolnay, p. 30; Thode 1908, II, p. 93). The "primo disegno" is generally dated 1516, before Michelangelo's meeting with the Pope in December, when the ten-figure scheme was presumably adopted (Geymüller 1904, VIII, pp. 5 ff.; Thode, pp. 89 ff.; Paatz 1952, II, pp. 531 ff.) The "first project" can be given an early date on internal evidence, too, because the design tends to evolve in clear steps toward a distinct mezzanine, a feature that is lacking here. Tolnay (*ibid.*, p. 31) ingeniously associated the "primo disegno" entirely with Baccio's model, which departed, we know, from Michelangelo's scheme. But as Baccio's model was supervised and corrected by Michelangelo, it could hardly have been so different as to dictate to him a new programme of sculpture, ignoring the Pope's demand for ten figures. Besides, the design, though not the best of the series, is strikingly original and must have been conceived by a superior artist.

The most fundamental of all decisions in the development of the façade has been overlooked: between the first two designs and the final version the façade changed from a veneer (or veneer=with=porch, Pl. 3d) attached to the old wall to a semi-independent narthex structure (see sec. 4 below). A similar duality had appeared in Giuliano da Sangallo's schemes: those made specifically for San Loranzo have a narthex, while those touched up for this purpose do not: Pl. 3a is inscribed "Sanza portticho".

That Michelangelo's earlier designs were for a veneer scheme is proven by (1) the absence of lateral façades in all the drawings so far cited; (2) the ten-figure decoration – a narthex scheme would have required at least fourteen; (3) the two-story central elevation flanked by one-story bays. To make a narthex of this scheme, the raised central portion would have to be structurally independent of the wings from the foundations up, as it is in the plan on the anonymous Uffizi 2048A, where communication within the narthex is thereby blocked off by heavy masonry supports, thus negating its value as an entrance-porch; (4) a report of 30 December 1516 (*Briefe*, p. 54), stating that on inspection the existing foundations were found inadequate; while it is plausible that a fifteenth-century support for a veneer façade would have been worth considering for Michelangelo's initial project, it is inconceivable that a narthex foundation suitable to the fragile style of Brunelleschi (or to the porch of the original Romanesque church) would have had dimensions close enough to a Michelangelo scheme to warrant excavation. Baccio's model was started in January and nearly finished in a form modified by Michelangelo on 17 February 1517 (*ibid.*, p. 61); the ten-figure scheme still obtained in early February. Therefore Baccio's model must have been for a veneer façade, and cannot be associated with the surviving model (Pl. 5b).

After finishing the clay model in the first week of May 1517, Michelangelo wrote (*Lettere*, pp. 383–384) that the cost would increase from 25,000 to 35,000 ducats. This huge difference is not likely to have been due merely to sculptural additions: it must be the result of the decision to substitute the narthex for the veneer. The evolution of this idea during March and April would explain why Michelangelo refused, in spite of constant urging from Rome, to proceed with the foundations, and why he began them (in July; *Briefe*, pp. 74–75) shortly after the narthex model was completed.

4. THE FINAL DESIGN: FIRST VERSION (Pl. 5a)

Since Pl. 5a (Casa Buonarroti, No. 43, D.85; F.211a) is an original drawing of the narthex scheme that provides for exactly the sculptural programme required by the contract of 1518 (though partly on a different scale), it must have been made after the first two groups. Without drastically altering the design concept, it elevates the wings to the height of the central portion, absorbing the independent outer tabernacles and central temple-front motif into a more unified grid. The mezzanine is revived, now divided by a cornice into two parts for horizontal emphasis; pilaster strips are used in the lower half, and pedestals in the upper; the latter may be read either as the termination of the mezzanine or the podium of the third order.

The drawing is the first to show the façade as a three-dimensional structure with lateral façades continuing the articulation of the front. The importance of the decision to give the façade three sides instead of one is demonstrated in three quickly sketched plan details by Michelangelo showing the façade as a building in its own right (as in the model: Pl. 5b); a narthex projecting not only forward from the old church but beyond its sides (Archivio Buonarroti, Vol. 1, fol. 157r, identified by Tolnay 1934, Fig. 7; 1954, Pl. 192. Casa Buonarroti, No. 77v, D. 113 [F. 268 shows only the *recto*]; and Casa Buonarroti, No. 113, D. 479, Geymüller 1904, p. 12). The last contains two plan-sketches for the façade with notes on alternative measurements for the relative widths of the portal- and statue bays. All of those cited must be studies for the first narthex scheme, before the proportions had been fixed. A clearer impression of the narthex is given by Aristotile da Sangallo in two plan-and-elevation drawings after Michelangelo (Pl. 4b: Munich, Kupferstichkabinett, No. 33258; Milan, Archivio di Stato; Geymüller 1904, VIII, Figs. 6, 7; Thode 1908, II, pp. 96–97; the Milan drawing was published as Michelangelo's by Beltrami 1901, pp. 67 ff.) which show that the new façade could no longer be merely a veneer for the old, since it had become one bay deep; Aristotile, in fact, removes the old façade entirely, but without assurance, since he notes "non so chome si stia di drento". Perhaps Michelangelo himself had not decided how to handle the ugly surface, which would now be brought indoors.

Antonio da Sangallo the Younger also made a drawing of this version (Pl. 4c: Uffizi, *Arch.* 790r, A. Bartoli, *I monumenti antichi . . .*, Rome, 1914, Fig. 453; analysed by D. Frey 1922, pp. 221–228) which is more convincing in proportions and has the advantage of showing the disposition of the free-standing sculpture: tall standing figures on high pedestals appear on the lower story, seated figures in the lower part of the mezzanine, and small standing ones in the niches of the upper story. The better-known drawing of the same project attributed to Bandinelli (Louvre; Tolnay 1934, Fig. 13; Thode 1908, II, pp. 93–94) is less accurate.

Aristotile's drawings represent a maturing of the ideas suggested in Pl. 5a; a still more accurate record is preserved in an anonymous half-elevation of the same generation (Uffizi, *Arch.* 205; Geymüller, Fig. 8). The fact that this is correct in scale and that Aristotile actually notes measurements indicates that Michelangelo must have developed Pl. 5a into a model or at least a large scale-drawing. Since there are two closely related versions of this scheme and two models, presumably of the same period – a clay one in the spring and a wooden one finished in December 1517 – it is tempting to associate this first version with the clay model (Geymüller, Thode, *loc. cit.*) The analysis of measurements and documents in the following section makes this link virtually certain.

5. THE FINAL DESIGN: SECOND VERSION

The only significant difference between the first and final version is that the mezzanine is unified by eliminating the cornice dividing it into two levels. The pilaster strips of the lower level are now given bases and rise the entire height of the mezzanine. As Thode recognized (pp. 97–98), the contract of 1518 demands the unified mezzanine since it calls for "a pilaster strip or pilaster six to seven braccia [*ca*. 3.6 m.] high . . . and on top of said pilasters runs a cornice from which spring 8 pilasters with socles, capitals and bases" (*Lettere*, p. 671). D. Frey (1922, p. 225) and Tolnay (1934, pp. 31 ff.) read the same passage to mean that the *two-level* mezzanine was still intended (interpreting "socles" to mean the membering of the second level, a reading which emphasizes the beginnings of anti-classical ambiguity in Michelangelo's design), but they neglected to take the measurements into account. On Aristotile's measured drawings of the first version, the lower level is marked 4 br. and the upper, 3 br., so that the *total* mezzanine height excluding the cornice is 7 br. This is to be expected, as Brunelleschi's mezzanine level along the side elevations measures approximately 7·2 br., translating from Geymüller's measured drawings. Furthermore, the wood model of the Casa Buonarroti (Pl. 5b) has the undivided mezzanine of the second version and its height is equivalent to 6·8 br. Therefore the pilaster 6 to 7 br. high called for by the contract could be adjusted only to an undivided mezzanine. The change allowed more room for the seated statues which the contract now required to be $4\frac{1}{2}$ br. high. The mezzanine in Michelangelo's block-sketch (Pl. 6b) is still higher: $7\frac{1}{2}$ br. In the lower part of this sheet he drew bases $1\frac{1}{2}$ br. high and pilaster strips 5 br. high. In the upper part he drew the cornice 1 br. high; it appears as a base for the socles of the third (pilaster) order (cf. Fig. 1). At first sight this upper part suggests the divided mezzanine again, but if this were so its overall height would be $9\frac{1}{2}$ to $10\frac{1}{2}$ br., making the mezzanine and the whole façade at least 2·7 br. (over $1\frac{1}{2}$ m.) higher than that of the model and Aristotile's sketch, and, what is more important, higher than the church behind.

A date for the change in the mezzanine may possibly be found in a contract with stone-cutters at Carrara of 16 August 1517, specifying "un altra figura a sedere di longheza brac. 3 e mezo con sua grosseza e fattezze . . ." (*Lettere*, p. 667). Seated figures $3\frac{1}{2}$ br. high would fit into the 4 br. lower level of the mezzanine in the first version, while the 1518 contract specifies $4\frac{1}{2}$ br. bronze figures. If the stone figures were ordered for the façade (they are too small to have been used on the Tomb of Julius II), the change from the divided to the undivided mezzanine must have been made in the final wood model initiated in the autumn. Consequently, the small model of May 1517, must have had the divided system, so it must have been from this model that the drawings of the first version were made.

The second version of the mezzanine appears, I believe, in one of two cross-section studies: an original sketch in the British Museum (Wilde 1953, No. 19v, p. 35; D.316; F.182. Wilde associates it tentatively with the project for Baccio's model; Thode and Tolnay, *loc. cit*., with the 1518 contract). The other section drawing, by an assistant? (Casa Buonarroti, No. 51; D. 464; F. 264), is a mixture of the two schemes in which most of the upper level of the mezzanine is pre-empted by an entablature as high as that of the lower story. An unskilled elevation of the lower part of half the façade could belong to this group (Casa Buonarroti, No. 41; D.462; F.30), but may be disregarded; it has elements, such as arched niches on the ground floor, probably never intended by Michel-angelo.

This view of the final version makes the model in the Casa Buonarroti (Pl. 5b) the closest record we have of Michelangelo's design, together with a seventeenth-century drawing probably based partly on it (Uffizi, *Arch.* 3697, by G. Nelli; Geymüller 1904, II, Fig. 11; Thode 1908, II, p. 98). Analysis of the contract and of the block-sketches shows that the model differs in proportion and detail from Michelangelo's ideas of 1518, but the differences are far less than modern criticism has wished them to be (cf. Pl. 5b, Fig. 1).

Only earlier writers accepted the model (Geymüller, Thode, *loc. cit.*) Some more recently have identified it with Baccio's rejected one (Tosi, *Dedalo*, VIII, 1927/1928, p. 326; Venturi, *Storia*, XI, 2, pp. 25 ff.; Paatz 1952, pp. 531 ff.; Schiavo 1949, Fig. 92) and some merely rejected any relationship to Michelangelo (Supino, *L'Arte*, IV, 1901, p. 256). The Michelangelo experts developed a subtler theory that the model is an academic copy (D. Frey 1922, pp. 226 ff.; Tolnay 1934, p. 33; Wilde 1953, p. 35n., with tentative attribu-tion to Dosio). This chorus of opprobrium is justified by the lifeless dryness of the model, but the fact remains that it is so close to Michelangelo's concept that it does not matter whether it was made for him or copied after his model or drawings. Tolnay (*loc. cit.*) rejected it on two grounds: because the mezzanine is undivided, which I have tried to prove is as it ought to be; and because there are no statue niches on the lower order. But the contract does not mention niches; they were unnecessary because the statues at ground level were to be placed on free-standing pedestals between the columns as in the Antonio da Sangallo and Louvre drawings from the preceding version (Pl. 4c). These pedestals were cut at Carrara and appear in one of the block-sketches exactly in this position (Pl. 6a). Small blocks like this could be lost from the model as easily as wax figures.

[After I had written this chapter and submitted it to Tolnay, he kindly informed me that he had previously discovered one remaining pedestal-block on the right lateral façade of the model, on which account he also is now convinced that the surviving model is substantially authentic.]

If the surviving model is the one referred to in the contract, it is strange that there should be even minor inconsistencies between the two (see B of the following section); so I prefer to say only that it is very close to Michelangelo's definitive design. We do know that there was "un altro, quasi simile modello, . . . ma più piccolo" that Nelli, according to the inscription on his copy, used for his representation of the reliefs of the upper story, and his statement is confirmed by the fact that two models remained in Michelangelo's possession in 1555 (letter in Vasari, *Nachlass*, I, p. 415). In Nelli's engrav-ing Medici arms appear in the mezzanine in place of figures, but the accompanying inscription tells us that these were a feature of the lesser model. This model, however, is the closer to the contract in showing a proportion of roughly 8–9–8 in the mezzanine reliefs (the last two observations I owe to Tolnay). Must we imagine a third model identical to the contract? Perhaps, but it is a clumsy solution, considering that only one was paid for and that it would have to be this one that was lost while two unofficial ones were preserved for posterity. (To avoid utter confusion I believe we must reject the fourth candidate, which appears in Empoli's portrait in the Casa Buonarroti of Michelangelo offering the model to the Pope [Steinmann 1913, Pl. 86], as a bad copy of one of the documented models.)

I have no final solution to the model problem: I expect that when it is made, the fact (pointed out to me by John Coolidge) that the surviving model is extensively restored and was originally made in two pieces, divided horizontally above the cornice of the first order, will play a part, because from the very start of the narthex scheme the first order remains virtually unchanged while the upper levels are altered. A number of alternative upper orders may have been placed successively on the same ground-floor base.

III RECONSTRUCTION OF THE FINAL DESIGN

A. DIGEST OF THE CONTRACT OF JANUARY 1518 (*Lettere*, pp. 671–672)

According to the contract, the specifications are "to be composed, ordered and according to the example and proportion of the wood model built with wax figures and made by and for said Michelangelo, which he sent from Florence last December".

Lower Order: 12 fluted columns (including 2 on each side façade) each about 11 br. high with 3 portals between them and 6 full-round statues (including 1 on each side façade) 5 br. high (Fig. 1:1), and certain relief panels, as in the model (Fig. 1:2).

Middle Order: Above the first cornice an Order of pilaster strips or pilasters 6–7 br. high framing 6 full-round figures (including 1 on each side façade), seated, $4\frac{1}{2}$ br. high, in bronze (Fig. 1:3).

Upper Order: At the summit of these pilasters runs a cornice from which spring 12 pilasters (including 2 on each side façade) with socles, capitals, and bases (Fig. 1:4), between which are 6 tabernacles (including 1 on each side façade) (Fig. 1:5), with full-round marble figures about $5\frac{1}{2}$ br. high (Fig. 1:6). Above the tabernacles are panels with life-size seated marble figures in high relief (Fig. 1:7).

Relief panels: In the "*compartimento*" of the model on the main façade, 5 rectangular relief scenes (Fig. 1:8) and 2 in *tondi*, of marble, in half relief (Fig. 1:9). Of the rectangular ones, 2 are to be about 8 br. long (Fig. 1:8′) and 1 about 9 br. (Fig. 1:8″), and the *tondi* are to be 6 to 7 br. in diameter. The figures are to be of life size or greater and the reliefs to be as deep as is necessary to make them "evident".

Pediment: To be placed over the central nave with its cornice and ornaments of arms and insignia as in the model (Fig. 1:10).

Ornaments that do not appear in the model are to be executed properly.

B. THE CONTRACT AND THE CASA BUONARROTI MODEL

To compare the surviving model (Pl. 5b) with the contract one need only translate the measurements of the former into Florentine *braccia* (*ca.* ·548 m.) A fairly accurate *braccia* scale is found by using the dimensions of the existing church and checking them against certain known dimensions of Michelangelo's project such as those of the contracts and block sketches. I have used the scale drawing published by Apolloni (1934, Pl. XXIII–XXIV).

Lower Order: No differences between the contract and model.

Middle Order: The order of pilaster strips in the model is $6\frac{3}{4}$ br. high from base to cornice; the panels between them before which the seated statues are to be placed are $4\frac{1}{2}$ br. high. Both measurements correspond to those of the contract.

Upper Order: The niches of the model are $6\frac{2}{3}$ br. high, while the contract requires statues $5\frac{1}{2}$ br. high. With allowance for pedestals, the measurements correspond.

Relief panels: The size of the *tondi* is the same, but otherwise differences appear. The model has space for the 5 rectangular panels required in the contract, but instead of 4 of 8 br. and 1 of 9 br. width, it has 2 of $6\frac{1}{2}$ br. over the *tondi* and 3 of about $8\frac{1}{4}$ br. in the mezzanine. Without any alteration, the model design could provide the four 8 br. panels, above and below the *tondi*, but not the 9 br. one, which obviously was to go in the centre over the main portal.

We see in the model the motivation for this change: the three mezzanine panels over the portals are equal in width and yet everywhere else the outer bays – those of the side portals and *tondi* – are actually *wider* than the central one, measuring the distance between pilasters. This differential is due to the fact that the central mezzanine panel is not recessed from the front plane of the façade as are the two outer ones, and hence is not narrowed by setbacks; thus, though the bay is narrower, the panel is not. Now if the bay were to be made equal to those alongside, its panel would then be larger, in approximately the proportion 9:8.

The choice, then, was between approximately equal portal bays (that is, intercolumniations on the lower Order) and equal mezzanine panels; or, to put it another way, between a consistent architectural system and a consistent sculptural one. Michelangelo chose the architecture, simplifying the composition of his first and third order from one that can be symbolized ABAcABA to one of ABABABA.

There is, then, an important difference in horizontal proportions between the contract and the model, but the elements of the design do not appear to differ significantly. Differences do appear, however, in analysing the block-sketches, which provide more complete measurements than the contract.

C. IDENTIFICATION OF THE BLOCK-SKETCHES

Michelangelo's notebooks in the Archivio Buonarroti contain many folios of drawings of blocks extracted from the quarries with their measurements. Tolnay discovered and identified a group of these as related to San Lorenzo and published them (1954, Pls. 145 ff.) prior to his anticipated volume on Michelangelo's architecture. The following descriptions are tentative identifications of the specific purpose of the blocks sketched. They provide sufficient information for a fairly accurate reconstruction of the lower two Orders of the final façade design. The folio numbers referred to are from Vol. I, Archivio Buonarroti, the plate numbers from Tolnay, 1954.

Fol. 128r; Pl. 145: Top: 6 bases for the statues of the lower Order. They are larger and higher than those shown on fol. 145r (Pl. 6a) but the design is approximately the same. Bottom: 6 dadoes and 12 socles for the columns of the lower Order; 12 small blocks, unidentified.

Fol. 128v; Pl. 146: Top: 6 unidentified blocks 4×2 br. and twelve $4 \times \frac{2}{3}$ br. Left: 10 setback strips to be used behind the columns of the lower Order (there are 12 columns but no setback behind the 2 flanking the central portal). Bottom: 6 cornices 3 to $4 \times \frac{1}{2}$ br., probably to be placed over the statues on the lower Order. The remaining drawings are cancelled; their identification is uncertain.

Fol. 129r; Pl. 147: Shafts (10 br. high with $2\frac{1}{2}$ br. flanges), bases, and capitals of the lower Order.

Fol. 130r; Pl. 148: Four 3-piece entablatures spanning 6 br. at the base and $9\frac{1}{3}$ at the top.

The above folios form a group drawn in a tighter hand than the following, suggesting that they may have been done earlier. This observation is borne out by the fact that blocks in fols. 128r and 130r differ in measurements from corresponding ones in the following folios. Finally, there are only four entablatures provided in fol. 130r to be placed over the pairs of columns on the lower Order; this indicates a date prior to the narthex scheme, which required six such entablatures, that is, during the construction of the Baccio d'Agnolo model.

Fol. 134v, 135r; Pl. 149 (Pl. 6b; Fig. 1a): Top: 6 cornices for the mezzanine and 12 socles for the pilasters of the third Order. Bottom: 12 pilaster strips of the mezzanine with a dado for each pair, and 8 setback strips. The lower drawing gives a clear idea of the mezzanine Order, but in the upper one, some measurements are lacking and some unclear (I do not know how much is included in the note "dua braccia el dado alto"). The width of the socles ($1\frac{1}{2}$ br.) is insufficient to support pilasters of adequate height; the pilaster bases of the model are $1\frac{1}{4}$ br. wide.

Fol. 136r; Pl. 150 (Fig. 1b): Top: architraves for the lower Order of the lateral bays and side façades; the pieces may be placed by their great depth ($2\frac{1}{3}$ br.), which is required only over the free-standing columns of the lower Order, but the measurements differ from those of fol. 145r.

Fol. 138r; Pl. 151 (Fig. 1c): 2 segmental ("quarto di tondo") pediments for the side portals with a chord of 9 br. and tympana of one piece.

Fol. 138v; Pl. 152 (Fig. 1d): Entablature of central portal.

Fol. 140r; Pl. 153 (Fig. 1e): Jambs of central portal.

Fol. 142r; Pl. 154 (Fig. 1f): 4 jambs for side portals: 2 lintels, cancelled, with a note that they appear on the following page.

Fol. 142v; Pl. 155 (Fig. 1g): 2 lintels for the side portals. 74 facing slabs for the wall alongside the jambs of the side portals; 33 facing slabs for the same purpose alongside the central portal.

Fol. 145r; Pl. 156 (Pl. 6a; Fig. 1h): Entire membering of the outer bays of the lower Order, main façade and for the lower Order, side façades.

Fol. 145v; Pl. 157: 2 lengths of "cornice" $11 \times 1\frac{1}{4}$ br.; purpose uncertain.

Fol. 155r; Pl. 171: Top: pieces for the entablature of the lateral bays, measuring as on fol. 145r but slightly less deep. Bottom: 5 unidentified slabs of varying sizes.

D. THE BLOCK SKETCHES AND THE CASA BUONARROTI MODEL

Table of comparative measurements in *braccia* (height, width)

	Model Measurement	Block Measurement	Source (Arch. Buon. fol.)
I. LOWER ORDER			
A. Colonnade			
1. dado	$1\frac{1}{4}\times7\frac{1}{2}$	$1\frac{1}{4}\times8$	128r, 145r
2. socle	$1\frac{1}{2}\times2\frac{1}{3}$	$1\frac{1}{4}\times2\frac{1}{2}$	,, ,,
3. base	$1\times2\frac{1}{4}$ to $1\frac{3}{4}$	$1\frac{1}{8}\times2\frac{1}{2}$ to $1\frac{2}{3}$	129r, 145r
4. shaft	$11\frac{1}{5}\times1\frac{1}{2}$	$11\times1\frac{1}{2}$	,, ,,
5. capital	$1\frac{3}{4}\times2\frac{1}{3}$	$2\times2\frac{1}{3}$	,,
6. architrave	$1\frac{1}{4}\times8\frac{2}{3}$	$1\frac{1}{4}\times8\frac{2}{3}$	145r, (136r)
7. frieze	$1\frac{1}{4}\times8\frac{1}{4}$	$1\frac{1}{4}\times8\frac{1}{4}$	,, ,,
8. cornice	$\frac{3}{4}\times10\frac{1}{2}$	$1\frac{1}{4}\times10\frac{3}{4}$	,, ,,
B. Portals, side			
1. jambs	$9\frac{3}{4}\times1$	$8\frac{1}{4}\times1$	142r, 145r
2. lintel	$1\frac{1}{4}\times6$	$1\times6\frac{1}{4}$	142v, 145r
3. pediment base	8	9	138r, 145r
C. Portal, centre			
1. jambs	$\frac{3}{4}\times11\frac{1}{2}$	$1\frac{1}{4}\times10\frac{1}{4}$	140r
2. lintel	$\frac{3}{4}\times6\frac{1}{2}$	$1\frac{1}{4}\times7\frac{2}{3}$	138v
3. frieze	$\frac{3}{4}\times6\frac{1}{2}$	$1\times7\frac{2}{3}$	,,
4. cornice, top	$1\times8\frac{1}{2}$	$1\times10\frac{1}{6}$	,,
II. MEZZANINE			
1. dado	$1\frac{1}{2}\times8\frac{1}{2}$	$1\times8\frac{1}{2}$	134v, 135r
2. base	$\frac{1}{3}\times8$	$\frac{1}{2}\times(8?)$	,, ,,
3. pilaster strip	$4\frac{1}{2}\times1\frac{1}{3}$	$5\times1\frac{1}{4}$	,, ,,
4. setback	$4\frac{1}{2}\times\frac{2}{3}$	5×1	,, ,,
5. cornice, top	$\frac{1}{2}\times9$	$1\times8\frac{3}{4}$	,, ,,
Total height	$6\frac{3}{4}$	$7\frac{1}{2}$	
III. UPPER ORDER			
1. socle base	none used	$1\times1\frac{1}{2}$	,, ,,
2. socle	$1\frac{1}{4}\times1\frac{3}{4}$	1 or $2\times1\frac{1}{2}$	,, ,,

(no further record available).

The blocks differ significantly from the model in the following respects:

Lower Order: The width of the column dadoes and of the side and central portals is increased. This may be due in part to the fact that the blocks were measured before final carving and polishing. Note, however, that the width of the central portal has grown substantially, for reasons explained in the analysis of the contract.

All the doors are apparently over 1 br. lower (see "jambs"), but it is not certain that a change was intended, since the jambs of the final version may have been cut to rest on bases (cf. Uffizi, *Arch.* 1945, Tolnay 1934, Fig. 9).

Mezzanine (Pl. 6b): The overall height is raised $\frac{3}{4}$ br. beyond that of the model, chiefly in order to lengthen the pilaster strips and consequently to give still more room to the seated statues.

Upper Order: The absence of adequate measurements and identifications makes it impossible to reconstruct the basement of the pilaster Order. Reading the note "due braccia el dado alto" to refer to the socle alone, we get excessive height – a Gothic kind of proportion. Conceivably, what I have called the socle and socle base is actually the lowest block of a pilaster (the $1\frac{1}{2}$ br. width would suit this interpretation) and its base; but in this case the third order would depart from the contract, and it would be lower than the model, allowing insufficient room for the *tondi* and panels.

The block sketches give no evidence of changes in the design accepted in the contract of 1518. They are incomplete, probably because the upper Order was not quarried at the time the project was abandoned, but for the lower stories they are sufficiently detailed to permit an accurate reconstruction (Fig. 1). The uncertain factors in Fig. 1 are (1) bay and portal widths on the lower order; (2) the degree to which the blocks would have been reduced in size by carving; and (3) the handling of the wall surfaces as distinct from the members.

Studies for the *Ballatoio* of the Cathedral of Florence
Ca. 1516–1520

In 1451–1460, after completing the lantern of the Cathedral dome, Brunelleschi's successor Antonio Manetti covered the eight-sided drum with marble incrustation and framed the great round windows (Paatz 1952, III, pp. 353, 464 ff., with bibliography). But the broad band between the drum and the base of the dome, where a combined gallery and cornice (*ballatoio*) was to be built, was barely begun when the campaign halted (see the view of the Cathedral in a panel representing the execution of Savonarola in 1498 in C. Ricci, *Cento vedute di Firenze*, Florence, 1906, Pl. LIX). Two fifteenth-century models for the drum and *ballatoio* are preserved in the Museo dell' Opera; one may be by Manetti, though the drum incrustation of both differs from the final design (P. Sanpaolesi, *La cupola di S. M. del Fiore* . . ., Rome, 1941, p. 12; Pl. IIIa, b; one model is ascribed to Brunelleschi and Ghiberti).

In 1507 a competition was held for the design of a facing; five models were submitted and the winning contestants – Cronaca, Giuliano da Sangallo and Baccio d'Agnolo – were instructed to collaborate with Antonio da Sangallo in revising their design to incorporate features of Manetti's model (C. Guasti, *La cupola di S. M. del Fiore*, Florence, 1857, pp. 122 f. Models from this period are preserved also; see L. M. Tosi, *Boll. d'Arte* VII, 1928, pp. 610 ff., Figs. 2, 3). In 1513, Baccio was appointed *caput magistrum* of the Cathedral, and in the following year the materials were ordered for constructing the *ballatoio* on one of the eight sides (*ibid.*, pp. 128 f.) It was completed and unveiled in June 1515 (Schiavo 1953, p. 157).

Vasari reported (V, p. 353) that Michelangelo, on returning from Rome (1516), objected so vigorously to Baccio's work – he called it "a cricket cage" – that construction was suspended. Michelangelo then made his own model, which he claimed was more in harmony with Brunelleschi's intention, but after much debate the project was abandoned by the *Opera*, and the *ballatoio* remains unfinished today.

Michelangelo's preparatory drawing for the model is in the Casa Buonarroti (No. 50r; D.92; F.173; Thode 1908, II, p. 139; III, No. 78; Tolnay 1948, pp. 211 f., No. 83).

The drum and part of the dome is sketched as a combined elevation and section, but with shifts in scale that make the intention obscure. An entablature and attic crowned by statues are carried by paired Composite pilasters on high pedestals; though the Order seems to extend downwards into the level of the drum, a more detailed sketch to the right shows it to be intended only for the *ballatoio*.

A sketch on the *verso* of this sheet, together with two similar drawings, has been identified as the elevation of one side of the drum facing (Casa Buon. Nos. 50v, 66r and v; D.92, 102, F.174, 123, 124; Thode 1908, II, p. 139; III. Nos. 78, 117). They all have a central oculus flanked on either side by a recessed vertical panel, which explains the association with the Cathedral drum; but the proportions are somewhat different, and there is no reason to suppose that Michelangelo intended to remove the Manetti incrustation to replace it with one that was less in harmony with the rest of the building. A fragment of a letter of 1520 appears on the most finished drawing, No. 66v. I have no alternative identification for the sketches; Tolnay's proposal (*loc. cit.*, No. 82) that they are early studies for the altar of the Medici Chapel might be correct, but is based only on their shape and date.

Florence, Windows of the Medici Palace
Ca. 1517 (Pl. 6c)

Speaking of Michelangelo's return to Florence in 1516, Vasari says (VII, p. 191) "Allora fece per il palazzo de' Medici un modello delle finestre inginocchiate (*i.e.*, supported on 'knees') a quelle stanze che sono sul canto", adding that a room behind was stuccoed and frescoed by Giovanni da Udine, and that Michelangelo designed "marvellous" blinds for the windows (now missing). In another account (VI, p. 557; Life of Giovanni), we are told that the occasion for the commission, given during the period of the San Lorenzo façade project (1517–1520), was the walling-up of an open loggia, and that the two windows (one for each of the two loggia bays) were the first of the *inginocchiato* type to be used on a palace façade. In a letter of 1534, Vasari dated the interior frescoes "in the time of Leo. X" (*Nachlass*, I, p. 29).

One would expect such a loggia to overlook the garden to the rear of the palace, but Karl Frey (1907, I, pp. 41 ff.), analysing a series of inventories of the building from the time of Filarete to 1531, discovered that the open chamber at the right of the main façade on the corner of Via Larga and Via de' Gori was referred to as a "loggia terrena" or "logieta" (see his plan, *ibid.*, p. 42). Michelangelo's two windows were inserted into the arches of this loggia; a third (of the same date?) is preserved at the opposite end of the original façade. I originally connected the commission with a garden loggia which also was part of the palace; Tolnay kindly corrected this error. The appearance of the open arches of the palace prior to Michelangelo's additions is recorded in Francesco Granacci's *Entry of Charles VIII into Florence*, Florence, Museo Mediceo, reproduced in M. L. Gengaro, *Umanesimo e Rinascimento*, Turin, 1940, Fig. 551 (brought to my attention by Wittkower).

A drawing (Casa Buon. No. 101; D.130; F.286, text, p. 131) of a similar window appears, as Frey suggested, to be a study for the Medici model. It resembles drawings of the period in style and is certainly for a palace (Thode 1908, II, p. 136, III, No. 156 suggested an altar-niche) because the section sketch shows steps leading to a platform *behind* the window, a typically Florentine device to enable the inhabitants to see over the extremely high sills.

The design, like that of the Castel Sant' Angelo front, makes use of conventional motifs in an unconventional way: the inner window frame is actually Quattrocento in form to harmonize with Michelozzo's arches; the pediment would suit a Raphael façade. But the attenuated volutes beneath the window make its stable form dynamic by giving it more "support" than it needs, and by accentuating verticals over horizontals. Vasari may not be right in crediting Michelangelo with the invention of "supporting" volutes – Antonio da Sangallo the Elder used them at about the same time in Monte-pulciano – but it is not so much the motif as the vigorous scale and proportion that attracts attention.

Florence, the Altopascio House, *ca.* 1518–1520?

Plate 6d, one of a pair of drawings for a large house (Casa Buon., Nos. 117, 118; D.139, 140) has the note "l'alto pascio". Thode (1908, II, 141, III, Nos. 166, 167) has suggested that the client was Ugolino Grifoni, owner of the Palazzo Altopascio, who later commissioned a palace from Ammanati.

The two sheets have alternate plans for a house like those built in Rome by Bramante and his school, with shops on the street, a tiny enclosed garden at the rear, and stairs in the middle. Plate 6d foreshadows the villa plans of Palladio in its symmetry; in the two plans on No. 118, the right-hand stairway is omitted. Both schemes have uninviting interior rooms without windows. Michelangelo used the *versos* of both drawings for studies of the dome of St Peter's in 1546–1547.

A more hastily-sketched plan (Casa Buon., No. 33; D.79; F.293) has been associated with this house (Thode 1908, II, p. 140; III, No. 100a). Tolnay, in publishing another version of this second sketch (Arch. Buon., Vol. XI, fol. 722v; 1928, p. 472, Fig. 76; D.36) which appears on the verso of a letter of 1518, believed that it was for a more modest dwelling, but has since, he tells me, placed it with the Altopascio group. The door frame sketched in chalk on Pl. 6d suggests a date of *ca.* 1520; its style is midway between the doors of the San Lorenzo façade and those of the Laurentian library.

An unpublished plan of the Florentine period in the Casa Buonarroti (No. 119; D.141) for a house or villa of about the same size has a large oblong court with a portico carried on rectangular piers. The proportions and planning method again prophesy Palladio.

Florence, San Lorenzo, The Medici Chapel, 1520–1534

I HISTORY

In the spring of 1520, just at the time when the project for the San Lorenzo façade lost momentum, the Pope and his cousin, Cardinal Giulio de' Medici, decided to build a family mausoleum in the same church (Pl. 15). Destined for the new sacristy (Fig. 3: 3) on the opposite side of the transept from Brunelleschi's sacristy (Fig. 3: 2) – which served as a model for its design – the mausoleum was to contain a chapel with an altar and tombs for four members of the family: the two "Magnifici", Lorenzo and Giuliano, fathers of Leo and the Cardinal, and the two recently deceased Dukes, also named Lorenzo and Giuliano of Urbino and Nemours. (On the history of the chapel, see Popp 1922, pp. 109 ff.: Tolnay 1948, esp. pp. 27 ff., 52 ff.; Wilde 1955.)

Vasari says (VII, pp. 192 f.) that Michelangelo came to Florence "and raised up the cupola that one sees there, which he had executed in varied ornament, and he commissioned the goldsmith Piloto to do a ball of 72 facets [for the lantern] which is most beautiful . . ." This would suggest that Michelangelo merely domed an existing structure. It is possible that Michelangelo was on hand when construction began (was resumed?) in March 1520 (as Wilde 1955, p. 66, believes), but since the Pope was still hoping to employ him at the Vatican in September (*Corr.*, pp. 12, 18 f.), it is more likely that his correspondence of November represents his first contact with the chapel (Tolnay 1948, p. 124, n. 2, 3).

The question of Michelangelo's part in the construction of the chapel has not been resolved; Tolnay (1948, p. 27) and Paatz (1952, II, p. 534) assigned everything on the exterior except the cupola and lantern to a period prior to his arrival, while Wilde (1955, pp. 55 f., Pls. 22, 23) attributed the whole building to him.

The basic evidence may be summarized as follows:

A. In favour of construction prior to Michelangelo's arrival:

1. Vasari's report, quoted above.

2. The exterior masonry below the level of the dome is indistinguishable from that of the church itself (Pl. 14a). Tolnay observed that the consoles of the second story are later than those of the lower story, but still late Quattrocento in style.

3. There is no logical relationship between the interior and exterior design of the third story: the entablatures are at different levels; the pendentive system is awkwardly disguised as a drum on the exterior; the exterior window frames are much higher than the interior windows, so that the upper half of the opening had to be walled up (Pl. 14a).

4. The sacristy appears as an exact counterpart of Brunelleschi's in a plan of San Lorenzo by Giuliano da Sangallo, which has not been discussed in this connection (R. Falb, *Il taccuino senese di G. da S.*, Siena, 1899, fol. 21v). The drawing pre-dates the façade competition of 1515, and may be earlier, since nothing in the sketchbook need be later

than a note of 1503. Since Giuliano's purpose was a thoroughgoing remodelling of the church with domes and a portico, he may have invented the new sacristy as a feature of his proposal (as suggested by Pommer, "Drawings for the Façade of San Lorenzo . . .", unpubl. thesis, N.Y.U., 1957, p. 81n.), but it is possible that he drew what he saw.

B. In favour of construction by Michelangelo (Wilde, *loc. cit.*):

1. According to the contemporary chronicler, Giovanni Cambi, a building pro-gramme was initiated shortly before March 1520. On 1 March, the Chapter allotted funds for the programme.

2. A letter from Rome of 28 November 1520 (*Briefe*, p. 161) acknowledges receipt of Michelangelo's "schizo della capella". (The wording suggests an architectural design, but may have referred to a tomb project.)

3. A view of the church by Leonardo, probably of 1502, shows the north transept without a sacristy (Wilde, Pl. 23a).

4. The chapel entrance wall must have been constructed especially to accommodate a deep tomb niche after the final designs of 1521. Its peculiar plan and angled doorway may be explained by the tomb.

The two arguments appear to be irreconcilable. The only evidence that is not open to varied interpretation is Leonardo's sketch, which proves that the chapel did not exist at the turn of the century. But one document, which has been used to support both views, remains to be examined.

A sheet in the Archivio Buonarroti (Vol. I, fol. 98; D.10; discovered by Tolnay 1928, pp. 379 ff.; 1948, p. 203, Pls. 79, 80; 1954, Pl. 120) contains a plan of the chapel by Michel-angelo (Pl. 12b) and an estimate in another hand of the cost of (carving or erecting?) stone membering. Wilde (pp. 65 f.) discovered that the estimate concerned the Old Sacristy and proposed that it was made early in 1520, with the intention of copying the Old Sacristy exactly. Michelangelo's plan is closer to Brunelleschi's than to the final form of the chapel: the "choir" has Brunelleschi's three niches; the great pilaster order and the columned door frames repeat on all four walls the system employed only on the choir wall of the Old Sacristy. The only new elements are two doodled chapels on the side walls, a fantasy that neighbouring structures and streets made impractical. Four tombs would have been put in the lateral bays of these walls, and a fifth on the entrance wall; monumental niche tombs were not yet considered. The sketch must date, then, from the beginning of Michelangelo's activity.

The plan could be Michelangelo's initial study for a new chapel or a sketch after a chapel already under construction. The former alternative (Wilde, pp. 57, 66) is appealing because it avoids the assumption that Michelangelo had to demolish parts of existing walls to suit his tombs; he would simply have delayed construction until the tomb de-signs were settled, after late December of 1520 (a free-standing mausoleum was still favoured at that time: letters in Tolnay 1948, pp. 226 f.) But construction reports weaken the argument: by 21 April 1521 the architecture of the first order was in place (*Briefe*, pp. 171–174). Assuming Michelangelo's authorship, the chapel would have to have been redesigned, and the membering carved and placed in a wholly new structure within the impossibly short span of three and a half winter months.

For this reason I assume that the lower Order of the chapel was substantially finished before the tomb designs, and then had to be remodelled to accommodate them. If Michelangelo had been in charge from the start, he would have delayed construction until the tombs were designed. The 1520 building campaign apparently continued earlier construction on the site, as indicated by the exterior masonry (paragraph A2 above).

The style of the interior shows that Michelangelo's active intervention as an architect began only at the pendentive level. The *pietra serena* Order of the lower two stories (Pls. 7a, 10) is superficially a copy of the Old Sacristy, but actually follows late Quattrocento models in the nave of San Lorenzo. Possibly Michelangelo found some members already carved during the previous months (as suggested by the estimate cited above) or even decades before (as suggested by the style). Some of the work, however, was done in Michelangelo's time. The insertion of simple piers between the pilasters and the tombs was not contemplated in Michelangelo's early drawings, so it was obviously his contribution. Since the piers are of a piece with the pilasters themselves (an observation I owe to Tolnay; see his 1948, Pl. 232), the latter cannot have been manufactured until the tomb designs were fixed.

So long as nothing of the exterior or interior articulation below the pendentive level – except for the marble architecture – bears the stamp of Michelangelo's style, it does not really matter for the criticism of his work whether it was built before or after his arrival. In either case the scheme is a copy of Quattrocento models, modestly altered to suit the requirements of the tombs.

In the upper stories (Fig. 2) there are clear signs of Michelangelo's intervention: the windows of the pendentive zone and the dome and lantern are unmistakably his (see an original sketch for the window, Casa Buon., No. 105; D.133; F.177B). There a copy of Brunelleschi was out of the question, because the Old Sacristy pendentives rested directly on the first story entablature, leaving space for but one row of windows. Michelangelo added another story between the main order and the cupola, changing the spatial character fundamentally.

In April of 1521 Michelangelo went to Carrara to supervise the quarrying of blocks for the tomb figures, which indicates the acceptance of a final design both for the tombs and for the architecture (*Lettere*, p. 582; Tolnay 1948, p. 160n). Meanwhile, in Florence, the *pietra serena* architrave was put into place (*Briefe*, p. 174) and pilasters set up (*ibid.*, p. 171); these may have been the small ones of the intermediate order (Popp 1922, p. 110). Michelangelo's deputy on the job had some trouble with the Cardinal over the entrance door and cornices (*Briefe, loc. cit.*), and the letters imply that the patron was insisting on the closest possible copy of Brunelleschi. There is no further record of construction until early in 1524, when the lantern was in place (*Lettere*, p. 424; its gilt polyhedron was mounted in 1525: Gronau 1911, p. 72) and the cupola was ready for stuccoing. Since a new scaffold had to be raised for this purpose (*Lettere*, p. 590), the actual construction of the cupola must have been finished long before and the original masons' scaffold removed (as proposed by Popp 1922, p. 113; her dating of the construction in 1521, however, is arbitrary). This stucco work must have been decorative (Michelangelo made a drawing for it: *Briefe*, p. 211) – anything as plain as the surviving coffer system would have been added at the conclusion of the masonry work. It was to be painted by Giovanni da Udine, but, although negotiations began in 1526, the paintings were not executed until 1532–1533 (*Briefe*, pp. 280 f., 283, 286 f., 288, 319 f., 331, 333. *Lettere*, p. 453). A Michelangelesque drawing for stucco reliefs and narrative frescoes in the coffers has been attributed to Giovanni da Udine (Casa Buonarroti 127, Tolnay 1948, p. 212; D.484 leaves the attribution "open"). According to Vasari they were not strong enough to make an impression at a distance and ultimately were whitewashed over (Vasari VI, pp. 560 f; *Corr.*, p. 104).

Some architectural details may have been unfinished at this time. In August 1533, the appointment of a foreman for work in *pietra serena* is mentioned in correspondence (*Corr.*, p. 114), but his job must have been a minor one. The tombs and marble architecture progressed as slowly as the building. Although some of the marble was quarried in 1521 (Tolnay 1948, p. 54), there was no concentrated activity until early in 1524, when Michelangelo promised to complete the tombs within a year (*Briefe*, p. 221). Before February he had sent the Pope a drawing of the lateral tabernacles and doors (*Briefe*, p. 211), and dispatches from Carrara report that these were being quarried from March on; by August they were nearly ready for delivery (Tolnay 1948, pp. 231 f., 234). But at this point some obstacle arose that prevented the stonecutters from blocking them out. Evidently Michelangelo considered changing the design; his indecision exasperated everybody and started off a shower of pleading letters which failed, however, to spur him into action for an entire year (Popp 1922, pp. 121 f.; Tolnay 1948, pp. 56 f.) But by June of 1524 the first of the tombs was far enough advanced to rule out any major alteration in design (*Briefe*, p. 230), and during the summer and autumn the pediments, entablatures and frieze of masks were mentioned in the records (*Lettere*, p. 596). This tomb was not completed until June of 1526 (*Briefe*, p. 285). It can be identified as that of Lorenzo; the details are more complex than those of the Giuliano tomb, which was probably executed sometime during the years 1531–1533 (Tolnay 1948, pp. 55 f.) The tomb of the Magnifici in the entrance wall was not started until August 1533 (*Corr.*, p. 114) although columns (which were not used elsewhere in the chapel) were already ordered from Carrara in January 1526 (Tolnay 1948, p. 238).

This again emphasizes the sporadic progress of the construction: work evidently slowed down or halted in 1522–1523, in 1525, and in 1527–1530/1531. During the last period, both patron and artist were distracted by political events; the Sack of Rome, and Florence's unsuccessful battle for independence, in which the two found themselves on opposite sides. The final hectic spurt of activity, which brought the chapel almost to its present condition before Michelangelo's final departure for Rome in 1534, was partly the result of the artist's fear of Medici retaliation for his loyalty to the Florentine Republic (Condivi, Ch. 38: "spinto più dalla paura che dall'amore").

Michelangelo left the statues strewn about the floor of the chapel, and visitors were not admitted until 1545, when Tribolo and Montelupo had finished the carving and put them in order (Paatz 1952, p. 578; on the history after 1534, see Frey, *Nachlass*, I, pp. 699 ff.) Even then the windows were not yet glazed, and in 1556 Vasari had to re-stucco the walls (*Nachlass*, I, p. 462). In 1559 some marble slabs left in Michelangelo's studio were fashioned into a sarcophagus to hold the remains of the Magnifici and to serve as a base for the statues on the entrance wall (Pl. 10; cf. Popp 1922, p. 118). An anonymous mid-sixteenth-century plan of the chapel (discovered by Tolnay 1948, p. 164, Pl. 165; now in the Metropolitan Museum) shows the architecture of this tomb completed with niches enclosing columns and framed by pilasters; if the drawing represents the actual condition of the chapel, as it appears to do, it is curious that the architectural members should have been removed later. By 1563, the chapel was again in poor condition (*Nachlass*, I, p. 712) and Vasari proposed to Duke Cosimo a restoration based on Michelangelo's original project, involving the addition of four allegorical statues, eleven frescoes, and stucco reliefs, to be executed by members of the newly formed Academy. Michelangelo's consent and assistance were solicited (*ibid.*, pp. 720 ff., 737 ff., 741 f.), but his response must have been cool, since posterity has been spared the results of Vasari's good intentions.

II THE DESIGN

Several of Michelangelo's drawings for the tombs have survived, but aside from the rapidly sketched plan (Pl. 12b), no actual architectural studies. In the earliest group of sketches a free-standing monument in the centre of the chapel appears together with sketches, probably the initial ones, of more modest wall tombs (compare analyses of Tolnay 1948, pp. 33 ff, and Wilde 1953, pp. 47 ff.; 1955, pp. 58 ff.) The free-standing monument was the subject of a lively correspondence between Michelangelo and the Vatican late in 1520 (*e.g.*, letters discovered by Tolnay, *ibid.*, pp. 225), in which the chief problem was to gain adequate scale without crowding the chapel; it was evidently insoluble, and early in 1521 Michelangelo turned again to wall tombs. While studying the free-standing scheme, Michelangelo could not have been much concerned with the architecture of the chapel itself; he would have used Brunelleschi's Sacristy to get a sense of the space, proportions, and colour, and the overall form of the free-standing tomb drawings suggests that they were conceived for a two-story Brunelleschian building, not the tall three-story one designed in 1521 (cf. Wilde 1955, p. 60).

The free-standing monuments evolve so consistently with wall tombs that we do not know in every case which is which (problematic, British Museum 26v [D.150; F.48]; Casa Buon., No. 88 [D.120; F.70]); but everyone agrees that there are two studies leading to the final solution for the Ducal tombs (British Museum, 26r; Pl. 11b [D.150; F.47]; 27r, Pl. 11a [D.151; F.55]) and two for the Magnifici tomb (British Museum, 28r, v, Pl. 12a, c [D.153; F.9a, b]; analysis and bibliography on the series in Wilde 1953, pp. 51 ff.)

Plate 11b is a double tomb for the two Dukes, perhaps planned for a scheme with double tombs on the side walls and a *sacra conversazione* facing the altar (Popp 1922, p. 127). Here the project is quite fluid, with inconsistencies of scale in both architecture and figures. Plate 11a, though it has nearly reached the final solution, also seems to be a double tomb, with the Dukes seated in niches alongside the single sarcophagus (Popp, *loc. cit.*, and Dussler, call it a single tomb). The central bay is broader than the one executed, the attic more ornate with its thrones and trophies, and the internal proportions somewhat different.

Plates 12a and 12c, two versions of the final scheme in which the Magnifici are assigned to the entrance wall along with the Madonna and Saints, presuppose a preceding and definitive design in which the Dukes are given single tombs on the lateral walls. In both these sketches the votive statues are in a kind of triptych in the upper portion, but the intermediate zone vacillates between seated statues of the Magnifici or of Cosmas and Damian (Pl. 12c) and an allegorical figure of Fame (Pl. 12a). Later developments of this scheme are documented in a group of drawings by Michelangelo's followers (Tolnay 1948, p. 40, Pls. 218–223; H.-W. Frey 1951, pp. 68 ff, Figs. 6–9; Luporini 1957, Figs. 1–3, 5, 8) which echo two further drawings of Michelangelo, now lost. These may not represent Michelangelo's final project; in the mid-century plan cited above (Metropolitan Museum, Tolnay, p. 164, Pl. 165) the columns are pushed back into wall niches as in the library vestibule, and the saints and allegories project forward in aediculas. Since the change is sympathetic to Michelangelo's interests in the mid-1520's, and since the author of the plan apparently found this construction *in situ*, it appears to be the definitive design.

The tombs in Pls. 11a and 11b are obviously wider than those in Pls. 12a and 12c. This is not chance, since both pairs are drawn precisely to the proportions of their intended architectural framework (as conclusively demonstrated by Popp, p. 125 and reconstructions on Pls. 5–8; my Fig. 4); the first pair, which is earlier, is conceived to fit a niche that occupies the entire space between the framing pilasters, while the second is contracted to allow room for the two *pietra serena* piers that in the final version are "inserted" (pier and pilaster are actually carved of one piece, see Tolnay 1948, Pl. 232) between the tombs and the pilasters. Fig. 4 shows that the existing central statue-niche is a version of the square central field of the early drawing (Pl. 11a) reduced in width by precisely the breadth of the two inserted piers.

Why did Michelangelo decide to use these two unconventional and rather unattractive piers when it involved a compromise in his design? Popp's answer (*loc. cit.*) was that in the period between the earlier and later pair of drawings Michelangelo decided to abandon the Brunelleschian two-story elevation for a more vertical interior space; the piers, then, helped both to verticalize the tombs and to articulate the added story by providing support for its arches. It seems equally likely that Michelangelo could find no way to avoid the piers. If the building preceded the tombs and was started as a copy of Brunelleschi's Sacristy, the pilasters would have been just where the piers are now. But Michelangelo wanted side bays narrower than Brunelleschi's, and moved the pilasters toward the corners, set them forward a little, and had the space that they had occupied filled with plain piers. Apparently he originally hoped to eliminate the piers for his broad tomb schemes (Pls. 11a and 11b) but was forced by economy and statics to retain them as a support for the relieving arches of the intermediate story which made the tomb niches possible. These arches probably had been carved before Michelangelo's time for a pendentive zone like that of the Old Sacristy (Pl. 7); the windows may have belonged to the same early scheme, though without the flat brackets beneath them they would just have fit the space between the two arches in the Brunelleschian design.

Whatever the process of reasoning, it appears likely that Michelangelo raised the entire elevation of the chapel when he changed from the broader to the narrower tomb scheme. This change greatly increased the light as well as the height of the chapel.

Among the surviving drawings of details of the tomb architecture the more important are profile studies (Casa Buon., Nos. 9, 10, 57, 59, 61 [D.57, 58, 95, 97, 99; F.163, 162, 282a, 175, vac.]); sketches relating to the friezes of masks (British Museum, 33; Windsor 12762 – connection questionable [D.159, 237; F.31, 212a]); and "thrones" that surmount the double pilasters of the Ducal tombs – the backs were truncated in execution (Casa Buon., No. 72 [D.108; F.266a]; for analysis and bibliography of the entire group see Tolnay 1948, pp. 41 f. and Cat. Nos. 72, 73, 76, 78, 81, 91, 93). Except for a sketch of the window of the pendentive zone (Casa Buon., No. 105 [D.133; F.177b]; Tolnay, Cat. 80), none of Michelangelo's many unidentified window-, tabernacle-, and door designs has been definitively associated with the chapel (but see Tolnay, pp. 209 ff.) A drawing by Dosio (Luporini 1957, Fig. 7) may reflect an early project for the lantern.

III THE PAPAL TOMBS

In May 1524, Jacopo Salviati persuaded Clement VII that the scheme of the chapel should be expanded to include another pair of tombs, for Clement himself and for Leo X (the history of this scheme may be traced in letters from Fattucci, Michelangelo's agent at the Vatican, *Briefe*, pp. 228–288, *passim*; summarized by Popp 1922, pp. 167 ff.; Tolnay 1948, pp. 76 ff.; H.-W. Frey 1951, pp. 49 ff.) The initial proposal was abandoned immediately, chiefly because one of the single Ducal tombs was too far advanced to change, and Michelangelo suggested putting the papal monument in "quello lavamani, dove è la scala" (*Briefe*, p. 230). This may be identified as the small sub-sacristy to the left of the chapel choir (Fig. 3); the washbasin and stairway are no longer there, but that the latter once existed is proven by a sixteenth-century plan in the Metropolitan Museum, in which the room is identified: "qui si va per un altra scala in su a chupola" (Tolnay 1948, p. 164, Pl. 165). In later correspondence (*Briefe*, pp. 283 f.), reference is made to *both* chambers flanking the choir, as if each were to contain a single papal monument (pointed out by H.-W. Frey 1951, pp. 50 ff.); we do not know whether this was projected from the start or represented a change in programme. Popp's hypothesis (1927, p. 391, accepted by Tolnay 1948, p. 76) that the intended site was the corresponding chamber in Brunelleschi's Old Sacristy was based on the present existence there of a stairway (right chamber) and basin (left chamber). This improbable proposal is disproven by Fattucci's recommendation that certain houses blocking the light of the "lavamani" in question be demolished (*Briefe*, p. 231); since the Old Sacristy overlooked the rear garden of the cloister (see Michelangelo's plan, Tolnay 1954, Pl. 194, and the site plan, Wittkower 1934, Fig. 6), only the Medici chapel could have been in the shadow of adjacent houses.

None of the numerous tomb sketches of this period can be identified with this scheme. A scale drawing formerly in Dresden (D.389) which Popp (1927, pp. 389 ff., Fig. 1; followed by Tolnay 1948, pp. 76, 207, Pl. 93) identified as the "lavamani" monument, can be eliminated by her proof that it would just fit the space in the Old Sacristy but not the slightly smaller area in the New (the measurements are contested by H.-W. Frey 1951,

p. 53); the authorship is questionable. Wilde (1953, p. 50) noted further that the arms on the Dresden drawings are not papal; in his view it belongs with the similar Casa Buonarroti No. 93 (D.125, with a summary of the problem and related drawings; F.125c) among the early studies for the free-standing tombs in the centre of the chapel. Wilde proposed (p. 75) that a drawing in Oxford resembling the Ducal Tombs (Ashmolean, No. 307; D.621; F.214a) was made for the "lavamani", but its proportions are poorly suited to the purpose (the longest wall of the chamber is only 3·85 m., which would make the sarcophagus on this sketch only 1·4 m. long).

From the start, Fattucci, speaking for Clement VII, insisted that the site selected by Michelangelo was too small and dark, and in July 1524 he suggested using the choir of San Lorenzo or some similarly important location (*Briefe*, p. 233). Popp (1927, pp. 395 ff.) found that the magnificent plan and elevation of a tomb (Pl. 13b; Casa Buon., No. 45 [D.87; F.14]; reconstructed by Popp 1927, Fig. 7 and Fasolo 1926/1927, Figs. 28, 29) was designed for the side walls of the choir; the proportions coincide with those of the walls (though Wilde 1953, p. 76, showed that the scale would be preferable if the tomb were to cover only part of the wall), and the monumental form suggests a papal commission. A precedent for placing important tombs facing each other behind the altar existed in Andrea Sansovino's monuments to two cardinals at Santa Maria del Popolo in Rome. Michelangelo's drawing is close in style to his contemporary projects for the Laurentian library (Pls. 19b, 21), notable in the use of recessed columns and projecting wall-masses. Several other drawings may be associated with this scheme: Casa Buonarroti, No. 46 (D.88; F.125b); British Museum, No. 39 (D.330; F.120a); and Archivio Buonarroti, V, fol. 38r (D.29 rejects any connection to the project) all seem to be for the choir tombs; British Museum, No. 38 (D.180), and Oxford, Ashmolean, No. 308 (D.345, with extensive analysis; F.143) are related in style but were not necessarily drawn for the same project (see discussions of the group in Fasolo 1926/1927, pp. 438 ff.; Popp 1927, pp. 405 ff.; Tolnay 1948, pp. 207 f.; H.-W. Frey 1951, pp. 68 ff.; Wilde 1953, pp. 75 f.; Dussler, *passim*).

The date of the choir drawings is not clear from the correspondence. In April 1525, an unidentified drawing of a single papal tomb was returned to Florence (*Briefe*, p. 250), and in June 1526, Fattucci again raised the question of the site (*Briefe*, p. 284), repeating his preference for the church over the chapel. Three months later the Pope warned Michelangelo that he intended to have his own way in planning the tombs (*Briefe*, p. 288). In view of the indecision of the correspondents it is curious that blocks for two papal statues should have been excavated at Carrara in August 1524 (letter discovered by Tolnay 1948, p. 235); probably they were destined for the "lavamani"; had they been for the church choir, Fattucci would not have had to insist on this site two years later. The existence of two blocks for the "lavamani" would explain Michelangelo's obstinacy. If these conclusions are correct, the choir drawings should be dated in 1526, after the Pope's ultimatum, rather than in 1524, when the choir was first proposed.

The political troubles of 1527 put an end to the project. After the Pope's death in 1534, Alfonso Lombardi was commissioned to do the tombs, using sketches by Michelangelo, and in 1536 Bandinelli replaced him, together with Antonio da Sangallo the

Younger, who was to design the architecture. They were built in Santa Maria Sopra Minerva, Rome. A number of splendid monumental tomb- or altar designs by Michelangelo (British Museum, No. 22v [D.160; F.106]; Arch. Buon., IX, fol. 539v [D.34]; Oxford, Christ Church, No. DD.24 [D.638]; cf. Tolnay 1948, Pls. 121–123) have been proposed as the models given to Lombardi (Popp 1927, pp. 407 f.; Tolnay 1948, pp. 78 ff. believes they were first drawn for the Julius Tomb in 1525; his dating is accepted by Dussler) but Wilde seems closer to the mark in dating them *ca.* 1516 for an unidentified project (1953, pp. 38 ff.): the similarity of the London sketches to the concept of the chapel in Castel Sant' Angelo favours an early date.

Florence, San Lorenzo, Reliquary Tribune, 1531–1532

I HISTORY

On 14 October 1525, Michelangelo was instructed by Pope Clement VII to design a ciborium in the choir of San Lorenzo for the storage and exhibition of the relics of the church, which were to be placed in urns from the collection of Lorenzo the Magnificent (*Briefe*, p. 260; further instructions, pp. 262, 265). The ciborium was to be in the form of a stone canopy over the altar, raised on four antique porphyry columns found in Rome. In the course of a long correspondence between Michelangelo and Fattucci, the Pope's administrator, the original project was abandoned in favour of a reliquary tribune or balcony constructed over the entrance portal on the inner side of the façade (Pl. 14c; for a detailed summary of the correspondence, see Thode 1908, II, pp. 102 ff.; for bibliography, Paatz 1952, II, 538n).

Michelangelo preferred the façade site from the start; the Pope was amenable, but feared that the relics might be raised too high to be visible, and asked that both sites be studied, together with one over the entrance to the Medici chapel (Letter of 29 November 1525; *Briefe*, p. 267). On 4 February 1526, drawings both for the ciborium and for a balcony arrived in Rome, and were corrected by the Pope (*Briefe*, p. 272); a surviving sketch for the projects (No. 1 below) has a notation of 8 February. A model for the ciborium requested in subsequent letters (*Briefe*, pp. 274, 278 f.) was not produced, and in November 1526, Michelangelo was asked to build a temporary ciborium in wood so that relics might be installed during the preparation of the marble structure (*Briefe*, pp. 291, 292, 293). Even the more modest plan was frustrated by the Sack of Rome, and correspondence resumed only in 1531, when the façade site was definitely accepted.

In October–November 1531, the materials and the form of the Medici arms were being discussed; a year later the columns had been raised and other essential members were on the site when the Prior of San Lorenzo wrote to Michelangelo, then living in Rome, for instructions on design details (*Briefe*, pp. 309, 331, 332; *Dicht.*, pp. 511 f.) The relics were installed in December (*Briefe*, p. 334; *Dicht.*, p. 512) and the finished "pergamo" was praised by the Pope in July 1533 (*Corr.*, p. 108).

II DRAWINGS

1. Casa Buon., No. 76; D.112; F.68, 69 (Thode 1908, II, p. 105; III, No. 131).

Recto: A measured plan of the central chapel of San Lorenzo showing a rectangular ciborium covering the altar under the entrance arch. It is raised on a platform that projects forward over the steps. Since only the column bases and the lintels are indicated, the elevation cannot be reconstructed. The sheet contains a *ricordo* of an unrelated financial transaction dated 8 February 1525 (=1526).

Verso: Front and side elevations of a portal framed by tall columns and surmounted by a tribune with a balcony of colonettes onto which a small door opens; studies of Tuscan and Ionic capitals, possibly for the same project. As Thode suggested, the sketches are probably studies for more exact drawings sent to the Pope on 4 February 1526. The scale of the tribune study on the *verso* can be estimated from the little door leading to the balcony, and identifies the drawing with the large façade portal rather than with the small entrance to the Medici chapel.

Tolnay (1928, p. 398, Fig. 16) published a perspective sketch in the Archivio Buonarroti (Vol. V, fol. 29v; D.28) as a preliminary study for the ciborium, and Thode (II p. 106) identified F. 107a–f (D.280–285; Casa Buon., Nos. 55, 56, 82, 83, 86, 87) as variations on the capital studies on the *verso* of No. 1. There is not enough evidence to warrant accepting or rejecting the suggestions.

2. Oxford, Ashmolean, No. 311; D.199; F.135. Pl. 14b (Thode II, pp. 106 f.; III, No. 432; Schiavo 1953, pp. 164 f.; Parker 1956, pp. 151 f., with bibliography).

A horizontal section through the centre of the church façade at the level of the tribune platform, showing a stairway and storage closets in the thickness of the wall, and balconies on both the exterior and interior. The design differs from the final solution (cf. Pl. 14c) in that the lateral doors are on axis with the supporting columns and are framed by thin pilasters; there are fewer balusters, and they do not alternate with posts.

The care with which the drawing is finished and inscribed suggests that it was prepared for the Pope. It was probably the project accepted in the autumn of 1531, since the correspondence mentions the exterior balcony; the *terminus ante* is Figiovanni's letter of 19 October 1532, which recommends shifting the side doors from their position in the drawing towards the centre, as in the executed structure.

The fact that a balcony was planned for the exterior as well as the interior (Pl. 14b; inscribed "il vano del pergamo di fuora") and that Figiovanni assumed (*Briefe*, p. 310) that "it would be of marble to unify it with the façade", is of interest for the history of the façade design, since the balcony could not be integrated with any of Michelangelo's façade projects. According to the final scheme of 1520, it would have been built inside a narthex, which would have destroyed its function as a place for the exhibition of relics to the congregation outside the church. But we need not assume that Michelangelo returned to an earlier proposal to face the Quattrocento wall with a marble veneer, because he probably considered the façade a dead issue, and had no expectation of building more than the balcony itself.

Tolnay (1951, Pl. 223) identified a door in the upper level of the northeast corner of the cloister as an entrance portal originally built by Michelangelo for the reliquary tribune. The door is ascribed, I believe rightly, to G.-A. Dosio by Wittkower (1934, p. 203, Figs. 62, 63) and Wachler (1940, pp. 159 f., Figs. 80, 81) on the grounds of Dosio's original drawing for it (Uffizi, *Arch.* 1946).

The existing tribune (Pl. 14c) is not an important example of Michelangelo's work. The columns and entablature are copies of their Quattrocento neighbours, and the upper parts, carved during Michelangelo's absence in Rome, are without distinction. I question whether Michelangelo prepared elevation drawings at all: the door frames are academic purifications of his library designs; the balustrade adheres to an anonymous Cinquecento formula, and the clumsy pilasters are totally alien to his style. Certainly, if Michelangelo had left instructions for the pilasters, they would have been carved alike, but disturbing differences in the capitals and the reliefs can be seen even from a distance.

Florence, the Library of San Lorenzo, 1523–1559

I HISTORY

The history of the design and construction of the Laurentian library (Pl. 15; Fig. 3: 7–8) may be reconstructed in detail, chiefly through Michelangelo's correspondence with his agent at the Vatican, Giovanfrancesco Fattucci (in 1523–1526) and, after a long period of inactivity during which Michelangelo moved permanently to Rome, with the executors of his design in Florence (1550–1559). In view of Wittkower's exemplary study of the library (1934), an outline of its history followed by a chronological study of the drawings will suffice here.

1523 *19 November:* Cardinal Giulio de' Medici is elected to the pontificate as Clement VII.

9/10 December: Michelangelo goes to Rome, where he apparently receives the commission to design a library for the Medici family collection somewhere on the site of the cloister of San Lorenzo. Returning to Florence, he has his assistant, Stefano di Tommaso, prepare and send to Rome a drawing, acknowledged by Fattucci on 30 December (*Briefe*, pp. 198–201).

1524 *2 January:* Michelangelo is asked to send a design by his own hand showing dimensions of separate libraries for Latin and Greek holdings, and providing sufficient light for the vestibule (*Briefe*, p. 204). He replies that he is still uncertain of the intended site (*Lettere*, p. 431, undated).

30 January: Answering a letter of 21 January, the Pope selects a site on the second story of the cloister, *volta a mezodì* (for interpretation see Section I of the list of drawings below), and requests a plan of the lower story. He wants the priests' quarters below to be: (1) kept intact with minimal demolitions; (2) unobstructed by the library foundations and (3) vaulted for security against fire. These orders are frequently reiterated later (*Briefe*, p. 209).

9 February: A new scheme is rejected because it involves demolition of some 14 rooms below; the Pope recommends an alternate site on the square before the church (*Briefe*, p. 211), requests estimate on purchasing property there.

February (late): New plans received in Rome, still involving demolition of cloister rooms (*Briefe*, p. 213).

10 March: Two further plans received; the Pope selects one of dimensions close to those of the final project (Gotti 1875, I, p. 165; additions by K. Frey, *Jhb. d. preuss. Kunstslg.*, XVII, 1896, p. 102, No. 73). Though the site on the square is still being discussed, the plan selected must be for the present site since (1) the floor of the vestibule is 6 br. below that of the library and (2) Fattucci, repeating his instructions on 3 April (*Briefe*, p. 221) indicates the Pope's approval of Michelangelo's request to use the site *"di verso la sacresta vechia"* (cf. Wittkower 1934, p. 218). Fattucci requests drawings of (1) the vestibule stairway, which was not drawn in the plan, (2) the foundations, (3) *qualche fantasia nuova* for the reading room ceiling, since the Pope does not like square coffers with deep recessions, and (4) four small studies at the corners of the reading room, for rare volumes.

13 April: Acknowledgement of drawing for reading room ceiling and library plan with a *crociera*, meaning "crossing" or "transept" (*Briefe*, p. 224). The Pope accepts both, but in August (*Briefe*, p. 234) instructs the architect to build the library in such a way that the *crociera* may be added at a later date.

29 April: Michelangelo is asked to design a lighter substructure which will not require thickening the walls of the priests' quarters (*Briefe*, p. 226); approval given for a vestibule stairway-scheme with two flights.

13 May: Structural solution approved that replaces the thick wall supports by a system of interior and exterior buttresses (*Briefe*, p. 227; Wittkower 1934, pp. 216 f.)

9, 21 July: Approval given to start foundations; estimates requested (*Briefe*, pp. 232 f.)

29 July–2 August: Michelangelo, having requested funds, receives them (*Lettere*, pp. 436, 438), and is told to proceed with haste (*Briefe*, pp. 234 f.). He is requested to add a structure (the one later identified as a chapel?) at the end of the library and to supply specifications for reading desks.

August/September: Baccio Bigio is appointed to direct construction so that Michelangelo may be free to carve figures for the Medici chapel (*Briefe*, p. 236).

September: The Prior of San Lorenzo complains that the new construction looks like a dovecote (*Briefe*, p. 237). Payments for demolition and foundations are recorded in January 1525 (Gronau 1911, pp. 68 ff.)

6 November: The Prior consults Michelangelo about technical problems relating to the buttresses (*Briefe*, p. 240). Work on the substructure continues through the winter.

1525 *3 April:* Entries in Michelangelo's account-books for the library construction: raising of the long walls; carving their exterior window frames (*Lettere*, p. 597; cf. payments in Gronau 1911, pp. 70 ff.)

12 April: Approval of drawings for windows and interior tabernacles of the library. Requests that the chapel at the end of the library be redesigned as a rare book room; that the vestibule stairway be made in a single flight "occupying the whole *ricetto*", rather than two flights; and that the ceiling design for the library be returned to Rome (*Briefe*, p. 250).

10 November: Approval of designs for the rare book room (*Briefe*, p. 265); the scheme demands the purchase and rental of new property to the south (*Briefe*, p. 269).

29 November: Michelangelo is prepared to start the vestibule, but his design is criticized on account of a novel proposal to light it through overhead windows (*Briefe*, p. 268: "one would need to commission two monks to do nothing but clean off the dust").

23 December: Approval of Michelangelo's proposal to light the vestibule from the sides by raising the walls two *braccia*; though the Pope is concerned for the safety of the substructure in view of the added weight (*Briefe*, p. 270; Wittkower 1934, pp. 133 ff.)

1526 *20 January:* The goldsmith, Piloto, writing from Venice, says that he has heard that the vestibule foundations have been started (*Dichtungen*, p. 506). On 23

February the Pope expresses his pleasure that Michelangelo can now turn his attention from the library to the tomb figures (*Briefe*, p. 274).

3 April: The Pope requests that the reading room floor and ceiling be designed to suit an arrangement of reading desks in two files with an aisle in the centre and one on either side (in the final scheme the side aisles are eliminated). Michelangelo, now prepared to design the frame of the entrance door, requests a decision on the rare book room at the opposite end, and is told to proceed on the assumption that it will be built after the vestibule (*Briefe*, p. 279).

18 April: Approval of design for reading room door, with particular praise for the proposed inscription. The drawings are returned 6 June (*Briefe*, pp. 280, 284).

17 June: Five of the vestibule columns are in place; the tabernacles are to be delayed another four months (*Lettere*, p. 453, misdated April; cf. *Briefe*, p. 285n).

17 July; 10 October; 1, 4, 10 November: Repeated instructions to cut down in expences, in favour of work on the chapel. Permission to proceed with the reading room ceiling withheld (*Briefe*, pp. 286 f., *Lettere*, pp. 454 f.)

1533 *3 August:* Clement VII wants to change the kind of wood chosen for the desks and ceiling (*Dicht.*, p. 519).

18 August: Michelangelo says he is ready to prepare the contract signed 30 August (*Dicht.*, p. 520).

23 August: The Pope gives Michelangelo permission to leave Florence for Rome providing he arranges for the execution of desks, ceilings, figures, and stairs (Gotti, I, 225).

30 August: Michelangelo gives a contract to five masons to erect the vestibule stairway and two doors, one at the entrance to the reading room (*Lettere*, p. 707; Wittkower 1934, pp. 167 ff.) The stairway is to follow the clay model executed by Michelangelo, and to be made of fourteen steps, of which at least the lower seven, those with "rivolte" (the curved side extensions of the final design?) are to be of one piece. The doors apparently were carved but only the one leading to the reading room was put in place (Wittkower 1934, pp. 186–195). Stones were carved for the stairway (Vasari VII, 236; *Lettere*, p. 550n), but none was used.

1534–1549: Vasari records an attempt by Nicolò Tribolo, during the pontificate of Paul III (1534–1549) to complete the vestibule stairway (VI, p. 92; VII, p. 236). After placing four steps, he seeks unsuccessfully to get instructions from Michelangelo – who now resides permanently in Rome – on how to proceed. Wittkower proposed (1934, pp. 169 ff.) that Tribolo's attempt was made in 1549/1550 (cf. *Lettere, loc. cit.*) and that evidence of it is preserved in the masonry behind the present stairway; his effort to erect these stairs against the south wall was in opposition to Michelangelo's intentions.

1549–1550: Probable date of execution of the reading room ceiling, redesigned with emblems of Cosimo I (1537–1574). The floor, which mirrors the design, and the desks, follow shortly (Vasari VII, p. 203; Wittkower 1934, pp. 196 ff.; Tolnay 1955, p. 239).

1555 *28 September:* (Michelangelo wrote "1 January" as well as "28 September" on the *verso*; but on the latter date he sent it via his nephew Leonardo): Michelangelo, in reply to a letter from Giorgio Vasari, who has been commissioned together with Ammanati to complete the stairway, says that he no longer recalls the original design (*Lettere*, pp. 312, 548, misdated; Vasari *Nachlass*, I, pp. 415 f., 419 f.) He describes and sketches a new scheme involving three flights; the central one ("for the signore") is oval and the sides ("for the retainers") straight, as in the final project. But apparently there is no landing midway: all three flights are continued to a landing before the reading room door (reconstruction by Panofsky 1922, pp. 262 ff.) The upper portion of the stairway bridges a passageway along the wall, so that the wall mouldings shall not be covered by the new construction.

1558   16 December–1559 29 January: The staircase plan proposed to Vasari having been abandoned, Ammanati is commissioned by Cosimo I to execute a new one with Michelangelo's advice. He sends sketches of two of Michelangelo's earlier designs to find which he prefers (Gaye, III, p. 11; Panofsky 1922, pp. 267 ff.), but Michelangelo makes a new clay model (*Lettere*, p. 344), which he sends to Florence (correspondence on the transportation: *Lettere*, pp. 348 f. misdated 1560; *Briefe*, pp. 358 ff.) In his accompanying letter (*Lettere*, p. 550), Michelangelo instructs Ammanati that (1) the stairway should be isolated from the wall except at the door, (2) the side flights should not have balusters, but "seats" on every other riser, (3) the staircase should fill the vestibule as little as possible, (4) wood may be used in place of stone. The design of details he leaves to Ammanati.

1559   18–22 February: Ammanati sends the model and letter to Cosimo I in Pisa, asking whether the stairway should be made in wood rather than stone (the Duke chooses stone for permanence), and whether he should get drawings of the ceiling and façade from Michelangelo (the Duke says "yes"). Funds are supplied for the construction (Gaye III, pp. 11–13). The choice of stone for the stairway makes it possible to employ steps for the centre flight carved in 1533–1534 (Wittkower 1934, p. 176).

1568: Date painted on windows of the reading room.

1571: Date of inscription over entrance door. Opening of the library to the public (Wittkower 1934, p. 200). Modern alterations include a remodelling of the façade which gave the vestibule its upper row of windows (Pl. 15). The completion of the articulation on the upper level inside the vestibule, and the addition of a circular reading room on the south of the library (see Wittkower, pp. 123 ff., 200 ff.)

II DRAWINGS

There are over thirty original sheets of drawings for the Laurentian library, more than for any other building by Michelangelo. This is due partly to the fact that dealings with the patron, Clement VII, were carried on entirely by mail, and partly to the nature of the design problem: the construction of a major building on two levels over an existing structure. Yet, the drawings are so varied in purpose that the development of the design remains conjectural at many points. I have attempted to arrange them in chronological order, so far as this is possible; *lost projects or drawings are indicated in the following catalogue by numbers in parentheses.*

I. THE SITE PLAN: JANUARY–FEBRUARY 1524

(1). 2 January: Plan with separate rooms for Latin and Greek books and a separate vestibule. The site is still not fixed. On 30 January, the Pope selects a site – probably recommended by Michelangelo – "volta a mezodì", which apparently means "on the south" as suggested by drawing No. 2, rather than "oriented N.–S."

2. Casa Buonarroti, No. 10v; D.58 (Tolnay 1935, p. 95, Fig. 2; 1951, p. 172). A site plan with the library orientated like the present one but on the S. rather than W. side of the main cloister, bisecting the smaller cloister to the left in Fig. 3:6, and Pl. 15.

3. Casa Buon., No. 9v; D.57 (Tolnay 1951, p. 172, Pl. 342). A sketch of the cloister showing the library on the E. side, oriented E.–W., on an axis parallel to that of the church.

Dr Wilde informs me that Nos. 2 and 3 were drawn on the same sheet and later separated. The decision of 30 January – which conforms to No. 2 – was retracted on 9 February in favour of a project – conforming to No. 3 – "che va in sula piazza e inverso il borgo Santo Lorenzo". The two drawings may have been sent to Rome at the same time, to become the basis for the decision of 9 February, or No. 2 may have been drawn in the period 30 January–9 February and No. 3 after 9 February in response to that decision.

4. Casa Buon., No. 81; D.117; F.235. A sketch showing the ownership of property before the church, probably made in response to the letter of 9 February, which requests estimates on purchasing the property.

5. Archivio Buon., Vol. I, fol. 121r; D.26 (Tolnay 1928, p. 466, No. 25; 1954, p. 156, Pl. 194). A plan of the rooms below the library at its present site. The sketch is a study for the buttress-system. Four buttresses similar to those actually built are drawn on the exterior of the W. wall at the vestibule end, and four corresponding ones on the interior of the E. wall. The drawings may be dated after the letter of 29 April 1524, and before that of 13 May.

II. DESIGNS FOR THE READING ROOM AND RARE BOOK ROOM, 1524–1533

(1). 10 March 1524: The Pope requests rare book studies at four corners of the reading room, and a sketch of the ceiling.

(2). 13 April: Michelangelo's plan for a reading room with a *crociera*; subsequently delayed and then abandoned (the *crociera* was probably an additional wing extending perpendicularly from the centre of the room on the W., where the modern rotonda appears in Pl. 15: a true cross-plan would have been prevented by the cloister on the E.).

(3). April–May: Studies of the support system.

4. Casa Buon., No. 42; D.84; F.199. Pl. 19b (identified by Tolnay 1928, p. 402n). Interior elevation of the reading room. Articulation begins at the floor, not at the level of the desk tops (cf. Pl. 16); recessed columns are employed as well as pilasters. The windows are on the second story, higher and farther apart than in the final project. Date: prior to the solution of the support system in the spring of 1524, since

the window design would determine where the walls had to be reinforced. Witt-kower places it early in the year (1934, pp. 145 f.), because of his deduction that the present low windows precede the first vestibule drawings.

5. Casa Buon., No. 96r, v; D.127 (Tolnay 1935, pp. 97 f., Figs. 5, 7). *Recto:* four handsome chalk sketches of framing elements related to No. 4; the door leading to the vestibule, flanked by encased columns; a semicircular niche (for the lower story of No. 4?); two windows close to the final design but still with crowning pediments. *Verso:* scale drawing of the door; its relatively conventional forms conform to those of Pl. 25b and recommend a date early in 1524.

(6). Michelangelo's sketch in response to the Pope's request for an unusual ceiling is well received on 13 April 1524, but the Pope believes that the intention to make the ceiling division the same width as the wall bays cannot be realized because the lateral panels on the sketch are too broad. The same problem arises in Pl. 19a (No. 7 below), but this must be an alternative study because the one sent to Rome had "small figures" in the panels.

7. Casa Buon., No. 126; D.146; F.266. Pl. 19a (Wittkower, p. 196). A study for one bay of the ceiling, similar to the final design except that the bay is broader, as it was in No. 6, which probably was done at the same time.

8. Oxford, Ashmolean, No. 308v; D.345 (identified by Tolnay 1955, pp. 237 ff.; Parker 1956, pp. 149 f.) A rapid sketch of the ceiling scheme. Indications of the wall pilasters demonstrate co-ordination of wall and ceiling in the same proportions as in the final solution. Tolnay placed it before Nos. 6 and 7, on the grounds that it is a hasty sketch, and that the ornamental motives in the rectangular fields are farther from the executed ceiling; he may be correct. I place it here on the basis of its more mature integration with the wall system, in which event it would date with the final wall design, before construction started in August, 1524.

(9). July 1524: The Pope agrees to "quella agiunta che viene in testa della libreria". This may be the chapel of No. 10.

10. Casa Buon., No. 89v; D.121; F.71. Pl. 20b (Wittkower, p. 181). The plan at the upper left – a rectangular room with an oval dome supported on corner piers and with pilasters on the long walls – is probably for the chapel to the S. of the reading room. This structure was cancelled in April 1525 in favour of a rare book room, but the drawing may be as much as a year earlier (see further comments, No. III, 6 below). The drawing published by Tolnay (1935, p. 101, Fig. 10) as a study for the chapel is for a much smaller structure which is too shallow for the purpose, though it appears to be of this period (D.180; Wilde 1953, No. 38r, p. 74).

(11). April 1525: Final (?) sketches for interior tabernacles and windows are sent to Rome.

12; 13. Casa Buon., Nos. 79, 80; D.115, 116; F.166, 167. Pl. 18b (Wittkower, pp. 182 ff.) Alternative plans for a rare book room of triangular form intended to replace the chapel at the end of the reading room. The base of the triangle is formed by the S. wall of the library; the angular sides solve the problem of neighbouring houses abutting the cloister. No. 12, rapidly sketched, has flat niches, free-standing corner columns, and an open central area: in No. 13 (Pl. 18b), which is more finished, the niches become more plastic, the columns are encased in the wall, and a round central desk interrupts the main axis. The strange cloister vault which can be visualized rising from the short, truncated angles and the long walls, is unique in Renaissance planning. These drawings were requested in April and accepted in November 1525, but construction was postponed in 1526 and later abandoned.

(14). In April 1526, the Pope asks that the reading room desks be arranged with aisles on the side as well as in the centre, with consequent changes in the floor and ceiling design. This results from a misunderstanding of Michelangelo's elevation, which was conceived for desks placed against the wall (Pl. 16; Wittkower, p. 145). The request must have been withdrawn.

15, 16. Casa Buon., No. 94; D.126, Fig. 150; F.269. Archivio Buon., Vol. I, fol. 101; D.14 (Tolnay 1928, p. 462, No. 13). Sketches of uncertain date for the reading desks. (Arch. Buon., Vol XIII, fol. 79v; D.38; Tolnay 1928, p. 472, 1954, p. 156, Fig. 190 [with different folio numbers] may also be a desk design).

17. British Museum, No. 37; D.157; F.117a, b. (Wilde 1953, pp. 73 f.) Frames for the main door of the reading room on the inner (*recto*) and vestibule (*verso*) side. Drawings for this door were approved in April and returned in June 1526.

18. Casa Buon., No. 111; D.478. Pl. 25b (Wittkower, pp. 186 ff., Fig. 49). Scale drawing of No. 17r. The principal elements were preserved in the actual door, but with substantial changes in treatment. Nos. 18, 19, 21 are working drawings, probably by an assistant.

19. Casa Buon., No. 98; D.474 (*ibid.*, Fig. 47). Scale drawing of No. 17v. On the vestibule side, the actual door is close to this drawing, but the slight changes are revealing (see Wittkower's analysis). The final design may date from 1533, when a contract was signed for the carving.

20. Casa Buon., No. 53; D.94; F.49, 50. Moulding profiles for Nos. 18 and 19.

21. Casa Buon., No. 95; D.472 (*ibid.*, pp. 190 ff., Fig. 51). Scale drawing of the exterior entrance door to the vestibule, related to Nos. 18 and 19. This door was partially carved, but not erected, in 1533.

No drawings are known for the reading room from the period following Michelangelo's departure from Rome in 1533. At this time the floor, ceiling and desks were not yet in place, though the library was roofed (Gronau 1911, pp. 74 ff.) The wall articulation of the reading room was probably complete; it appears in its present state in a group of drawings made in the building by Battista da Sangallo, probably in the period 1535–1540 (Lille, Musée des Beaux-Arts, Nos. 889–901, subsequently copied by Oreste Vannocci, Siena, Bibl. Communale, S. IV. 1, fols. 28v, ff. On Uffizi, *arch*. 1944r and v, Battista also drew the interior elevation and a measured exterior window frame. For the dating see Ackerman 1954, pp. 208 f.) The rare book room had not been started, and the exterior façades remained unfinished (Ammanati requested a design for the latter in 1559: Gaye, III, p. 12).

III. DESIGNS FOR THE VESTIBULE AND STAIRCASE

(1). March 1524. In the first plan for the present site, the vestibule is 6 br. (3·5 m.) lower than the reading room (now, 3·03 m.) The stairway is not shown.

(2). 29 April 1524. Approval of a stairway of two flights.

3. Arch. Buon., Vol. I, fol. 101, pp. 3, 4; D.15 (Tolnay 1928, p. 400, Fig. 17; Wittkower, p. 128, Fig. 20). A sketchy vestibule plan (*verso*) with flights of stairs against the E. and W. walls rising to a platform along the breadth of the S. – reading room – wall.

4. Haarlem, Teyler Museum, No. 33v; D.298; F.315; Pl. 20a (Wittkower, pp. 146 ff.; rejected by Tolnay 1928, p. 402; 1935, p. 102). An elevation of the W. wall of the vestibule with a flight of steps; the elevated principal Order is first drawn with three bays and corrected above to four bays, of which the one on the right is not drawn. Whether an original or a copy, No. 4 reflects an initial phase of the elevation, when an attempt was made to carry through a version of the final reading room elevation, with its plain base and low windows, into the vestibule. The solution was quickly abandoned due to its high, dull base and to the fact that the niches or windows, while level with the reading room windows, would have been much narrower. The date is probably shortly after No. 2.

5. Casa Buon., No. 89v; D121; F.72 (Tolnay 1928, p. 402; 1935, p. 102; Wittkower, pp. 153 f.) Another four-bay elevation; the scheme proved to be impractical. If the S. wall has four bays, then the central pillar splits the reading room entrance into two small doors; if, to avoid this, the S. wall is given three bays and the other walls four, the consistency of the articulation system is lost. In addition to this anomaly, motifs used here are strange to the library projects; possibly the sketch belongs with the contemporary group of tomb projects discussed on pp. 29 f.

6. Casa Buon., No. 89r; D.121; F.71. Pl. 20b (Tolnay 1928, pp. 400 ff.; 1935, p. 102; Wittkower, pp. 156 f.) Plan of the vestibule (lower centre) in which the wall flights are shorter than in Nos. 3 and 4, rising 8–9 steps to platforms in the S. corners, from which 3–4 steps continue to a central platform and 2–3 to the door. Corner piers jutting in at the S. corners support a vault. The shortened flights, heavy piers, and similarities to the chapel plan on the same sheet suggest a 3-bay elevation. Although, as Wittkower notes, a sketch of the steps in this plan appears in No. 12, of 1525, Michelangelo is not likely to have considered projecting corner piers after the supports had been started in the summer of 1524.

(7). 12 April 1525. The Pope agrees that "if it seems advisable to you, change (the stairways) from two, to one that fills the whole *ricetto*". The decision was partly prompted by the difficulty of getting a uniform elevation on the side and entrance walls with wall flights.

8. Casa Buon., No. 48r; D.90; F.234. Pl. 21 (Tolnay 1928, p. 402; 1935, p. 103; Wittkower, pp. 128 ff.) Elevation of the W. wall of the vestibule, which is vaulted and has a free-standing stair. The attempt to restrict the total height to that of the reading room explains differences from the final scheme (Pl. 17. See Wittkower's analysis): the main story, being much less high, has correspondingly smaller recessed

columns and hence space is left for pilasters flanking the niches. The low elevation emphasizes horizontality, which is accentuated by a strong entablature and by the absence of verticals in the upper story. Light comes only from the vault (Wittkower, pp. 133 f., Fig. 12). The drawing may be dated between Nos. 7 and 10.

9. Casa Buon., No. 48v; D.90 (Tolnay 1935, pp. 102 ff., Fig. 9). A quickly sketched tabernacle framed by two columns (or pilasters?) on the left and four on the right. The system is the same as that on the *recto*, No. 8; I agree with Dussler that the drawing is too rough to support Tolnay's view that it represents a step toward the final solution in which the tabernacles are framed by pairs of recessed columns.

(10). November 1525. Michelangelo's answer to the lighting problem is to use round overhead windows in the ceiling (ochi di vetro nel palco) under skylights in the roof, but the Pope objects that collecting dust would cause a maintenance problem. The word *palco* suggests that by this time the plan to vault the vestibule has been abandoned. Michelangelo next proposes to raise the walls by 2 *braccia* to gain clearance for wall windows. Though in Rome there is doubt about the ability of the structure to sustain the added weight, the walls eventually are raised still higher since the abandonment of the vault eliminates the structural problem. This scheme is accepted in February 1526. Evidence of the heightening of the vestibule appeared in the exterior masonry before its modern restoration (see Fig. 6 and Wittkower, pp. 123 ff., Figs. 2, 3).

11; 12. Casa Buon., No. 92r and v; D.124; F.164, 165. Pls. 22, 23 (Tolnay 1928, pp. 406 ff.; 1935, pp. 102, 104; Wittkower, pp. 156 ff.) Sketches for the staircase and for base mouldings. The staircase drawings evolve methodically from the original wall-type of Pl. 20b (No. 12, top) to projects with a central concave flight filling the breadth of the vestibule in response to No. 7 above (No. 11, left centre, No. 12, bottom); then to flights extending obliquely from the reading room door (No. 12, centre), and ultimately to a unified free-standing stairway in which the side flights are still distinguished from the centre (No. 11, right centre; bottom). The sheet was drawn shortly after No. 7: April 1525?

13; 14. British Museum, No. 36r and v; D.173; F.118, 119 (Wittkower, p. 154; Wilde 1953, pp. 71 f.) The *recto* (Pl. 25a) has a careful study of the base and lower part of the main story of the vestibule, in transition from No. 8 to the final project. Volutes have been added to the base, but almost touch the bottom moulding, indicating a lower overall elevation; recessed panels appear in the base beneath the tabernacles. The drawing is done over earlier jottings, including a wall section close to No. 8: the main story still has the complete entablature surmounted by a low second story (lower than in No. 8) and a vault. The *verso* contains mouldings similar to those of Nos. 11 and 12. The wall section appears to be contemporary with No. 8 or earlier; the principal drawing, of the base, may be, as Wilde suggests, of the last quarter of 1525. Profiles for the wall mouldings, etc. of about this period appear on Casa Buon., No. 62; D.100 (Tolnay 1928, p. 475, Fig. 82).

15. Casa Buon., No. 39r and v.; D.82; F.209, 210 (Wittkower, p. 140). Two sketches for windows in the clerestory. Framed by paired pilasters, they are closer in their tall proportions to the final scheme than to No. 8. Since the present windows may not be Michelangelo's, No. 15 could be nearer to his intentions. The high clerestory, obviously of more than two *braccia*, is subsequent to No. 10 and the section sketch of No. 13, and is therefore late in 1525 or early in 1526.

16. Casa Buon., No. 37r and v; D.81 (Tolnay 1928, p. 433, Figs. 39, 40). *Recto:* another window, nearer the final solution. *Verso:* uncertain (Tolnay and Dussler propose a pedestal of the stair railing).

17–19. Uffizi, *arch.* 816, 817, 1464. (Wittkower, pp. 161 ff.; Figs. 28, 27, 26). Copies by Antonio da Sangallo the Younger of alternative designs for a free-standing stairway with interlocking steps – variations on No. 11, bottom (Pl. 22). Sketches by Battista da Sangallo (Lille, No. 885; Wittkower, pp. 165 f., Fig. 32) and Oreste Vannocci (Siena, S. IV. 1., fol. 65r; *ibid.*, p. 162, Fig. 31) may or may not reflect authentic designs. The series is perceptively analysed by Wittkower.

(20). Final vestibule scheme, accepted in February, partly executed in June 1526. No progress on the stairway at this time.

(21). A clay model of the stairs by Michelangelo serves as the basis of the contract of August 1533. The lower seven steps are to be designed with "rivolte". Wittkower's demonstration (pp. 175 ff.) that some of the existing central steps were probably cut in 1533–1534 leads to the identification of "rivolte" as the lobed side projections (cf. *contra*, Tolnay 1935, p. 104n).

When Michelangelo left Florence in 1533, the vestibule was complete through the main story but apparently unfinished above. The drawings of Battista da Sangallo cited at the end of section II show the clerestory level as rough masonry. Michelangelo is thought to have completed one wall at this level up to the cornice (Wittkower, p. 203), but it is unlikely that Battista would have drawn it as he did if he had had an authentic model. Possibly both the design and the execution are post-Michelangelo. Most of the door frames required by the 1533 contract were carved but not set in place (Wittkower, pp. 167 ff., 186 ff.)

22. Cod. Vat. 3211, fol. 87v; D.225 (Panofsky 1922, pp. 262 ff.; Tolnay 1927, p. 157; Wittkower, pp. 171 ff., Figs. 33, 34). A rough sketch illustrating Michelangelo's letter of 26 September 1555 to Vasari, showing the stairs in a front and a side elevation in a form approaching that of the final solution.

22a. Lille, Musée des Beaux-Arts, No. 94v; D.301v. As recently suggested by Tolnay (1960, Catalogue No. 247), the quick-sketch in the lower corner of a stairway plan with oval treads closely resembles the sketch on No. 22, and may be another scheme jotted down in the Autumn of 1555. Dussler noted the resemblance to the actual stairway but discounted it for reasons that are not clear.

(23). December 1558. Michelangelo executes a second clay model for the stairway, used as a guide by Ammanati in building the existing stairway (see the historical outline under 1558).

Fortifications of Florence, 1528–1529

I HISTORY

A republican government was established after the banishment of the Medici from Florence in 1527; early in 1529 the Medici Pope, Clement VII, enlisted the help of the Imperial forces to regain the city by conquest (see Cecil Roth, *The Last Florentine Republic*, London, 1925). Michelangelo was appointed to a committee called the *Nove della Milizia*, established in January 1529, to complete the fortifications begun by the Medici in 1526, and on 6 April he was raised to the post of Governor General and Procurator of Fortifications (*Lettere*, p. 701; for accounts of his activities of 1529–1530, see Gotti 1875, I, pp. 182–200, II, pp. 62–74; Gaye, II, pp. 184–222; Milanesi, in Vasari, VII, pp. 366–376; summaries in Tolnay 1948, pp. 10 f. and Schiavo 1953, pp. 247 ff.) He had been engaged in the improvement of the fortifications before the emergency arose; in September 1528, the Gonfaloniere Capponi called him from Settignano to a conference on the defences of San Miniato (*Briefe*, p. 296). *Ricordi* of July and September 1528, appear on drawings for the bastions of the Porta and Prato d'Ognissanti.

In July 1529, Michelangelo consulted with the defenders of Pisa after visiting the Leghorn fortifications, and on 2 August he was in Ferrara under government orders to inspect the fortifications there, reputedly the most efficient in Italy. He returned directly to Florence, but on about 25 September deserted his post and fled to Venice, arriving there on the 28th with the intention of continuing to France (overtures to Francis I were made through the French ambassador; L. Dorez, *Bibliothèque de l'École de Chartres*, LXXVIII, 1917, pp. 209 ff.) He justified the flight as an escape from a plot against his life (*Lettere*, p. 457), but contemporary accounts claim that he had been forewarned of the treason of the Florentine commander, Malatesta Baglione (which brought about the fall of the city a year later), and escaped for fear of Medici reprisals. On 30 September he was declared a rebel by the Balía. Urged by his friends Battista della Palla and the Florentine Orator in Ferrara, Galeotto Giugni, he returned to Florence at the end of November and immediately started repairing the damaged campanile of San Miniato (Gaye, II, pp. 209 ff.; Gotti, I, pp. 90 ff.; Varchi, Bk. X, pp. 133 f.; Condivi, Ch. 37; Vasari, VII, pp. 198, 369 ff.; *Briefe*, p. 301). The siege of the city had started in October, and ended in capitulation in August 1530. Michelangelo went into hiding to evade the ensuing terror, which brought about the death or imprisonment of leading patriots, among them della Palla; his pardon from the Pope in November (Gaye, II, pp. 221 f.) must have amounted to a sentence of enforced labour on the Medici chapel, though Clement was more disposed than Michelangelo to forget the past (*Corr.*, p. 42).

Apart from the aberration which prompted his brief desertion, Michelangelo devoted his entire energy to the fortifications throughout the war; his value to the defence is indicated by the reluctance of the Balía to spare him for more than a few days (Gaye, II, p. 199), by its willingness to restore him to his post after his desertion, and by the urgency with which allied cities requested his aid (*ibid.*, pp. 184 ff., 206).

Contemporary accounts agree that Michelangelo was occupied mainly with the defence of the hill of San Miniato. Varchi says (Bk. X, p. 146) that he took charge of the fortifications, "e principalmente quella del Monte . . . di San Miniato": an anonymous contemporary reports (Gotti, I, p. 183; Milanesi, in Vasari VII, pp. 367 f.): "di primo aspetto attese a fortificare il poggio di San Miniato et Santo Francesco". Both authors add that he found the Medici bastion foundations of 1526 too extended for proper defence and decided to shorten the lines, including in the fortress only the church and monastery of San Miniato, whose campanile provided an ideal observation post over the southern approaches. Here he raised "due piuttosto puntoni che bastioni" (Varchi, *loc. cit.; puntoni* are probably simplified salients of a triangular trace). These were defended in turn by "un alto e fortissimo cavaliere" (a new defensive device to raise part of the artillery on a platform above the bastions to increase its range). Curtain walls with bastions and ditches had to be built up the slopes of the hill to bring the fort within the defensive perimeter of the old city walls along the banks of the Arno (Pl. 25c). Construction was under way in April 1529 (letter in Vasari, VII, p. 366).

The project for defending San Miniato was opposed by two successive Gonfalonieri, Capponi and Carducci, the first of whom reputedly was motivated by treachery. Michelangelo claimed that, in spite of the support given him by other members of the government, his inspection trips out of the city were used as ruses to undermine the project, and that on his return from Ferrara his labourers and materials had been removed (Letters of Battista Busini, ed. Milanesi, Florence, 1860, pp. 103 f., 115; Gotti, I, pp. 186 f.)

The San Miniato defences were experimental in design, as were all bastioned systems in the 1520's, and were criticized for their great number of flanks and artillery positions and for the restricted range allowed to the cannon (Varchi, *loc. cit.*; anonymous chronicler, Gotti, I, p. 183); but the professional soldier who wrote the anonymous account defended them with the comment that too many positions were better than too few, and that the defences were placed "marvellously" accordingly to the nature of the terrain. The only fault, he said, was that the government did not assign a military adviser to Michelangelo, adding "but what can mere merchants understand of war, which requires no less experience than all the other arts?"

The fortifications were temporarily constructed of packed earth mixed with straw and revetted with unbaked bricks made from soil strengthened by a mixture of oakum and dung (Varchi, *loc. cit.*) After 1534 the Medici replaced them in masonry; it was the later, permanent defences that Vasari painted in his fresco of the siege in the Palazzo Vecchio (ill. Schiavo 1949, Pl. 156, with Vasari's preparatory plan, Pl. 155, and a schematic plan of the walls of the city, Pl. 157). Vasari wrote that the permanent fortifications followed Michelangelo's design (Vasari, *Ragionamenti*, in *Vite* VIII, p. 195; Schiavo, *loc. cit.*), but his claim is hard to substantiate. The fresco, and later plans of Florence (cf. G. Boffito and A. Mori, *Piante e vedute di Firenze*, Florence, 1926, especially the Stefano Bonsignori bird's-eye facing p. xxiv) show a conventional early Italian system that only vaguely reflects Varchi's description; it is apparent that the shortcomings of the temporary earthworks mentioned by Michelangelo's critics were eliminated, though the advantages of ingenious siting probably were retained.

Condivi (Ch. 38) and Vasari (VII, p. 200) report that Michelangelo, on returning from Venice, devised a protection for the damaged campanile of San Miniato consisting of wool mattresses and balls hung from the cornice; but Milanesi (Vasari, *loc. cit.*, note) discovered that the makeshift was invented in October, during Michelangelo's absence (Varchi, Bk. X, p. 153, attributes the device to the defenders).

Contemporary reports do not assign more than the San Miniato defences to Michelangelo. His position as Governor General and his drawings for various points along the city perimeter imply that other fortifications were built after his designs, but his name does not appear in Varchi's descriptions of them (Bk. X, pp. 147 ff.) I shall discuss below the paradox that while all the written sources refer to San Miniato, none of the drawings can be associated with these defences.

II DRAWINGS

Michelangelo's surviving drawings for the fortifications of 1528–1530 are preserved in the Casa Buonarroti. Listed by Gotti (1875, II, pp. 185 ff.) and Thode (1908, III, pp. 79 f.), they were classified and analysed first by Tolnay (1940, pp. 131 ff.) Their dynamic formal character has been discussed by Scully (1952, pp. 38 ff.)

All the drawings are studies for bastions at the city gates and angles of the medieval walls (Pl. 25c). By checking site notations in Michelangelo's hand with sixteenth-century plans of the fortifications, Tolnay was able to localize some of the projects.

I. IDENTIFIED DRAWINGS

A. Bastion for the angle at Prato d'Ognissanti, at the western limit of Florence on the city side of the Arno. As the most acute angle in the medieval enceinte, unprotected by flanking walls, it required the most elaborate fortification. The new designs incorporate the medieval Torre delle Serpe into the system.

a. Cancroid Trace

Four groups of studies (Casa Buon., Nos. 17, 17v, 16, 16v; D.64, 63; Tolnay, 1940, Figs. 15, 14, 16; *idem* 1951, Pl. 353) for a final, pen-and-wash drawing (Casa Buon., No. 15; our Pl. 26a; D.62; Tolnay, Fig. 17). The basic proposal is to construct claw-like curved salients on either side of a central recessed concave form. The initial studies on Nos. 16 and 17 have the drawback that the forward curved faces of the salients cannot be covered by fire from the flanks. In the final scheme this is remedied by protruding orillons on the flanks. The trace is unorthodox because it has no provision for covering the curtain walls on either side; instead, the curtains are given protruding orillons. No. 17v has a *ricordo* of a loan dated September 1528; No. 15 (Pl. 26a) shows a Medici bastion of 1526 a little to the east (left) of Michelangelo's, as recommended by the report of Machiavelli cited below.

b. Stellate Trace

Two groups of studies (Casa Buon., No. 30, 13v; D.77, 60; Tolnay, Figs. 18, 19) for a final pen-and-wash drawing (Casa Buon., No. 13; Pl. 26b; D.60; Tolnay, Fig. 20). The concave core of the first trace is retained, but the curved flanks become acute triangular salients expanding from the centre like the points of a star. The ditch also is star shaped. In this trace the curtains may be covered from the flanks of the bastion, though the curved faces of the outermost salients are still unprotected. Because of its close connection with the Porta al Prato bastion, Pl. 26b seems to be the final solution. One of the salients of No. 13v is labelled "pietra".

B. Bastion of the Porta al Prato, the city gate immediately to the north of the above angle. The gate is identified in a note on Casa Buon., No. 14.

Two groups of studies (Casa Buon., No. 20, 20v; D.67; Tolnay, Figs. 25, 24) for a final pen-and-wash drawing (Casa Buon., No. 14; our Pl. 27a; D.61; Tolnay, Fig. 21). The trace is a condensed version of A2, lacking the concave core, and has the same blind spots at the faces of the salients. Casa Buon., No. 14 has a *ricordo* of July 1528, on the *verso*.

C. Bastion for the Porta alla Giustizia, the easternmost gate on the north bank of the Arno, just across the river from the Colle San Miniato.

One study (Casa Buon., No. 19; D.66; Tolnay, Fig. 22), rapidly washed in, but still tentative in form, identified "la porta alla iustitia". An irregular trace with curved and angled salients overlooking the Arno, and minimal protection on the side away from the river. The scheme apparently influenced Antonio da Sangallo the Younger in his study for the same bastion (ill. Scully, 1952, p. 44).

D. A sketch (Casa Buon., No. 11v; D.59; Tolnay 1951, Pl. 352) of the existing medieval wall "dalla torre del miracolo insino al bastione di San Piero Gattolino" (the present Porta Romana, the southernmost city gate, at the far right in Pl. 25c). Below, a bastion with two irregular salients, smaller and simpler than those used for gates.

2. UNIDENTIFIED DRAWINGS

A. Bastion for a gate in a straight stretch of city wall. The gate, flanked by short buttress walls on the city side, may have been arched, but probably had no tower. It could have been the Porta San Miniato, as suggested by Tolnay, but there is no internal evidence for an identification.

Casa Buon., Nos. 24 and 22r; D.71, 69 (Tolnay, Figs. 9, 8) are crustacean schemes with three curved, claw-like salients on either side of the bastion. They are probably the earliest in the series, being of a complex construction with a maximum of unprotected face and a minimum of mobility and range for the artillery. The trace is simplified in Casa Buon., No. 21; D.68 (Tolnay, Fig. 7) and Casa Buon., No. 23; D.70 (Tolnay, Fig. 6), which is the closest to later sixteenth-century traces, such as those of Maggi and Paciotto; the claw design gives way to two angled salients with straight faces and orillons, and straight flanks covering the curtains, but the centre of the bastion is crowded with a concave rampart inhibiting flexibility and range.

B. Bastions for other gates

Claw-like salients are used in several fantastic studies on Casa Buon., 22v; D.69 (Tolnay,

Fig. 10); and in a finished drawing, Casa Buon. 25; our Pl. 27b; D.72 (Tolnay, Fig. 13).
Casa Buon. 26; D.73, and 18; D.65 (Tolnay, Figs. 12, 11) have simpler traces with straight
faces and flanks.

Groups 2 A and B appear to be the earliest in the collection; they are the tightest in
style and the least practical in trace.

C. Later drawings for gate bastions. Two sheets for unidentified gates developing
further the traces for the Porta and Prato d'Ognissanti.

Casa Buon., 27v, 27; our Pl. 28a; D.74 (Tolnay, Figs. 27, 26) are similar schemes for a
towered gate, of which the *recto* is more highly developed. Here ravelins (outworks)
appear for the first time (a separate study of ravelins *per se* appears on Casa Buon.,
No. 29; D.76 [Tolnay 1951, Pl. 351]); the bastion is designed in three independent sections: a polygonal core at the centre between two salients with acute angles and curved
faces. The passages to the gate are covered by casemates in the curtains. Fantastic variations on the trace are sketched in chalk at the top of the sheet.

Casa Buon., No. 28 (Tolnay, Fig. 23), 28v (Tolnay 1951, Pl. 350); D.75. The *recto* is a
bastion for a gate similar to the Porta al Prato and the *verso* a bastion for an angle of the
walls near a gate which is not shown. These are the only drawings in the series in which
no curves are employed, and No. 28, a simplified version of No. 27 (Pl. 28a), is the most
practical in the collection from a military standpoint; it resembles the "tenaille trace"
of the seventeenth century.

For the criticism and dating of the Casa Buonarroti drawings it is essential to determine how they were to have been used. For several reasons I believe that they are studies
for permanent fortifications in masonry:

1. The same wash technique is used to indicate the new bastions and the medieval
masonry walls. (2) Where earthworks are planned, they are not shown in wash, but are
labelled "terra" (Nos. 14, 19, 23, 27, 27v; Pls. 27a, 28a). (3) One drawing (13v) has the indication "pietra" on the foremost salient. (4) Most decisive is the fact that the complex
forms and fine detail used in every drawing could not be constructed except in masonry;
thin cannon embrasures, pointed salients, and sharp angles are sufficient proof.

Extensive permanent fortifications could not have been contemplated after the start
of the war and the formation of the Nove della Milizia in January 1529. When the siege
started ten months later, vast stretches of defences had been raised and bastions placed
at every major gate (Varchi, pp. 147 ff.) Given the speed of activity, only temporary
construction such as Varchi described for the San Miniato bastions is conceivable;
Varchi also spoke of the packed-earth technique in describing the bastion of the Porta
alla Giustizia and its adjoining walls, and mentioned masonry only once: at the angle bastion of the Prato d'Ognissanti "outside, opposite the tower, they *began* to wall a powerful
cavalier all in stone, as can still be seen" (*loc. cit.*) Apparently even this could not be
completed.

It would have been fruitless for Michelangelo to design elaborate permanent structures during the period when he was raising temporary defences under the pressure of

an imminent attack. A more likely explanation of his drawings is that they were made in 1528 when he was a consultant on fortifications (see above, p. 43). Before the war had started, the Florentines probably felt that there was time to raise a permanent system of defence, since the Pope was still reeling from the effects of the Sack of Rome. The two *ricordi* of 1528 jotted on the drawings support, if they do not confirm this assumption. The difference of a few months in the dating of the drawings is not itself important, but it helps, first, to explain why there is no relationship in form and construction between them and the temporary fortifications described by the chroniclers; second, to demonstrate why the surviving defences do not resemble the drawings; and third, to remove the implication that Michelangelo was amusing himself with impractical experiments at a time of emergency. The absence of drawings for the temporary fortifications at San Miniato and elsewhere can be explained by the pressure of time: the problem was no longer primarily one of design, but rather of the organization of a large labour force.

That the fortifications planned by Michelangelo adhere to a project proposed to the Medici in 1526 is shown by a little-known report of Machiavelli ("Relazione di una visita fatta da Niccolò Machiavelli per fortificare Firenze", *L'Arte della guerra e scritti militari minori*, Florence, 1929, pp. 207–212) which records the opinions of the engineer Pietro Navarro dictated to Machiavelli, at that time Cancelliere dei Procuratori delle Mura. Here too, San Miniato is recognized as the weak point, and a strong fort is proposed for the summit of the hill; bastions are recommended before all the gates, of the same general type as those described by Varchi. Two of Navarro's suggestions for the angle of the Prato d'Ognissanti were put into effect before Michelangelo started to work: the diversion of the Mugnone river for use as a ditch (p. 211; cf. Michelangelo's drawing, Pl. 26b: "mugnione fuor di letto suo"; also Pl. 27a) and the erection of a new bastioned enclosure outside the Porticciola al Prato, just east of the angle, to include the mill there (p. 210; cf. No. 16: "e bastioni facti" [i.e., made prior to Michelangelo's appointment] outside the "porticciola"). Other suggestions could not be acted upon before the expulsion of the Medici, but were adhered to closely by Michelangelo: to make at the angle itself "un gagliardissimo baluardo in su quel canto, che difendisse e verso la mulina e verso la porta al Prato" (Pls. 26a, b), and to enclose the Porta al Prato in a bastion (Pl. 27a).

Baldassare Peruzzi was another distinguished forerunner of Michelangelo in fortifying Florence; he drew a careful plan of the medieval walls and bridges (Pl. 25c), no doubt in preparation for designing new bastions (C. Ricci, *Cento vedute di Firenze*, Florence, 1906, Pl. XI; Boffitto-Mori, *op. cit.*, p. 20). The plan is probably prior to Peruzzi's voluntary participation as a military architect for the Florentines in the war of 1529–1530 (Gaye, II, pp. 207 ff.; he had refused the Pope's invitation to serve on the Imperial staff). It may have been drawn just before the Machiavelli report.

Rome, Piazza and Palaces of the Capitoline Hill
1538–

Throughout the Middle Ages the Capitoline hill had served as the focus of the political life of Rome. As early as the twelfth century a Senate house was built on the ruins of the ancient Tabularium overlooking the west end of the Roman Forum; in 1299–1303, and again in 1348, this structure was enlarged on the model of North Italian communal palaces, and given an interior court, projecting corner towers, and a high campanile. The fourteenth-century palace (Pl. 30a, left) was oriented away from the Forum; an open loggia on the *piano nobile* (Pl. 30b) led by a broad flight of steps to the irregular plateau that was later to become Michelangelo's piazza. Around the turn of the fifteenth century a second palace was started on the south border of the plateau, across from the church of Santa Maria in Aracoeli; it was intended to house the *bandieri*, who kept the banners of the several *rioni* of Rome, and offices of the major guilds and of the Conservators – legislators elected annually to exercise whatever powers the Pope left to the citizens. Under Nicholas V in the mid-fifteenth century, the Palazzo dei Conservatori was remodelled in the style of the Roman Renaissance with an arcaded colonnade along the façade (Pl. 30a, right). (For the early history of the Campidoglio, see E. Rodocanachi, *Le Capitole Romain*, Paris, 1904; T. Ashby 1927, pp. 159 ff.; C. Cecchelli, *Arch. R. dep. rom. di storia patria*, LXVII, 1944, pp. 209 ff.; Siebenhüner 1954, pp. 24 ff., with bibliography.)

The haphazard form and ragged condition of the two palaces in the early sixteenth century is revealed in a series of drawings of *ca.* 1536 by Marten van Heemskerk (Pl. 30a; Siebenhüner 1954, Figs. 7–9, 24–25), which also show a collection of ancient monuments – columns, an obelisk, sculptural fragments – mounted casually about the unpaved central opening. In a city which was becoming the architectural model of Western Europe, the need for a more impressive centre of civic life was urgent, and shortly after Heemskerk's visit Pope Paul III took the initiative in planning a programme of rehabilitation.

I HISTORY: THE MID-SIXTEENTH CENTURY

(In the following outline, for the sake of brevity, the Palazzo del Senatore at the head of the piazza to the east will be referred to as the "Senatore" and the Palazzo dei Conservatori on the right and to the south as the "Conservatori".)

1537 22 September; 26 October: A meeting of the representative council of the city decides to restore the Conservatori. A month later the deputies appointed for the construction appoint a foreman of the *fabbrica* at 5 scudi monthly. Political problems and lack of funds thwart the project (Lanciani 1902, II, pp. 68 f.; Pecchiai 1950, pp. 36 f.)

Autumn: Paul III proposes to move the bronze equestrian statue of Marcus Aurelius from its site before the Lateran Basilica to the Campidoglio. The Lateran chapter protests in November and again in January, to no effect (Appoloni 1912, p. 10). In a letter from the Urbinate ambassador to the Duke, Michelangelo is quoted as having objected to the project "since it seemed to him to be better where it was, and if he had not strongly dissuaded the Pope, His Holiness would also have taken the two horses and statues from Monte Cavallo" (Gronau, *Jhb. pr. Kunstslg*, 1906, *Beiheft*, p. 9; the Monte Cavallo, or Quirinal, statues appear in our Pl. 76a).

1538 January: The statue of Marcus Aurelius is moved from the Lateran to the newly levelled piazza of the Campidoglio between 9 January and 25 January, when Biagio de' Martinelli describes a visit of Paul III to "locum capitolii noviter explanatum cum aequo aenea Constantini ex Laterano translato in platea Capitolii" (Pastor, *Geschichte*, V, p. 755; Künzle 1956, p. 350, proposes 18 January. On the identification of the statue as Constantine and similar errors, see Ackerman, *Renaissance News*, 1957, pp. 69 ff.) The statement in the diary of Cola Colleine that the statue was placed on 23 March (Appoloni, p. 10) may be in error; perhaps it referred to the consecration (Künzle, *loc. cit.*) The inscription on the base of the statue recording the removal and consecration is dated 1538.

1539 22 March: The Conservators set aside 320 scudi to be spent "partim in reformatione statue M. Antonii in platea Capitolii existentis secundum iudicium d. Michaelis Angeli sculptoris et partim circa muros fiendos in dicta platea" (Lanciani, II, p. 69). The nature of Michelangelo's alterations to the statue will be discussed below. Probably the "muros" in the piazza are the retaining walls against the slope below Santa Maria in Aracoeli (Pl. 31a).

(Ca. 1539): A drawing inscribed SIC ROMAE in the Escorial sketchbook of Francisco de Hollanda (Pl. 32; fol. 7v. E. Tormo, *Os disenhos das antigualhas que vio Francisco d'Ollanda*, Madrid, 1940) shows the Marcus Aurelius mounted on its existing base with the Quattrocento Conservatori appearing behind. The river gods, which Michelangelo later used at the base of the Senatore steps, appear before the arcade. The entrance portal to the Conservatori, erroneously inscribed SENATUS, is a sixteenth-century type, probably added in the reconstruction ordered in 1537 (Siebenhüner's contention, p. 61, that the whole façade was remodelled in 1538 ff. is negated by Pl. 31b, where the condition of the building is the same as it had been at the time of Heemskerk's visit). Francisco's version of the inscription on the statue base is accurate except for the omission of the last line (ANN. SAL. M. D XXXVIII). The drawing may be dated between Michelangelo's design of the base in 1538–1539 and Francisco's departure from Rome in 1539–1541. An engraving of the statue and base from the opposite side (the Emperor's left) was made in 1549 by Nicola Beatrizet (Tolnay 1930, p. 28; Siebenhüner, Fig. 42).

1544: Prospero Boccapaduli, deputy of the "fabbrica del Campidoglio . . . et in specie alla nuova scala del Palazzo del Senatore" opens his account books for the decade 1544–1554 (Pecchiai, p. 85n). (In evaluating these and later accounts we must keep in mind that payments are made only after completed work has been measured and estimated by the supervising architects, and that payments may have been made long after the execution of a given job.)

3 March: A mason is paid for work on the peperino loggia of three bays at the summit of the flight of steps leading from the rear of the piazza toward the transept of the Aracoeli (Pls. 31a, 36a; Pecchiai 1950, p. 41). An undated document "probably before, or at least not after 1547" (*loc. cit.*) records what seem to be the finishing touches. Siebenhüner proposed (p. 67) that the construction of the steps may have begun shortly after 1542, when the obelisk standing on the site (Pl. 30a) was removed to the piazza. Documents of May 1548 and October and December 1549, may be either for this stairway or the one leading to the southern loggia (Pecchiai, p. 42).

1547 12 October: Payments for the demolition of the old loggia on the façade of the Senatore and for completed work on the right half of the new stairway ("schala nova del palazzo del Senatori verso la consolazione"; Pecchiai, pp. 77 f.) These are followed by undated payments (*ca.* 1550?) for a "primo fondamento del muro che fa parapetto della scala verso la consolazione"; "pezo di muro che farrà parapetto alla loggia"; "cornizia del pilamidone (cornice over the central pilasters)" (Pecchiai, pp. 84 f.)

(1547): An engraving published in H. Cock, *Operum Antiquorum Romanorum* . . . Antwerp, 1562 (Pl. 30b) gives a retrospective view of the condition of the palaces in 1547. It shows the left half of the new Senatore stairway under construction, with the statue of the Nile in position before it. The "Tiber" remains by the Conservatori; it was moved only in 1552. Work on the right side of the stairway, mentioned in the preceding document, has not begun. In representing the balustrade on the upper story of the façade, Cock was deficient equally in historical and in practical perspective. The balcony, completed by July 1554, could not have been built before the reconstruction of the right half of the façade.

1551–1552: The Rome plan of Bufalini (1551; Siebenhüner, Fig. 31) shows the stairways leading to the three-arched loggias on the north and south but not the loggias themselves; the stairways leading from the piazza toward the Forum; the retaining wall on the side of the piazza by the Aracoeli, with its central niche; and the cordonata, or entrance ramp, without steps (later views do not show it). The Senatore stairway is not represented.

Ligorio's plan (1552; Siebenhüner, Fig. 32) shows in addition the northern loggia and the Senatore steps, but not the cordonata.

1552 21 May: The last payments are recorded for carving on the Senatore steps. Further payments for balusters and for moving and mounting the second River-god (Pecchiai, p. 85; Siebenhüner, p. 66).

1553 8 November: Payments for work on the southern three-arched loggia (Pecchiai, pp. 41 f.) The loggia bears the insignia of Julius III (1550–1555). It appears in a drawing by G.-A. Dosio of 1561–1564 (Siebenhüner, p. 68, Fig. 35; for the dating, Ackerman 1956, p. 55). The stairway to this loggia may have been built before

1547; it appears in Pl. 30b which, however, is too inaccurate to trust without substantiating evidence.

1554 April–August: Estimate of the completed central doorway of the Senatore (25 April; Pecchiai, pp. 86 f.; Siebenhüner, pp. 69 f.), illustrated in the Dosio drawing cited above and in Pl. 31b; it was removed in the remodelling of the 1590's. On 17 August, a payment for dismantling "del coritore et refarlo con balaustri sopra al portone" (Pecchiai, *loc. cit.*) This is the balcony cantilevered from the third story of the palace. The alternation of balusters and posts follows the design of balustrades elsewhere in the piazza. The medieval "coritore" appears in Heemskerk's views to have been an enclosed passage supported on modillons (Pl. 30a; Siebenhüner, Figs. 8, 9).

(1554–1560): A drawing in Brunswick (Pl. 31a; Tolnay 1930, p. 27) shows the completed stairway and balcony of the Senatore and beyond, the earlier retaining wall, loggia, and stairway by the Aracoeli. It was executed after the construction of the 1554 balustrade and before the construction of the oval steps and front balustrade of the piazza, finished in 1561.

Another sketch (by the same hand?) in the Louvre (Pl. 31b; Egger, *Röm. Veduten*, II, Pl. 10) shows the condition virtually unchanged; the appearance of the new Senatore portal and balustrade confirms the proposed *terminus post quem*. There is no sign of sixteenth-century construction on the Conservatori or of the initiation of the cordonata.

In Pl. 31a, Marcus Aurelius is placed forward of the centre of the piazza and the base is incomplete; in Pl. 31b, the statue is centred and the base appears in its present form. The differences will be analysed below, and a more precise dating of the drawings will be suggested tentatively.

1555–1559: During the pontificate of Paul IV construction virtually is halted. The accounts of the period contain expenditures averaging under 200 scudi annually (Pecchiai, pp. 42 f.; Siebenhüner, p. 78).

1561: Payment for "quattro membretti con la guida, imbasamento, et cornice con le doi teste et tutto altro aggiunto al posamento del cavallo [Marcus Aurelius statue]; giornate messe in aiutare ad smurare detto posamento" (Tolnay 1932, p. 249, Docs. 1, 4; the precise date is not transcribed).

30 April: Payment for the front balustrade of the piazza (Tolnay, Doc. 2). The construction was accompanied by costly preparatory work on the cordonata and retaining walls along the slopes of the hill (Pecchiai, pp. 42 f., cites expenditures of 5316 scudi in the period 1554–1565). See the further payments of 24 April 1564.

30 July: Payments for the three oval steps in the piazza and for travertine platforms at the foot of the Senatore stairway and at the summit of the cordonata; a final payment is made on 24 April 1564 (Tolnay, Docs. 2, 17).

15 October, 5 November: Pius IV demands that building be begun and that the cordonata be finished, and suggests using the tax on university students as a source of revenue. The use of these funds promotes a controversy that is not settled until they are assigned by a papal *motuproprio* of April 1565 (Pecchiai, pp. 44 f.; 221), after which time construction proceeds rapidly. For the moment, 600 scudi are assigned to clearing the forward slope of the hill and 600 "per fabricar in detta piazza" (Tolnay, Doc. 5). At the second meeting the Pope asks that at least the Senatore be repaired as the interior is being damaged by inadequate roofing; 1000 scudi are assigned to the project (*ibid.*, Doc. 6; Pecchiai, pp. 44, 87). Completion of this project is recorded in April 1564.

(1561?–1563): An anonymous engraving published by Lafreri showing the piazza from the west (Siebenhüner, Fig. 36). Highly inaccurate, it adds only one detail of interest to the information provided by Pl. 31b: the oval ring of steps appears complete, but without the three concave recessions designed by Michelangelo (Pl. 36b); gaps appear in their place. The engraving was made after the completion of the steps in or before 1561 and before the demolition of the old Conservatori portico in 1563.

(1562 15 April): The Conservators ask for three "disegni di studio" to be made by Vignola, Nanni (di Baccio Bigio) and Guidetto (Guidetti) (Tolnay 1932, p. 250, Doc. 8; Lanciani 1902, II, p. 70). The "Studio" was the seat of the University of Rome (Sapienza), the remodelling of which was the Conservators' responsibility (Pecchiai, pp. 44 ff., 224); the document is cited here because it has been associated mistakenly with the Campidoglio.

1563 1 February: Payments for walls and roofing of the Senatore and for work on the two corner towers and the bell tower. The fee is estimated by Giacomo della Porta, who appears for the first time at this date (Tolnay, pp. 239, 250, Doc. 10; Pecchiai, pp. 87 f.) Completion of the programme is recorded in the documents of April 1564.

11 March: Pius IV asks that the construction of the Conservatori be begun (Pastor, *Geschichte*, VII, p. 604), and attends a banquet in the palace on 21 March. Prior to 8 June, orders are given for shoring up the old façade and for stripping off the decorative membering and roofing (Pecchiai, p. 123). Apparently the existing building was left as much as possible in its original state as a core for the new construction which, by this device, could be executed by completing each bay from the base to the cornice before undertaking the next.

8 June: Foundations for the first pier of the portico of the Conservatori, on the right, western, end (Pecchiai, pp. 123 f.)

26 July: Payment to Guidetto Guidetti "quale si è preso per eseguire li ordini di M. Michelangelo Buonarruoto in la fabrica di Campidoglio" (Tolnay, Doc. 12; Pecchiai, p. 230).

10 December: Guidetto paid for time spent during 1563 "in far disegni della fabrica di Campidoglio così in pianta come ancho della facciata" and for designing internal bracing for the "archi piani" (flat arches) of the portico, templates, and centring (Tolnay, Doc. 13; Pecchiai, *loc. cit.*)

1564 24 April: Payment for "tutti li lavori fatti nel palazzo del Sr. Senatore dal fondamento insino a summo secondo il nuovo designo di messer Thomao del Cavalieri approvato da Nostro Signore, computatoci li tetti, le prigioni, et ogni altra cosa"

(Pecchiai, p. 89); elsewhere the construction, costing 727 scudi, is referred to as following "il nuovo designo restato presso di m. Thomao del Cavalieri", which suggests that the project may not have been designed actually by the official (Tolnay, Doc. 16; Siebenhüner, p. 70, implies that the former document was of 1554).

Whether the façade as well as the interior and roof was affected by this campaign is uncertain. A drawing in Stuttgart (Siebenhüner, Fig. 46), done after the mounting of statues in the Conservatori in 1567 and before the destruction of the campanile in 1577, shows an orderly row of windows on the upper story and new construction on the south tower (both missing in Pl. 31b). But all of this may have been done by della Porta in his reconstruction of 1574 ff., as the small dimensions of the windows suggest. 727 scudi would not have supported an ambitious campaign.

24 April: Payment for walls of "the parapets under the balusters" of the cordonata (Tolnay, Doc. 15); followed by another of 5 June for removing earth on either side of the ramp during the period since April 1562 (*ibid.*, Doc. 19; Pecchiai, p. 43). The report of Flaminio Vacca that Pius V (1559–1565) placed the pair of Egyptian lions at the foot of the cordonata (C. d'Onofrio, *Le fontane di Roma*, 1957, p. 124) must be mistaken, since the balustrades that support them were not built until 1577–1578. The drawing of 1567–1577 cited immediately above shows the cordonata unpaved, without balustrades, and substantially shorter than della Porta's.

26 April: Payment for masonry work in providing a permanent foundation under the statue of Marcus Aurelius: "muro del fondamento fatto sotto il posamento del cavallo di metallo quando fu rialzato", and for the wood cradle required for raising the statue (Pecchiai, pp. 46 f.) Later payments for the same work ("per levare la statua et cavallo . . . et mettere in opera il posamento dessa") are made on 17 May and 16 July 1565 (*loc. cit.*; Tolnay, Doc. 25). The domical form of Michelangelo's central oval required that the statue be raised before the paving could be started.

26 April: Payment for foundations and walls at the right corner of the Conservatori "sino al piano del primo cornicione" (*i.e.*, up to the top of the ground floor portico; Tolnay, Doc. 18, Pecchiai, p. 123).

31 October: Payment for the travertine facing "del portico nuovo del palazo de' Sri. Conservatori dal piano del primo cornicione in giù . . . et per tutte doi li primi pilastri con li suoi riscontri" (Tolnay, Doc. 20).

A drawing in the Albertina, Vienna (Ital. Arch., Rom, No. 30, unpublished) shows the first two bays of the façade under construction. Two-plus bays of the portico are complete but of the upper story only the partially-completed pilaster-piers may be seen. The *verso* contains a measured plan of the bays. Another sixteenth-century plan and elevation of the palace is preserved in the same collection (No. 31, unpublished). No upper story is shown.

12 December: Giacomo della Porta is paid as "architetto succeso doppo la morte de m.o. Guidetto" (Tolnay, Doc. 21; Pecchiai, p. 230). Michelangelo had died in February and Guidetto, the executor of his design, in the late summer or autumn.

1565 Early?: Payment for "doi pilastri dinanzi et un altro verso li caffarelli" (Tolnay, Doc. 26). The Caffarelli property, adjacent to the Conservators' garden, must have been to the southwest, since the road built later by the cordonata was referred to in the same words (Pecchiai, p. 54). So "dinanzi" must refer to the long piazza front and "verso li caffarelli" to the short façade overlooking the city.

Payments for two windows already erected (Tolnay, *loc. cit.*) and, on 26 July, for capitals of the pilasters (Tolnay, Doc. 28). If windows and capitals were in place, the western bays must have been complete to at least the height of the entablature.

24 August: Payment for a wood model "del cornicione et del capitello del pilastro nel cantone della facciata del palazzo"; also identified: "il quale modello serve alla fabbrica del palazzo delli Sri. Conservatori" (Pecchiai, pp. 125 f.) The purpose of Porta's cornice model will be examined below.

31 December: Porta is paid for a design "del cornicione in forma propria [to full scale?] nel salone del Sr. Senatore" (Tolnay, Docs. 22, 29; Pecchiai, p. 231). Tolnay proposed (p. 240; followed by Pecchiai, pp. 92 f., and Künzle 1956, *loc. cit.*) that this cornice was intended for the *salone* of the Senatore, executed in 1574–1575. But Siebenhüner gives the more credible interpretation (p. 94n) that both documents refer to the Conservatori model, which was merely stored in the *salone*. The design of the *salone* cornice presupposes the project to raise the hall to a height of two stories. Had this been accepted in 1565, there would have been no purpose to the publication of Michelangelo's designs in engravings of 1568–1569, where the hall remains one story high. Furthermore, no funds were spent on the Senatore in 1564–1573.

(1565–1566): A drawing ascribed to Vignola (Uffizi, *Arch.* 7922; Siebenhüner, p. 85, Fig. 50) shows the elevation of the two western bays of the Conservatori complete to the architrave; the frieze, cornice, and balustrade are still absent, as would be expected from the two foregoing documents (though the appearance of pilaster capitals leaves unexplained the need for a model of these capitals). An accompanying detail of one of the portals within the portico leading to the guild offices (Uffizi, *Arch.* 7923, *ibid.*, Fig. 51) has notations and measurements clearly taken from the building rather than from preparatory drawings, and suggests the identification of both drawings as accurate documents of work in progress. The draughtsman does not show the ironwork rinceaux in the pediments of these portals, which were put there in 1566–1568 (Pecchiai, p. 124).

A group of sketches in the Metropolitan Museum, New York (49.92.27, 64, 69, 70, *etc.*) probably dates from the same period: the plans of the Conservatori show only two bays, and the office-portal is without ironwork in the pediment.

II HISTORY: POST-MICHELANGELO

Only those elements of the Campidoglio that had been begun by 1564–1565 followed Michelangelo's design. After this, della Porta and his successors felt free to improvise wherever new construction was to be started (for a critique of these changes, see H. Sedlmayr, "Das Kapitol des della Porta", *Zeitschr. f. Kunstges.* III, 1934, pp. 264 ff.) A condensed summary of the later history therefore will answer our purpose.

PALAZZO DE' CONSERVATORI (Tolnay 1932, pp. 244, 252 f.; Pecchiai, pp. 122–181; Siebenhüner, pp. 93–97).

In 1567 the first four statues on the cornice balustrade at the western corner were installed, and stucco reliefs were executed in the first three portico vaults. Della Porta designed the central window and door in 1568; by December of that year a model of the window had been mounted experimentally, and by April 1569, carvers were working on the frame itself (Tolnay, Docs. 33–37). Existing inscriptions in the portico recording the reconstruction of the palace are dated 1568, although a year later the builders had reached only the fifth pilaster. In 1576 iron tie rods were bought for "the last arch of the portico", but the crowning balustrade was not complete until 1583; the last statues were set up in 1584.

I recently found in the Albertina, Vienna (Ital. Arch., Rom, No. 29, unpublished) a working drawing for the construction of the court, apparently by della Porta. Except for a proposed colonnaded portico surrounding the court on all sides, the design is close to the existing building.

Meanwhile construction began about the interior court in 1570–1573, with the building of rooms by the garden at the rear and of the principal stairway on the east. Porta directed the decoration of the stairway, in which Domenico Fontana took part in 1572. In 1583 construction based on a model still continued around the court, which was paved finally in 1587.

After the campaign of 1563–1587, the only substantial alteration to the palace was the addition of a second bay to the short western front overlooking the city in the pontificate of Alexander VII (1655–1667) (Siebenhüner, p. 96).

The three rooms over the portico on the *piano nobile* were remodelled while construction was in progress. The westernmost Sala dei Trionfi was decorated in 1568–1571; the central Sala dei Capitani in 1568–1594; and the Salone Grande to the east in 1581–1619. A chapel on the rear of the façade wing overlooking the court was finished in 1575–1578 (Pecchiai, pp. 147–175).

PALAZZO DEL SENATORE (Pecchiai, pp. 90–105; Siebenhüner, pp. 107–114).

Construction on the Senatore began only toward the close of the Conservatori campaign. The remodelling of the *salone* on the *piano nobile* into a great two-storied vaulted hall (see the cross-section in Ashby 1927, p. 38) was begun in 1573–1574. Payments of 1575 cover work on the walls, the vault, the interior cornice, the vault windows (those of the third story of the façade), the doors, and decorative work in stucco and on the marble tribunal and curved benches (Tolnay 1932, Doc. 50; Pecchiai, pp. 91 ff.); the work continued until 1579. In making a single two-storied hall where Michelangelo had planned two stories of equal height, della Porta had to alter fundamentally the design of the Senatore façade; while he kept the proportions of Michelangelo's design for the second-story windows, he had to reduce the upper row at the level of the vault to small rectangles (Pl. 29). The façade was not completed actually until the 1590's, but the final design must have been anticipated, if not fully developed, at the time of the interior remodelling. The Tempesta plan of 1593 (Siebenhüner, Fig. 60), published before the renovation of the façade, shows the exterior frames of the second-story windows, which probably were put in place during the 1570's. In 1577 to 1579 the prisons on the lower story were remodelled, and payments for the prison chapel were made in 1583.

In August 1577, the palace campanile was destroyed by lightning; the Conservators decided to replace it in February 1578, and discussed in June a model and design by the papal architect Martino Longhi, which appears on a medal of 1579 with the Pope's portrait (Gregory XIII; Pecchiai, Pl. 10; Siebenhüner, Fig. 59). The tower, which departed from Michelangelo's design, was completed in November 1583 (cf. a contemporary account in A. Fulvio, *L'antichità . . .*, Venice, 1588, p. 74v). The palace façade, as it appears on the medal, has windows begun by della Porta, but colossal pilasters only on the corner towers; at the centre, Michelangelo's baldachin is raised to a height of two stories so as to continue the vertical accents of the tower through the façade. These changes must represent Longhi's attempt to extend his influence over the Campidoglio project.

Michelangelo's design was further compromised in 1588–1589, when a fountain designed in competition by Matteo da Castello was built about the base of the triangular stairway (Pl. 29), after Sixtus V had directed the extension of the Aqua Felice to the Campidoglio (d'Onofrio, *Fontane di Roma*, pp. 125 ff.) In 1592 the central niche of the stairway received the seated statue of Minerva as *Roma*, in place of an earlier and larger one installed in 1583. Michelangelo's plan to place a Jupiter statue in the niche (Vasari, VII, p. 222) never was realized.

The Senatore façade was given its present membering in 1593 (or 1598, the date inscribed on the central portal) – 1612 (Siebenhüner, pp. 109–112, reviews the campaign). The design has been attributed to both della Porta and Girolamo Rainaldi, who completed the work after Porta's death in 1602. As "Architect of the Roman People", Porta is the more likely author; his work of 1573–1579 on the interior predetermined the essentials of the design by fixing the size, placement, and proportions of the windows. The low relief of the membering, the feeble detailing, and the surfaces of sandstone and stuccoed brick emasculate the vestiges of Michelangelo's conception.

THE CORDONATA AND PIAZZA (Lanciani 1902, II, pp. 71 ff.; Pecchiai, pp. 54–62; Siebenhüner, pp. 100–106).
In 1576 the area at the foot of the cordonata was enlarged by demolitions; a year later the Conservators, meeting with a group of architects, decided to lower the area in order to extend the ramp beyond the entrance to the Aracoeli steps. In September 1578, a new cordonata design by della Porta was chosen in a competition involving Longhi, Lippi, and three lesser architects. The new project gradually diminished the width of the ramp toward the base, probably not to produce a perspective illusion, but to avoid blocking

the access to the Aracoeli steps. In other respects Porta apparently adhered to the Michelangelo project. The date of execution is unknown. In 1581–1582 a second access was added
to the right of the cordonata, and in 1585 the first of the Dioscures was mounted by the
top of the ramp (C. Pietrangeli, *Capitolium*, 1952, pp. 41–48). The second followed in
1590, at which time the mileposts from the Via Appia and the so-called "Trofei di Mario"
were raised on the balustrade. In 1588, two Egyptian lions were installed as fountains
at the base of the cordonata (the present lions are copies of these). No documents have
been published on the paving of the piazza; the pavement with radiating bands which
existed prior to the reconstruction of 1940 (Pl. 36a) appears in Cruyl's view of 1665
(Siebenhüner, Fig. 73), but not in early Seicento views.

THE PALAZZO NUOVO (Rodocanachi 1904, pp. 126 ff.; Siebenhüner, pp. 115 ff.)
In 1595, the statue of a River-god known as the "Marforio" was installed as the centre-
piece of a fountain designed by della Porta in the niche that had been built earlier on the
side of the piazza toward Aracoeli (Pl. 31a). The third palace planned for this site by
Michelangelo (Pl. 37) was founded in June 1603, by Clement VIII. But construction of
the "Palazzo Nuovo" halted after the laying of the foundations, and was not completed
until 1654.

III MICHELANGELO'S DESIGN

In spite of rich documentation on the building history of the Campidoglio, important
questions concerning Michelangelo's participation remain unanswered, particularly the
date(s) of the design and the extent to which the architect formulated his intentions in
drawings or models. The problem may be introduced by examining a posthumous set
of engravings (collected first by Tolnay 1930) purportedly based on original drawings
which have not survived.

A. THE ENGRAVINGS

1. Plan (Pl. 36b) published by B. Faleti; dated 1567 and inscribed: "Areae Capitolinae . . .
ex Michaelis Angeli Bonaroti architectura ichnographia". It represents a project for
the piazza alone, showing only a small portion of the stairways leading up from the
base of the hill and down from the lateral arched loggias, nothing is indicated of the
portions of the three palaces other than what would be visible from the piazza. The plan
differs in several respects from the one executed: for the complex stellate pattern within
the oval, with its recessed steps at three points, a simple system of eight radiating bands
was substituted until replaced in 1940 by a dry version of the engraving (Pl. 35b; the
restoration preserved the paths at the four corners of the square – Pl. 36a – which Michelangelo had not intended). Alongside the main portal of the Senatore are two piers
designed to support the baldachin pictured in Pl. 37; although they were built, they no
longer are preserved (but beginnings of one of the corresponding pair attached to the
balustrade opposite are still visible: Schiavo 1948, Figs. 75–76). In other respects the engraved plan was closely followed, the greater part of it having been started under
Michelangelo's supervision. The fact that the porticoes of the flanking palaces and the

offices behind them are somewhat shallower than in the executed work is due probably to the restrictions of the engraver's plate.

2. Perspective of the piazza from the west by Dupérac, dated October 1568 and inscribed: "Capitolii quod S.P.Q.R. impensa ad Michaelis Angeli Bonaroti eximii architecti exemplar in anteiquum decus restitui posse videtur tabula accuratissime Stephani Duperac . . . opera delineata . . ." (Tolnay 1930, pp. 22 f., Fig. 11; Siebenhüner, pp. 85 f., Fig. 47). See Fig. 8.

The buildings correspond in elevation to the plan (No. 1) and show the projected rather than the executed design. Differences between this engraving and the one of 1569 (Pl. 37; No. 3) are: (a) the placement of two Constantinian statues on the pedestals at the summit of the cordonata where in No. 3 spheres are set (the Dioscures with their horses do not appear); (b) the window aediculas of the Senatore. While the frames of No. 3 have segmental and triangular pediments in alternation, those in No. 2 are segmental on the *piano nobile* and triangular on the upper story; the latter are broken at the apex and filled with an ornamental motif (Fig. 8).

3. Emendation of No. 2 by Dupérac, dated 1569 and inscribed "Capitolii sciographia ex ipso exemplari Michaelis Angeli Bonaroti . . . accurate delineata" (Pl. 37).

Two Dioscure groups are mounted facing one another on pedestals at the summit of the cordonata. They are not (as Tolnay reminded me) those discovered in 1560 and later erected in this position, but are modelled on the Dioscures of Monte Cavallo. This need not indicate a revival of Paul III's plan to bring the latter pair to the hill, but, I believe, only the probability that the recently discovered statues were not accessible to the engraver. The second pair were not mounted as Dupérac shows, but stand facing the city on independent bases resembling the base of the Marcus Aurelius statue (Pl. 29). The executed elevations differ from those of Nos. 2 and 3 in: (a) Porta's enlargement of the central window of the Conservatori (Pl. 35b); (b) the façade design of the Senatore, which lost plasticity in every detail – by weakened drafting on the lower story and alterations in its windows and cornice; by the elimination of window balconies and the central baldachin; by reducing the projection of pilasters and pilaster-strips, and by increasing the height and width of the campanile (cf. Pl. 29); (c) the addition of a second bay to the short façades of the flanking palaces.

4. Elevation of the right side of the Conservatori (Pl. 35a) published by Faleti, dated 1568, showing three-plus bays of the façade, and inscribed "porticus et palatii Capitolini aspectus accurate commensuratus studiosorum bonarum artium commoditati delineatis". This engraving does not belong quite in the preceding group: the inscription, in which there is no reference to Michelangelo's design, implies that the source was the building itself rather than drawings or a model – an interpretation confirmed by the fact that in 1568 construction had advanced exactly as far as the engraving indicates. The fact that the engravings were produced three and four years after Michelangelo's death makes it imperative to distinguish what *must* have been Michelangelo's design from what *may* have been supplied by his successors.

No. 3 was copied at the end of the century by Duchet, who added the Senatore fountain and the "Trofei di Mario" (Siebenhüner, p. 87, Fig. 53); a drawing based on the engraving (of the 1570's?) appears in a volume attributed to Dupérac formerly in the Dyson Perrins collection (Ashby, *Topographical Study*, Pl. XII; the stellate design in the oval is lacking), and another by an anonymous draughtsman is in the Uffizi (*Arch.* 2702; Siebenhüner, p. 86, Fig. 52). Professors Lane Faison and John McAndrew inform me that another view is frescoed in the theatre at Sabbioneta.

To the knowledge of the original design derived from the engravings, the description of Vasari in 1568 (VII, pp. 222 f.; the 1550 edition, pp. 997 f., refers only in passing to "il disegno del Campidoglio") adds some minor points: the Senatore façade was intended to be built of travertine, like the flanking palaces; a statue of Jupiter was to occupy the central niche of the double-ramped stairway; the portico of the Conservatori was "piena di colonne e nicchie, dove vanno molte statue antichi, ed attorno sono vari ornamenti e di porte e finestre, che già n'è posto una parte"; the balustrade of the cordonata as well as that of the piazza was to support "tutta la nobilità delle statue, di che oggi è così ricco il Campidoglio". The mention of statue niches in the portico arouses suspicion of Vasari's accuracy, since there are none in the project supervised by Michelangelo in 1563; perhaps Vasari recalled the niches of the earlier portico. which appear in Pl. 30b. Elsewhere Vasari mentions (VI, p. 449; cited by Thode 1908, II, p. 191) Michelangelo's intention to employ Aristotile da Sangallo in the Campidoglio construction, which was frustrated by the latter's departure from Rome in 1547. Presumably he would have supervised the construction of the Senatore stairway, which was under way in that year.

B. DRAWINGS BY MICHELANGELO, POSSIBLY FOR THE CAMPIDOGLIO

Three original sketches that may be associated with the Campidoglio are mere jottings that defy precise analysis. The recently discovered Oxford No. 332v (Pl. 34b; D.206; Tolnay 1956, pp. 379 f., Fig. 41; Parker 1956, pp. 171 f.; D.206) contains plans – and elevations? – of a corridor with encased paired columns on the exterior and the note "porta" on one of the interior openings. Tolnay interpreted the sheet as a group of studies for the ground floor portico of the Conservatori and for an interior elevation of the dome of St Peter's; though the proportions, the position of the "porta", and the number and vaulting type of the bays recommend the identification, the exterior apertures appear to be doors or windows rather than the open bays of a portico. Oxford No. 333v (D.352; F.273; Parker 1956, pp. 172 f.) contains the elevation of a palace façade with a colossal Order embracing arched apertures on the lower story and pedimented windows on the upper. The system is closer to that of the Campidoglio palaces than to other Michelangelo projects, but the connection cannot be verified. The two Oxford sketches appear on the *verso* of contemporary windows designs, probably of the late 1540's, close in style to those of the Farnese palace court (Pl. 46b). If the first proves to be for the Conservatori, we could conclude only that the existing palace elevation was not contemporary with the plan of 1538/1539, and remained unsettled in the late 1540's. Casa Buonarroti No. 19 F. (D.50; Tolnay, *loc. cit.*, and 1948, pp. 208 f., Figs. 124 f.; Wilde 1953, p. 109) contains a roughly sketched elevation of a double-ramped stairway which has been associated both with the Senatore and the Belvedere (see p. 115).

IV PROBLEMS OF CHRONOLOGY AND AUTHORSHIP

A. THE 1539 DESIGN AND THE MARCUS AURELIUS STATUE

Although Michelangelo objected in 1537 to the proposed removal of the Marcus Aurelius statue to the hill, he was called in 1539 to advise on its placement or mounting. At or before this time he must have designed the existing base, because it appears – in a somewhat simpler form – in Francisco de Hollanda's sketchbook of *ca.* 1539 (Pl. 32; the significance of this drawing for the chronology of the design was brought out by Ackerman 1956, pp. 54 f., and Künzle 1956, p. 350). The way in which the statue is placed in Francisco's sketch implies that it was to be on the central axis of the piazza, and that the principal entrance to the area also was to be on this axis, facing the Emperor. Furthermore, the semi-cylindrical short ends and slightly curved sides of the base, which make it quasi-clliptical in plan, imply that the oval form of the piazza already had been determined. In March, 1539, the Conservators provided funds for adjusting the statue and for walls "in said piazza", which must be those of the embankment against the Aracoeli (Pl. 31a). These walls, which complete the trapezoidal plan of the square, which enclose a central niche that determines the cross-axis, and which fix the position of the lateral stairways from the square to the three-arched loggie above, would not have been started before a comprehensive plan had been accepted.

Indeed, the elements of the plan engraved in 1567 (Pl. 36b) are so interrelated that few of them can have been absent from the 1539 project. If the statue base implies the oval and the cordonata or a similar entrance way, the oval implies the double-ramped stairway leading to the Senators' hall, since no other form would have left sufficient space for it (the concave recessions in the steps of the oval also presuppose the stairway, but need not have been proposed in the original plan). The stairway, in turn, would force the architect to treat the lower story of the Senatore as a basement; hence its drafted masonry in Pl. 37 and Fig. 8. Finally, the oval could function visually only if a second palace were placed at a tangent to it, opposite the Conservatori.

We do not know whether designs for the palace elevations were made in 1539, since the construction was not started until the 1560's. We shall see that the style suggests a date just prior to the St Peter's project of 1546/1547. The key to the elevations is the design of the Conservatori, for the choice of structural method was determined by the need to add a monumental portico and façade onto the Quattrocento palace: the new design had to conform to the proportions of the old and, what is more important, to its orientation. The remarkable shape of the piazza is due to the irrational axis of the pre-existing buildings. The Quattrocento Conservatori appears to be seven bays wide in Pl. 32, twelve in Pl. 31b, and eighteen in Bufalini's plan of Rome in 1551. Faced with such a range of inaccuracy, we cannot ascertain securely whether Michelangelo increased the length of the existing palace; probably he did not, since two contemporary records (Bufalini's plan, a drawing by Dosio: Siebenhüner, Figs. 3, 35) show the left corner of the old palace in the same position as the corner of Michelangelo's: in line with the stairway leading up to the three-arched loggia (cf. Pl. 36a).

In Francisco's drawing (Pl. 32), the statue of Marcus Aurelius is incorrectly placed with respect to the cross-axis of the piazza, being in line with the rear corner of the old Conservatori. By contrast, in the views of 1547 (Pl. 30b) and 1554–1561 (Pl. 31a), it appears too far forward of the cross axis, which is marked by the niche; furthermore, in both cases, the base appears without its semi-cylindrical ends. The ends appear again in Pl. 31b, which is close in date to Pl. 31a, and in all subsequent views, and from this time on the monument is shown in its present position. Since it is unlikely that the statue and portions of its base were hoisted about three times without purpose, we may consider an alternative explanation: first, that Francisco's drawing was taken from Michelangelo's sketch or model in which the exact position of the statue was not indicated; this explains why not only Francisco, but Beatrizet – whose engraving of 1548 presumably was based on the same source – omitted the small piers at the angle where the curved sides meet, and perhaps why the former omitted the date, 1538, at the close of the dedicatory inscription; second, that the statue was mounted shortly thereafter in the position shown in Pls. 30b and 31a, but the base was left unfinished, without its curved ends; and finally, that after Pl. 31a but before Pl. 31b the curved ends were added and the statue was moved to its present position. The weakness of this hypothesis is in the assumption that when Michelangelo placed the statue in 1539 he deliberately put it in the wrong spot; but it has the advantage of trusting the author of Pl. 31a, who was a meticulous observer, and of explaining an otherwise mystifying document cited above. This is a payment of 1561 for the carving of additional details on the base (Pl. 33): "4 small members (the angle piers omitted by Francisco?) with the guide (raised courses?), base, and cornice with the two head-pieces (the semi-cylinders) and everything else added to the pedestal of the horse, and for work in helping to dismantle the pedestal (to centre it in the piazza?)". Since the document clearly speaks of "adding" these details, the core of the pedestal must have remained unchanged.

Other payments of 1561 cover the front balustrade of the piazza and the three steps forming the central oval. But this progress does not show in Pl. 31b, where the complete statue base is illustrated in its final position. To explain this contradiction, we may assume that the additions to the base were made a year or more before, but paid for only in 1561, when the Conservators diverted large sums to building.

In April 1564, and July 1565, workmen were paid for a "foundation wall under the pedestal of the metal horse when it was raised again (=*rialzato*, also used simply in the sense of "raised"). Evidently when the base was remodelled before 1561 it was merely set on the ground, so that it had to be dismantled a second time to give it permanent footing at the precise level demanded by the domical form of the oval pavement.

If these hypotheses are correct, they clarify most of the apparent contradictions in the documents and also permit a more precise dating of Pls. 31a and 31b. If the statue base was completed and centred in *ca.* 1558–1560, then Pl. 31a was drawn in 1554–1558/1560 and Pl. 31b in 1558–1560 (allowing a year for the building of the balustrade and oval steps).

B. DESIGN AND CONSTRUCTION IN THE 1540's AND 1550's

The first actual structure to be erected in accordance with Michelangelo's plot-plan was the arched loggia by the Aracoeli (before 1544 to 1547; Pls. 31a, 36a). The curious fact that it was not designed by Michelangelo may be explained by the intervention of Pope Paul III, whose insignia, fleurs-de-lis, appear in the spandrels. Michelangelo, because of his hatred of the Pope's favourite architect, Antonio da Sangallo, was not employed in any architectural capacity by the Holy See until Sangallo died in 1546. The loggia, and its twin to the south of the piazza (*ca.* 1553) were attributed to Vignola until Coolidge proved (1948, pp. 69–75) that the tradition was based on a misreading of Baglione (*Vite*, 1642, p. 7), who clearly assigned to Vignola only the doors at the rear of the porticoes (not yet erected in Pl. 31a; perhaps done around 1562, when Vignola made a "disegno di Studio" for the Conservators). Coolidge suggested Nanni di Baccio Bigio on stylistic grounds, an attribution supported by the present hypothesis that the Pope was committed to Sangallo, in whose atelier Nanni was the leading figure, and further by the Conservators' choice of Nanni as a competitor with Vignola in 1562.

Probably the loggias were not worked out in elevation in Michelangelo's plan of 1538–1539, which apparently concentrated on the effects of the piazza itself (Pl. 36b). Michelangelo may not have wanted loggias at all, though he must have planned the broad stairways leading to the two summits prior to the construction of the retaining wall shown in Pl. 31a.

Sometime between the opening of the account-books in 1544 and the payment of October 1547, the double-ramped stairway before the Senatore was begun. Its design must have been determined at least in plan in the late 1530's. The left side, which was built first (Pl. 30b), was placed against the wall of the medieval palace. Prior to building the right side, the eccentric loggia and stairway of the old palace had to be dismantled, and a new façade, symmetrical with the left half, built in its place. The last payments for the stairway were of May 1552, but payments for reconstructing the palace still were made in 1554, when the doorway and balustrade above it were finished. The additions appear in Pl. 31b, where the southern tower appears incomplete. This drawing raises the question of Michelangelo's intentions for the façade; if he already had produced an elevation project, it either was fundamentally different from the one illustrated in the engravings of 1568–1569 (Pl. 37; Fig. 8), or was ignored by the anonymous author of the restoration programme (Nanni again?). The fact that the soberly classical central door and the smaller one above it (best illustrated in Siebenhüner, Fig. 35. See also C. Hülsen, *Das Skizzenbuch des Giovannantonio Dosio*, Berlin, 1933, Pl. CXV), designed with cornices but no pediments, was inconsistent with Michelangelo's style is not the chief problem; they were at least of a size and position that did not conflict with the engraved design. But other elements of the new façade (Pl. 31b) did not in any sense conform to that design: (1) the ground floor window of the south tower is not the small square aperture of the engravings but a tall vertical one which invades the area of the ground floor cornice; (2) the projecting balcony of the upper story forestalled the construction of a colossal pilaster Order. The anomaly of the balcony has escaped notice, probably because it was believed to be a feature of the medieval building. But the style – in addition to the document of August 1554 – certifies at least the balustrade as a recent addition: balusters interrupted at regular intervals by square posts bearing spheres are Michelangelo's invention and appear throughout the Capitoline scheme (Michelangelo's are less conventional, more sculptural, than these Sangallesque forms). Yet this balcony gives the façade a placid character inconsistent with Michelangelo's principles; like the central portal and window, it appears to result from the effort of a minor architect to improvise something in harmony with the stairway. While the stairway of 1547–1552 obviously followed a detailed model or elevation sketch by Michelangelo, the façade construction of 1552?–1554 must have bumbled along without such guidance. Exactly the same situation arose at the Vatican Belvedere in 1551, when Michelangelo produced another double-ramped stairway and left the façade behind it to a minor architect. In the second building campaign at the Senatore, of 1563–1564, based on designs by or in the hands of Tommaso Cavalieri, changes were made in the prisons, roofing, and walls; we cannot tell whether the façade was affected or whether Michelangelo was involved.

C. THE 1560's AND THE PROBLEM OF THE ENGRAVINGS

In 1563 the foundations of the Conservatori were laid at the Pope's request; Guidetti was employed to supervise construction under Michelangelo's direction, as Calcagni had done at San Giovanni de' Fiorentini. New plans and elevations were required including detailed studies of the Conservatori portico, and specifically for the "flat arches". Again it appears that no model had been produced, but in this case, Michelangelo's active participation leaves no doubt of the authorship. Having held the commission for nearly thirty years, Michelangelo must have made studies that only now required translation into working drawings; in the process important changes may have been made.

In October 1528, shortly after Guidetti's death, the first two bays of the portico were completed, at least "from the first cornice down" (*e.g.*, the ground floor only), and two pilasters were in place. The upper cornice was still missing; it does not appear in the "Vignola" drawing of 1565–1566. In August 1565 della Porta, who succeeded Guidetti, finished a model of the cornice and a pilaster capital. If Porta had to make a model, I presume that here, as at St Peter's, Michelangelo had left no definitive cornice design. Porta's model either was based on sketches by Michelangelo or was designed without any help from him (I exclude Siebenhüner's alternative, p. 94, of a "counterproject" by Porta, for which there is no evidence). In this case, the engravers of 1568–1569 would have had no recourse but to interpolate Porta's design.

Dupérac's inscriptions claim for his engravings the authority of Michelangelo's drawings. But analysis of the building campaigns has indicated that Michelangelo left no decisive sketches for parts of the elevation that he did not execute. Here, as at St Peter's and the Porta Pia, the engraver may have been forced by Michelangelo's working habits to compose a pastiche of authentic and imagined solutions – how else can we explain the publication of two different versions? Changes made five years after Michelangelo's death in the Senatore façade windows and the statuary at the front of the piazza must have been due to the absence of a clear mandate from the master.

The engraved Conservatori elevation (Pl. 35a) always has been accepted as a record of Michelangelo's design, and the absence of the central window has been taken as an indication that there existed a completed model or drawing from which Porta departed. But there is no evidence of such a design apart from Dupérac's engravings, the authority of which already has been challenged. Indeed, the elevation of 1568 suggests that the engraver, having no drawings to refer to, was forced to illustrate only what had been built (in 1568 exactly three bays, complete with statues, had been finished). He had to stop short of the central bay not only because construction had not reached that far, but because its window and portal just were being designed by Porta (see Part II above). The publication of $\frac{3}{7}$ of a building design would be odd in any era, but particularly so in the symmetry-loving Renaissance, unless it were unavoidable. Thus the engraving published by Faleti, far from recording part of a complete drawing or model by Michelangelo, suggests that no such record existed. If Faleti's engraver was uncertain about the intended design, Dupérac must have been, too; but the latter, being impelled to represent the whole perspective, apparently decided on his own to repeat the first three bays all along the façade (Pl. 37). This hypothesis puts della Porta's designs of the central window (Pl. 35b) and portal in a new light; rather than being departures from Michelangelo's project, they would be the first and only decisive proposals for the central bay. In the context of Michelangelo's intentions for the whole composition (cf. the analysis, Vol. I, pp. 62–65), Dupérac's reconstruction remains more convincing than the existing building; della Porta's emphasis on the cross-axis represents the same passion for dramatization that prompted him to elevate the dome of St Peter's. The extent to which Dupérac is reliable in other respects – for example, in the design of the campanile (not a persuasive record of Michelangelo's work), and in the choice and placement of the statues on the forward balustrade – cannot be established on documentary grounds. Fig. 8 is based on Dupérac's 1568 version, which appears more authentic, first, because the Dioscures at the head of the cordonata (Pl. 37) cannot have figured in Michelangelo's early plans, and second, because the window pediments of the Senatore are better suited to the scheme of the lateral palaces (Tolnay 1930, p. 23) and those in the upper row are especially original in conception. The fact (mentioned to me by Tolnay) that the 1568 engraving is described as "accuratissime" and the 1569 as "accurate" probably is not significant, for the latter term is used for the elevation plate which, by Renaissance standards, is remarkably accurate.

D. CONCLUSION: THE DATE OF THE ELEVATION DESIGNS

The foregoing observations on the elevations lead to two conclusions: first, that they cannot be dated on documentary grounds and second, that they were not clearly recorded at the time of Michelangelo's death. The simplest explanation of all the chronological problems is that Michelangelo did not start to design the façades until construction began in the 1560's (Siebenhüner, pp. 81 ff.) This solution has one vitiating weakness: the design is wholly foreign to Michelangelo's late style, and suitable in every respect to a period preceding St Peter's and the Farnese palace (cf. the reviews of Siebenhüner's book: Ackerman, Künzle, Tolnay, 1956). The point is illustrated readily by comparing details on the Conservatori façade and the apses of St Peter's (1546; Pls. 35b, 64): the colossal pilaster Order and entablature are generically alike; the second-story windows, however, provide an exact parallel in the balcony projecting at the base framed by pedestals for engaged columns which support a segmental pediment with a recessed base. The baluster designs are nearly the same; where the frames differ in detail, St Peter's is the more complex – a garland hangs from its column capitals, and a bracket appears below the pediment. A large shell in the Conservatori pediment became a double garland at St Peter's, but the fact that the shell appeared in the St Peter's model (Pl. 59a) indicates a progression from the Campidoglio to the model to the basilica itself. Comparison with the Farnese palace windows (1547/1548, Pl. 46a) confirms an evolution in the late '40's toward complexity and fantasy of detail, supporting the impression that the Conservatori, as the most conventional in detail of the three designs, is therefore the earliest. Finally, only the Conservatori preserves motifs from the Florentine schemes of the 1520's; the door frames within the portico (Pl. 35a) recall both the vocabulary and the crisp, linear conception of the Laurentian library tabernacles (Pl. 24).

Structural analysis strongly sustains this hypothesis. A study of the façade system of the Conservatori (p. 64 Vol. I) reveals that the loads are borne by broad piers into which the pilasters are carved; but in order to give the illusion that the pilasters bear the loads alone, Michelangelo disguised the visible portion of the piers alongside the pilasters as ornamental strips or bands that seem merely to frame the brick wall (a drawing of the construction in progress, Albertina, Ital. arch., Rom, No. 30, shows that the piers – pilasters plus "strips" – were constructed before the wall was started). The motif was used with variations on the apses of St Peter's; but there the stability of the structure is achieved entirely by the wall masses, so that the pilaster-strips serve a purely expressive function, independent of the structure. It is unlikely that this extraordinary motif was invented for formal effect and subsequently found to solve an unforseen technical problem; the relationship of the two designs makes more sense if the motif was inspired first by the structural imperatives of the Conservatori façade and later adapted to St Peter's. Analysis of both style and structure therefore supports the conviction that the Conservatori façade was worked out essentially before 1546, though certain details may have remained unsolved at Michelangelo's death. 1538/1539 is the most probable date, since there is no reason to suppose that the plan and elevation were not contemporaneous.

The same reasoning does not apply to the Senatore façade where, as at St Peters, the pilaster piers of the Conservatori were applied to a structurally self-sufficient wall. Further, since none of the work was executed under Michelangelo's supervision (other than the stairway and foundations for the baldachin), the validity of the engravings is uncertain. The architect who reconstructed the medieval façade in 1552?–1554 did not follow the design engraved by Dupérac or any other by Michelangelo, which suggests that none existed at that time. Since the style of the engraved façade is not more advanced than that of the other palaces, it is improbable that Michelangelo returned to the Senatore façade in the '50's or '60's. To resolve this paradox we may suppose Dupérac's two versions to have been based on a number of sketches for window- and door frames dating from 1538/1539; the differences in the two engravings could then be explained by the hypothesis that Michelangelo sketched various ideas for the windows without composing them into a complete elevation. The colossal Order may not have been drawn at all; the engraver could have reconstructed it from the Conservatori façade provided he knew from the sketches or even from hearsay that Michelangelo had intended to use it.

Rome, Farnese Palace, 1546–

When Michelangelo was appointed as architect to the Farnese palace in the autumn of 1546, the building already had been in progress for nearly thirty years. To appreciate his contribution, it is first necessary to review the early history of the palace under Antonio da Sangallo the Younger.

I SANGALLO'S PALACE FOR CARDINAL ALESSANDRO FARNESE, 1517–1534

1495: Cardinal Alessandro, the future Pope Paul III, purchases property near the Campo di Fiori and partially on the site of the present palace (Navenne, *Revue des deux mondes*, 15 September 1895, pp. 382 ff.; Lanciani 1902, II, p. 150).

1509: The Cardinal is living on the Via della Regola, near the present palace (Albertini, *Opusculum de Mirabilibus . . .*, ed. Valentini-Zucchetti 1953, p. 552).

1517: Fra Mariano di Firenze (*Itinerarium urbis Romae*, ed. P. Bulletti, Rome, 1931, p. 64) reports: "the Cardinal began this year sumptuously to reconstruct his palace from the foundations . . . with a straight street from the palace door to the Campo di Fiori". The Cardinal moves to Trastevere, relinquishing the site to the builders (Gnoli 1937, p. 204).

1519: Pope Leo X visits the site and stops "ante novum palatium Cardinalis de Farnesio" (Diary of Paris de Grassis quoted by Gnoli, *loc. cit.*)

1520: Leonardo Furtembach, a German contractor, agrees to furnish lime and travertine (Lanciani 1902, I, p. 198; II, p. 152).

These documents are supported by Vasari's account (Life of Antonio; V, p. 450): "Antonio already had acquired a name as an ingenious architect, and one who had an excellent style in building; and for this reason Alessandro, first Cardinal Farnese, later Paul III, had the idea of restoring his old palace in which he lived with his family. Antonio, desirous of gaining a reputation through this work, made numerous designs in several styles; one of which, with two apartments, appealed to his most Reverend Lord, since he had the intention of accommodating in the building Signor Pier Luigi and Signor Ranuccio, his sons. And the work having started, a certain amount was built systematically each year." Vasari suggests the date of this event by listing it as Sangallo's first commission as an independent architect after the death of his master, Bramante, in 1514: the design was made perhaps in 1515–1516 when Sangallo was appointed as assistant to Raphael in the Fabbrica of St Peter's.

The last sentence of Vasari's report indicates that the new construction proceeded slowly; no more is heard of it until the mid-1530's, except that the family continued to purchase property in the neighbourhood (Navenne 1914, pp. 159 ff.), particularly around the square before the palace, not only to make room for the new building, but to house the army of retainers, which numbered 306 in a census of 1526, and continued to grow (Lanciani 1902, II, p. 157).

II SANGALLO'S SECOND PALACE, 1534–1546

I. THE CHANGE IN PLAN

The election of Cardinal Alessandro to the papacy in 1534 brought about a complete change in the palace project, which is also recorded by Vasari (V, p. 469):

> "Paul III while he was Alexander Cardinal Farnese had built a good part of his palace, having made a portion of the first window-row (*i.e.*, second story) on the front façade, the public room behind, and started one arm of the court. But it was not, however, so far advanced that its completion was in sight; so that when Alexander was created Pope, Antonio changed the whole original design, seeing that he had to make no longer a cardinal's but a pontiff's palace. So having razed some of the neighbouring houses and the old stairway, he remade it anew, and more commodious, enlarging the court on every side and similarly the whole palace making public rooms (*sale*) of greater size and more numerous and magnificent private rooms (*stanze*), with the most beautiful inlaid ceilings and many other ornaments."

The differences between the Cardinal's palace and the Pope's are not specified by Vasari, and modern writers either have discredited the account or have assumed that the original building was destroyed entirely or hidden in the remodelling. Recently Wolfgang Lotz uncovered conclusive evidence of the form of the original palace which he generously has permitted me to summarize here.

An architectural sketchbook in Munich (Staatliche Bibliothek, cod. icon., 195, fols. 1, 8) contains plans of the palace before and after the enlargement referred to by Vasari. The early palace has a façade of eleven bays with shops on the ground floor; piers with paired pilasters separate the bays. A simple passageway leads from the main portal to a court with the same piers as the present palace, but with only three arches on each side. Although the court portico appears to be finished, rooms are shown on only the front and left sides. The second drawing shows the start of a transformation into the existing palace; only the façade wing is drawn, substantially in its present form, though some rooms are arranged differently and the main staircase does not appear. The new design preserves intact some of the piers of the original court but it sacrifices the façade, since the front of the palace now extends some 14′–16′ farther into the piazza. Lotz found support for the evidence of the drawings in the building itself: in the court, the original bays can be distinguished from those added after 1535, and the foundations for the original façade can be identified in the palace cellar.

Lotz's attribution of the drawings to Philibert de l'Orme (supported by A. Blunt, *Philibert de l'Orme*, London, 1958 [Vol. I of the present *Studies*], pp. 15 f. The drawings formerly were attributed by Geymüller to J. A. du Cerceau, who came to Rome only in 1539) permits an exact dating, since the architect was in Rome only during the years 1534–1536; the early palace would have been sketched shortly after the election of Paul III in 1534, and the later one toward the end of the sojourn. Work on the new palace may have begun in 1535, the year in which the Maestri delle Strade ordered the enlargement of the piazza (Navenne 1914, p. 413). The accuracy of this schedule is confirmed by the diary of a German, Johannes Fichard, who visited Rome in the summer of 1536 and spoke of the "elegant and splendid palace" as less than half finished ("Italia . . .", *Frankfurtisches Archiv . . .*, II, 1815, p. 26).

The construction, which proceeded so rapidly until 1536, slowed down during the next five years (no documents are preserved from this period), and in 1540 the Pope's granddaughter, Vittoria, was injured in a fall from the provisional wooden stairway which evidently was still the only means of access to the upper floor (Navenne 1914, p. 251).

A contract of March 1541, between the Pope's son, Pier Luigi, then Duke of Castro and Nepi, and a construction firm (published by Gnoli 1937, p. 209), indicates the start of an energetic new campaign which continued without further interruption until the Pope's death in 1549. Besides establishing the customary division of responsibility between the client, the architects (Sangallo and Meleghino), and the contractor (Baronino), the document contains valuable indications of the state of the palace: some ceilings and roofs (of the original palace) still had to be torn down; a price is set for the finishing of *old and new* vaults; and in some parts, foundations still had to be laid. Sangallo had not yet produced a complete design, because the agreement on prices for the construction of roofs and ceilings and for the carving of certain mouldings is deferred to a later date "since now one cannot determine how they are to be made".

Construction started soon after the signing of the contract: Baronino gave a banquet for the masons and carvers in August 1541 (Bertolotti, *B. Baronino*, Casale, 1876, p. 11, where the date is transcribed mistakenly 1540; the correction is from Rome, Archivio di Stato, *Camerale* I, *Tesoreria Segreta* 1290, fol. 30r) and in the following year the Pope appealed to Pier Luigi for financial assistance in continuing the work (Pastor, *Geschichte*, V, p. 814; letter of August 1542 from Serristori to Cosimo I).

2. SANGALLO'S DESIGN

The palace designed by Antonio in 1535–1545 can be reconstructed partially from the large numbers of drawings of this period preserved in the Uffizi (the majority are reproduced in Giovannoni 1959, Figs. 43, 99 ff.) I summarize here those features which clarify Michelangelo's contribution to the palace.

Knowledge of Antonio's plan is founded on a scale drawing by an assistant (Pl. 47a; Uffizi, *Arch.* 298) inscribed in Antonio's hand on the *verso* "Palazzo del Duca di Castro" (repeated in a later hand on the *recto*). The inscription dates the drawing prior to 1545, when the Duke's acquisition of Parma made the title obsolete. Pl. 47a may be the plan used for the contract of 1541; the scheme is close to that of the present building (Fig. 9); significant differences appear only in the rear wing. Sangallo probably built only the left corner of that wing (Fig. 10): the narrow corridor, the stairway, and the small corner room are features of the present palace which already were fixed in Pl. 47a, and which, therefore, were probably started under his supervision.

We know more of Antonio's court design from the existing building than from drawings. There is a large and carefully executed elevation (Uffizi, *Arch.* 627; partially reconstructed in Letarouilly 1849–1866, II, p.303) showing arcades with five *open* bays on each level, but measurements prove it to be an early project (*ca.* 1535?) that was superseded in the construction of the late '30's or early '40's. We do not know whether Antonio's final design proposed open bays on the upper stories or window-bays, as in the present palace.

Drawings for the façade elevation show that Antonio first intended to join the two upper stories by an Order of giant pilasters at the corners (Uffizi, *Arch.* 998r [Letarouilly, p. 289], 1752), but later decided to use the existing quoins. Since the overall height is considerably less than in the present building, the uppermost story is reduced to mezzanine proportions. A cornice decorated with fleurs-de-lis is smaller than Michelangelo's but not fundamentally different in form. The windows of the uppermost story, which were not built until Michelangelo's time, appear almost in their present form in Antonio's sketches (Uffizi, *Arch.* 998, 1109).

The drawings contain valuable evidence on the suite of rooms along the façade on the *piano nobile* (cf. Pl. 49b, a later plan of this story). Sketches for the great *sala* at the left corner (Uffizi, *Arch.* 998r, 1009r, and v) suggest that Sangallo planned to make it two stories high, as it is today. The overall height of the stories was less, but a drawing for the ceiling shows that the plan-dimensions were the same. We know from these projects that Michelangelo's enlargement of the *sala*, referred to by Vasari (see below), can have affected only its height.

Plans and ceiling projects for the rooms at the centre and right half of the *piano nobile* are close to the existing scheme and show that Antonio must have been decorating this suite at the time of his death (Uffizi, *Arch.* 734, 1000; Letarouilly, pp. 287, 318). The ceiling sketch for the room just right of centre which has the arms and inscription of the Duke of Castro and Nepi, must have been drawn before the change of title in 1545. The central window of the façade appears in plan with two free-standing columns in the opening, which helps to clarify Michelangelo's remodelling of the window (four columns appear in Pl. 49b). Antonio's design for the elevation of the central window is known from an anonymous drawing to be discussed below.

3. CONSTRUCTION PRIOR TO SANGALLO'S DEATH

In June 1545, fifteen months before Sangallo's death, the Duke's agent contracted for extensive carving in travertine (5000 scudi for materials alone). Drawings of Doric arches appended to the contract indicate that the construction in question was to continue the ground floor portico of the court (Bertolotti, *Artisti bolognesi*, Bologna, 1886, p. 22; Lanciani 1902, II, p. 152). Evidently only the one side behind the façade had been finished previously (and one arch of the left wing shown in de l'Orme's drawing of 1536).

On 9 January 1546, a stonecarver, Nardo de' Rossi, wrote to Antonio in Rieti, appending two drawings of the second-story façade windows (Uffizi, *Arch.* 302; the letter on the same sheet is transcribed by Milanesi in Vasari, V, pp. 487 f.):

"Now I send you the windows sketched here together with the measurements – that is, those of the corner: one on the piazza side and one on the side toward the Tedeschi [left]. The corner, which you assigned to me when you left, I finished to a height of 35 *palmi* [7·7 m.] from the cornice that makes a parapet for the windows on up. And I began the four store-room windows that look out on the garden, the ones at socle level [?*dalla banda del zocholo:* under the rear ground-floor windows are small openings to light the basement store rooms below] and the kitchen door is almost done and soon will be finished.

"You should know that Jacopo Meleghino has been here at the palace and told me that the Pope said I should make architraves that go on the pilasters of the side entrance on the San

Girolamo side [right, towards the church of San Girolamo della Carità], and that I should make the cornice there separately because there are no proper stones. Now please advise me what I must do."

The first part of the letter indicates the upward progress of the building nine months before Antonio's death; thirty-five *palmi* is just the height of the *piano nobile* today, measuring from the base of the parapet to the base of the course separating the upper stories, so Nardo must have finished this story, at least on the left corner.

Progress toward the rear is indicated by Nardo's other activities: the kitchen door is the last one on the left under the ground floor portico on Pl. 47a. The four store-room windows toward the garden are probably those on the left side of the rear façade; the lintel of these basement windows is 2·1 m. above ground level, and presumably the rear walls on this side had not risen above that height, since Nardo speaks only of the "banda del zocholo". The entrance portal that the Pope wanted finished is the central one in the right wing.

Altogether, the drawings, the contract, the letter and Mochi's report of 1547 quoted below, form a picture of the palace in 1546 as decreasing by steps from a height of two stories on the front half of the façade wing to just above foundation level at the left corner of the rear wing (Fig. 10). Probably the ground floor of the forward half of the palace had been completed as far back as the side entrances; Nardo was working on the ground floor of the rear half on the left wing, but had reached only the central portal on the right. Wherever Antonio's plan (Pl. 47a) differs from the plan of 1549 (Pl. 47b) it is probable that construction had not started: on the rear half of the right wing, and on the central loggia and right side of the rear wing. So much remained unfinished that Vasari commented in the 1550 edition of his *Lives* (p. 881; ed. Ricci, IV, p. 325): "it never will be unified nor seem to be by the same hand".

Knowing that Nardo wrote in January and that Antonio died in September of 1546, it is hard to accept Vasari's story that the architect finished the whole façade except for the cornice (V, p. 470). If it required eleven years to build the two lower stories, eight months cannot have been enough time for the third. Moreover, there are other difficulties in Vasari's report; immediately following the above statement in Sangallo's biography appears a story that the Pope called Perino del Vaga, Sebastiano del Piombo, Michelangelo, and Vasari himself to present cornice designs in competition with those proposed by Antonio, who would then be required to execute the best – an embarrassing situation for any architect. Michelangelo's design was selected, much to Antonio's annoyance. This anecdote is missing from the Life of Michelangelo and from the 1550 version of Antonio's Life, when the events would have been fresh in Vasari's mind; possibly Vasari, writing fifteen or more years later, made an error in chronology – calculated to discredit Sangallo and to glorify Michelangelo? – which actually involved only a few weeks. A more credible sequence would be as follows. January–September 1546: start of the third façade story under Antonio; brief pause following his death in September. Autumn 1546: the "competition"; selection of Michelangelo as architect. Winter 1546/1547: completion of the third façade story using Antonio's windows.

III MICHELANGELO'S DESIGN

I. THE FAÇADE

On 2 March 1547, shortly after Michelangelo's appointment, Prospero Mochi, the agent of Pier Luigi Farnese in Rome, wrote a report on the progress of the construction (Gotti 1875, I, pp. 294 f.; Rocchi 1902, pp. 252 f.):

> "The front façade is almost completed up to the top windows; only the cornice is missing . . . a piece of which has been put up on the S. Geronimo [right] side as a trial to satisfy His Holiness whom we accompanied on a stately tour inside . . . The colonnade all around is in place [court portico]. And the [second story] rooms on the San Geronimo side are almost finished with the chapel at the head of the corridor [completed only under Card. Alessandro Farnese, 1565–1585] and shortly will be habitable. And on the Catena and Tedeschi side [left], the servants dining hall and commissary [*tinello* and *dispensa*; cf. Pl. 47b] and the public and private kitchens are done, and the majority of storage rooms with the water storage [in the basement], the largest and most convenient that I have ever seen . . . so that, if all goes well, it will shortly be finished."

Some of the progress reported here was due to Sangallo, but we know from Vasari (VII, p. 223) that it was Michelangelo who "had a wood (cornice) model made, six *braccia* (3·5 m.) long and to full scale and placed it on the corner of the palace to show the effect it would have when built; which pleased His Holiness and all of Rome, and then was carried out".

The new cornice (Pl. 40) started a battle between adherents of the two architects; in May 1547, Michelangelo was told that Sangallo's pupil, Nanni di Baccio Bigio, was spreading the story "that you have made a model of a cornice for the Farnese palace of such size that, though it is of wood, it has been necessary to buttress the façade. He suspects (*spera*) that anyhow you are out to ruin the palace and that some wreckage is bound to ensue" (letter from Giov. Francesco Ughi; Gotti 1875, I, p. 310). Aesthetic as well as practical objections were raised: an extensive Vitruvian criticism, perhaps by Giovanni Battista Sangallo, has been preserved in a copy by Michelangelo himself (published by Gotti I, p. 292; S. Meller 1909, pp. 1 ff., proved that Michelangelo was the object, not the author of the attack). The secret of the passions raised by the cornice is revealed by Giovanni Alghisi, a military engineer employed by Michelangelo; he reported (*Delle Fortificationi*, Venice, 1570, III, 2; Navenne 1914, pp. 11, 413 f.) that the stone lintels and architraves in the façade cracked when the cornice was begun, due to the poor foundations which had been built on weak antique walls, and that a costly rebuilding had to be undertaken (confirmed in the Diary of Flaminio Vacca quoted by Bonanni 1699, I, p. 214). Defenders of Sangallo countered that the failure was due to the excessive weight of the cornice. The heat generated by this debate may have twisted Vasari's account of the "competition". The cornice was completed at least partly in July 1547, when Paul III again inspected the palace (Navenne 1914, p. 427).

Vasari attributed other alterations in the façade elevation to Michelangelo (VII, pp. 223 f.): one was the design of "the great marble window with beautiful *mischio* columns, above the main portal, with a big coat of arms, beautiful and original, of Paul III". Sangallo had already built the central window in completing the second story. His design is preserved in an anonymous drawing of the façade (Munich, Graph. Slg., No. 34356;

identified by Tolnay 1930, p. 35, Fig. 22; Siebenhüner 1952, p. 152, Fig. 135. The central window in our Fig. 10 is taken from this drawing.), an alternative to Sangallo's scheme with a remarkably inept proposal for a fourth-story attic surmounted by a feeble cornice. Since all the second-story windows have triangular pediments, the drawing must pre-date the placing of the existing windows with alternating pediments in January 1546; therefore it cannot be one of the "competition" projects. Here the central window has free-standing and applied columns as they exist today, but they support two concentric arches framing a coat of arms (Pl. 4a). Since the drawing does not follow Sangallo consistently in other respects, the window arches might be discarded as a fantasy of the draughtsman, but for the fact that they can be traced by breaks in the existing brickwork and in the masonry of the lintel (cf. Anderson photo No. 6472). Sangallo's authorship of the free-standing and applied columns is confirmed by stylistic evidence (Tolnay, *loc. cit.*); they are typical examples of his classic manner. Michelangelo's only contribution to the window frame as seen from the piazza was therefore the single block of masonry that spans the opening as a lintel. He also added a second pair of *mischio* columns (Pl. 49b) behind the first for structural rather than for expressive reasons (Antonio's drawings, Uffizi, *Arch.* 734, 1000, show only the outer pair), which explains Vasari's reference. Though the changes were modest, the suppression of the arches, and particularly the monumentalizing of the arms, altered the entire effect of the façade. The two lesser arms were later glosses to Michelangelo's design.

Michelangelo's window appears in several contemporary representations: two medals of 1548 celebrating the revised elevation (Bonanni 1699, I, p. 214, Nos. XVI, XVII; Schiavo 1949, Fig. 42); an engraving by Nicolas Beatrizet dated 1549 (Pl. 41; Tolnay 1930, pp. 37 f., Figs. 23, 24); and a drawing of May 1549 (Pl. 42a). All but the last must have been made from drawings, before the window actually was changed; the medals and engraving show a balustrade at the base of the window that is missing from Pl. 42a, which was sketched on the site (we do not know whether a balustrade was built; in Pl. 49b, of 1558–1568, it is sketched only in chalk, which may indicate that it was not executed yet; Baroque views show the window with and without it, and the existing balcony was not there in Letarouilly's time: 1849–1866, Pls. 119, 120, 125). Moreover, Beatrizet (Pl. 41) adds projections to the entablature that are structurally meaningless; he must have misread the drawings. Lotz drew my attention to a correction in the engraving: a darkened area around the papal arms indicates that Sangallo's arches were incised first on the plate and later removed – a further indication that Michelangelo's remodelling post-dates the preparation of the engraving.

The anonymous draughtsman of 1549 visited the palace after the arches were suppressed and the lintel added, but before the papal arms were in place. His sketch (Pl. 42a; Uffizi, *Arch.* 4939) is inscribed "questa è la metà della facciata del palazzo di Farnese in Roma. E come stia il cornicione, e le modinature delle finestre per l'appunto si vede nel mio primo libro à carte 35 e 101" (Lotz pointed out that the traditional attribution of the sketchbook in which the drawings appear to Giorgio Vasari the Younger, nephew of the biographer, who was active in the early decades of the seventeenth century, is chronologically improbable). The inexact cornice of Pl. 42a is drawn more correctly on

fol. 35 of the sketchbook, as the author says (Uffizi, *Arch.* 4629; a detail, lacking the ornaments in the frieze and cyma).

In supervising the construction of the third story, Michelangelo apparently made no
change in the window design. Preparatory window sketches appear in Sangallo's drawings (Uffizi, *Arch.* 998, 1109) and the carving of the frames probably started before his
death. But another change in the elevation is intimated in Vasari's passage quoted below
which mentions Michelangelo's enlargement of the great two-story *sala* on the left of
the façade wing. Sangallo's drawings (*Arch.* 1009r and v) prove that the existing plan of
this room was established before Michelangelo's time (Pl. 49b). Michelangelo's "enlargement", then, can have been only upward; if the room was made higher, the façade
would have been raised, too. While Sangallo intended to follow Florentine tradition by
progressively reducing the height of the stories, Michelangelo raised the third approximately to the height of the second to compensate for the compressive effect and the cast
shadow of his enormous cornice. The colossal proportions which this change produced
in the *sala* itself are unique in the Renaissance (Schiavo 1949, Fig. 45).

2. CHRONOLOGY OF CONSTRUCTION UNDER MICHELANGELO

1546 Autumn: Michelangelo's appointment.

1547 2 March: Façade completed, somewhat raised in height; wooden cornice model
set up; second-story suite and chapel on front and right wings nearly ready for
occupation; kitchens, *tinello*, and *dispensa* on left half of the rear wing at least
partly finished (letter of P. Mochi).

1547 July: Paul III visits the palace to inspect the cornice.

1548 to May 1549: Reconstruction of the central window; arms not yet in place (medals,
engraving, 1549 drawing).

The following records are from the sole surviving account-book of the palace construction, for the year 1549 (Rome, Archivio di Stato, *Camerale* I, *Fabbriche*, No. 1515.
Following the Pope's death in November 1549, the costs could be defrayed no longer
by the Camera).

1549 January to June: Total expenses for the "Palazzo nuovo", 8964 scudi; June to
December, 5108 scudi (fols. 1 f.; 23v). Throughout the year, payments are made
for quarrying, sculpting, carpentry, "lavori di muro", the carving of wooden
ceilings, and work in alabaster and marble (fols. 11, 12).

1549 5 January: Payment to a mason for "mattonato ch'ei fa nella camera del cantone
verso S. Hieronimo", the second-story corner of the façade on the right
(fol. 11).

1549 4 May: 17 metal ties supplied "per il camino di mischio del salotto del cantone"
(fol. 18v).

24 April: a neighbour is paid compensation for the razing of his house "to make
a street alongside the palace of the Farnese family toward San Geronimo" (fol. 18).
6, 18 July: "a maestro Gio. Pietro falegname a buon conto del modello delle
loggie del palazzo verso il giardino" (fols. 23, 24v). That is, a model for the rear
wing, presumably after Michelangelo's design, in the form of loggie. Since the

design of this wing presupposes final decisions on the court elevations, Michelangelo's palace project apparently was complete by this date.

1549–1550 Start of Vignola's activity at the palace. In 1547 Vignola was hired by Pier Luigi Farnese to take Sangallo's position as chief architect for the family projects at Piacenza and Castro. On arriving in Rome in the winter of 1549/1550, he immediately began to work at the palace, and appears in documents of the period 31 May 1550 to 9 March 1552 as paymaster and architect supervising the purchase of materials for the tomb of Paul III, which was being sculpted by Guglielmo della Porta (Léon Cadier, "Le tombeau du pape Paul III Farnèse", *École fr. de Rome, Mélanges*, IX, 1889, pp. 86 ff. Lotz brought these documents to my attention). At this time Vignola must have joined or, more likely, succeeded, Michelangelo as chief architect.

1550 on: No further evidence of Michelangelo's participation. As at St Peter's, he probably declined to supervise construction during the 1550's on the grounds of infirmity.

1551: Rome plan of Bufalini. The cartographer inaccurately completed the palace plan, including the rear wing, anticipating later construction, perhaps from the evidence of Sangallo's foundations (F. Ehrle, *Roma al tempo di Giulio III*, Rome, 1911).

1552: The French Ambassador refused to stay in the palace because "there were too few rooms and the house was all open". In the following year Cardinal du Bellay moved to the Cancelleria for the same reason (Navenne 1914, pp. 523, 527).

Ca. 1554–1560: Sketch of the court by an anonymous Fleming (Pl. 42b; Brunswick, Herzog Anton-Ulrich Museum; Tolnay 1930, Fig. 27. The drawing is on the *verso* of Pl. 31a executed in 1554–1560, cf. p. 52). The rear wing has not been started; only the ground floor portico and the socles of the second-story pilasters above appear. Beyond the portico to the left appears a wall – faintly indicated alongside the great pier in the foreground – which suggests that the construction of the rear portion of the left wing had been completed to a height of at least two stories (compare Pl. 49b). The absence of any sign of construction, such as scaffolding, implies that there had been a temporary abandonment of the building programme.

1555: Rome plan of Pinardo. No rear wing appears, but arcades – without their brick walls or windows – are shown on the first two stories of the front and side wings. The representation is inaccurate; it fails to show the third façade story, and if only two stories of the lateral wings had been finished, they would not have been roofed. The engraving is useful only as an indication that some of the upper galleries were done in 1550–1555.

1558–1568: The palace was surveyed at some point in these years by an anonymous draughtsman whose sketches (Pls. 48b–49) will be analysed shortly. We can deduce from the drawings that there was no major departure from Michelangelo's project during the 1560's, but we cannot distinguish the portions completed under Michelangelo before 1550 from those added later.

Ca. 1560: Cardinal Ranuccio Farnese calls conferences to discuss the design and cost of the rear wing (letter of Guglielmo della Porta discussed below).

1560: Engraving (Pl. 43b; Tolnay 1930, p. 41, Fig. 26) of Michelangelo's project for the rear wing of the court, probably after the model of 1549. The publication indicates that construction had not yet started on the existing rear wing.

3. MICHELANGELO'S PROJECT FOR THE COURT AND REAR WING

Following his report on Michelangelo's additions to the façade, Vasari continues (VII, p. 224): "Inside he continued upwards from the first Order of the court, the other two Orders, with the most beautiful, ingenious, and gracious windows and crowning cornice that ever have been seen; whence, by the efforts and genius of that man, there has arisen today the most beautiful court in Europe. He enlarged and made greater the grand *sala*, and arranged the *ricetto* before it, and with an ingenious and new kind of arch in the form of a half oval he carved out the vaults of this *ricetto*." The *ricetto* is the second-story gallery built upon the ground floor portico to provide circulation around the court. It is structurally independent of the outer rooms, so that Sangallo could build two stories of the façade without starting the second story of the court (Fig. 10). But Antonio must have supervised the carving of the Ionic columns and arches, since except for the frieze of garlands and masks, the style is characteristically his, and wholly different from Michelangelo's uppermost story (Pls. 45 and 46a). That Vasari correctly assigned the building of the *ricetto* to Michelangelo is proven by its flattened, "half oval", vaults – a wholly new invention, not anticipated by Sangallo, and a hallmark of Michelangelo's late work. The vault had to be flattened to accommodate a mezzanine for servants' quarters between the second and third stories, which left no room for a conventional barrel vault (Pls. 43a–b). The mezzanine was built only in the two lateral wings; on the front and rear, where the *ricetto* arches were left open toward the court (Pl. 43a), there was insufficient space for it, since the springing of the vault had to be substantially higher (Letarouilly 1849–1866, Pls. 125, 130; Schiavo 1949, Fig. 47; Tolnay 1951, Pl. 243).

The court façades were praised especially by Vasari in his essay on architecture (I, p. 123): "But more than any other master, Michelangelo ennobled this stone (travertine) in ornamenting the court of the Farnese house, having used it there with marvellous judgment to make windows, masks, brackets, and many other such fantasies, all worked as if in marble, so that one cannot find any similar ornament done more beautifully . . ." The fantasy and marble-like treatment praised by Vasari are illustrated in the second-story frieze and in the whole of the upper story (Pl. 45), but the second-story windows, with their dryness of treatment and reserved simplicity, are wholly different in style. They are too distant from ancient and Renaissance conventions to admit attribution to Sangallo; the detached panel-like bands alongside the jambs and the strange volute-like brackets above them are unparalleled in his work. These very motifs were favourites of Vignola (cf. *Regole delle cinque ordini*, Amsterdam, 1617, Pl. XXX), who began working at the palace in 1549/1550. Michelangelo, who was occupied elsewhere during the 1550's, may have left the design to his younger successor; it appears in the engraving of 1560 (Pl. 43b). A fascinating alternative study for the court elevation now in the Kunstbibliothek in Berlin (Hdz. 4151, fol. 81v) was published by Letarouilly (1849–1866, II, p. 272) from the Destailleur collection. It is a perspective section-elevation in which the windows of the *piano nobile* have alternating pediments and those of the upper story flat pediments; there are no mezzanine stories. The sheet carries an old attribution to Vignola; Letarouilly ascribed it to Sangallo; but I agree with Lotz that it should not be used for documentary purposes without further study, since it has a suspiciously nineteenth-century appearance.

The uppermost story (Pl. 46a), entirely uninhibited by Sangallo's bequests, succeeds remarkably in importing the style of St Peter's into the court without disrupting its homogeneity. Two chalk sketches in Oxford (Nos. 332, 333; D.633, 634; F.271, 272; Parker 1956, pp. 171 ff.) have been called original studies for the windows; No. 332, which has a cartouche with an inscription, probably is unrelated, but No. 333 (Pl. 46b) is reasonably close to the final version and may be Michelangelo's sole surviving sketch for the palace. The *verso* (see p. 124) contains a façade elevation too faintly preserved to assess. It could be related either to the Farnese or to the Conservatori palace.

A remodelling of the early nineteenth century (Letarouilly, p. 279, calls it "assez récente") filled in the open gallery arches on the second story of the front and rear wings (Pl. 43a, rear wing; for the front wing see Pl. 49b and a drawing by Annibale Carracci, Frankfurt, Städelsches Kunstinstitut, No. 4064; brought to my attention by Lotz), making them uniform with the side elevations except for the original balustrade, which projects from the concrete screen (Pl. 45). Perhaps Michelangelo intended to leave the front elevation as it appears in Pl. 49b, but he did not plan the five open arches that his successors also built in the rear wing. His design as seen in the engraving of 1560 (Pl. 43b, Tolnay 1930, p. 41, Fig. 26; Siebenhüner 1952, pp. 156 f.), which probably represents the model of 1549, shows only three open bays; the outer two continue the design of the side elevations, including the use of a socle rather than a balustrade at the base of the windows.

The engraved project eliminates the central block of Sangallo's rear wing (Pl. 47a); it is only one bay in depth and permits construction of a semi-transparent screen of three superimposed loggias. Michelangelo did not contemplate the destruction of the rear corner started by Sangallo (Fig. 10) and finished in Pl. 49a; the garden façade may be visualized as a ⌊_⌋, the base of which is formed by the loggias and the arms by two projecting blocks conforming – with some restriction in width – to Sangallo's foundations. Vasari explains (*loc. cit.*) that the open loggias were related to an overall plan involving the palace garden with an ancient sculptural group called the *Farnese Bull* to be used as a fountain on the central axis, a bridge across the Tiber, and a second garden on the far side of the river, all designed to be seen from the main entrance of the palace. The scheme was not carried out; the loggias were suppressed by Michelangelo's successors, the *Bull* was housed in a temporary shelter, and the bridge never was started.

A number of sixteenth-century plans of the palace indicate that Michelangelo's open-loggia scheme was only one of several proposed. The interpretation of the 1549 plan (Pl. 47b) is made difficult by its inscription: "Questo è la pianta del Palazzo di Farnese di Roma di mano di M. Antonio da Sangallo, con l'aggiunta di Michelangelo Buonarroti, et di quello che vi mancha [*i.e.*, unexecuted as well as existing portions are shown], fatto oggi questo dì 12 di Maggio 1549". Presumably the Michelangelo additions are to be found in those portions which differ from Sangallo's earlier plan (Pl. 47a): the centre and right half of the rear wing and the rear half of the right wing. But this conclusion is unacceptable on stylistic grounds: the substitution of a long, narrow corridor for Sangallo's garden loggia and the disagreeable proportions of the resulting interior spaces is a perversion of the original scheme and certainly not characteristic of Michelangelo's planning. Some light is cast on this paradox by inscriptions in the two rooms to the left of the rear corridor: "tinello", and "dispensa", which recall the passage in Mochi's letter of March 1547: "e verso la catena e Tedeschi è facto il tinello e dispensa et cucina palese et segreta". If Sangallo himself designed the long, narrow *dispensa*, then he, and not Michelangelo, would have been responsible for replacing the loggia with a corridor. But Mochi seems to have been only partly accurate; in Pl. 49a, of 1558–1568, the *dispensa* is still unfinished – there are walls only in the forward half. The problem of loggia-or-corridor must have been so important that the construction of the *dispensa* was halted at a point where either solution remained possible. The model of "loggie verso il giardino" was made just two months after Pl. 47b; we have assumed that it was Michelangelo's and that it was copied for the 1560 engraving (Pl. 43b); if this is so, then Michelangelo's solution was a third alternative that required the elimination of everything but the *tinello*, and furthermore, Michelangelo can have contributed to Pl. 47b only the relocation of the stairways in the front and right wing.

In other projects of the period, the loggia-or-corridor alternatives reappear. One, by Vignola (Vienna, Albertina, Ital. arch., Rom, No. 1073, unpublished. I first knew of this drawing from Dr. Thelen, via Dr. Lotz), retains the corridor of Pl. 47b, but eliminates the doorway into the *dispensa* and the one opposite, in order to enliven the corridor walls with rows of niches copied from those of the main entrance. The *tinello* wall is moved farther to the right than in Pl. 47b, so as not to obstruct the façade window; and the stairway in the right wing appears again in the corner room, where Sangallo had placed it.

Sangallo's loggia appears again in three plans that must have been done after Vignola's, since they incorporate his innovations, such as the niches (in the passageway to the loggia), and the corner stairway, though adding the stairway of Pl. 47b. One is Pl. 48a, Uffizi, *Arch.* 3450, attributed to Ammanati. A slightly different plan in the Albertina (Ital. arch., Rom, No. 1075) was discovered by Lotz, and another has been acquired recently by the Metropolitan Museum in New York (No. 49.92.61; probably a copy of the 1560's). The Metropolitan group also contains a project for the garden (No. 49.92.74; these drawings, identified by Tolnay and presented by Janos Scholz, were brought to my attention by Mr. Hyatt Mayor and Sir Anthony Blunt) in which the Sangallesque central loggia of the rear wing is repeated on the other three sides of the garden enclosure to establish a symmetrical system of a sort used by Vignola in garden plans (both drawings reproduced by Blunt in the *Metropolitan Museum of Art Bulletin*, Summer, 1960. pp. 15 ff.)

The date as well as the authorship of these projects is uncertain. Vignola's palace plan, a refinement of the 1549 solution (Pl. 47b), may have been drawn when he first came to the palace in the winter of 1549/1550. But, since so little building was being done during

the 1550's, it may be that all the post-Michelangelo drawings are related to the conferences held by Cardinal Ranuccio around 1560 on the design of the rear wing and
loggia. Perhaps a competition was held at that time; this would explain the publication
of Michelangelo's project of 1549 in an engraving of 1560 as an effort to influence the
Cardinal in his decision. Like the engravings of St Peter's and the Campidoglio, it may
have been sponsored by Michelangelo's friends in an unsuccessful attempt to assure
adherence to the master's intentions. As a result of the discussions, Vignola must have
abandoned the long corridor in favour of a solution closer to Sangallo's; he was probably
the author of the existing rear wing, which incorporates elements of all the plans (compare Pls. 47b, 48a; Fig. 10).

IV COMPLETION OF THE PALACE

Cardinal Ranuccio Farnese (1530–1565), called Cardinal Sant'Angelo, was the first mem-
ber of the family to live regularly in the palace. He is responsible for the decoration of
the second-story suite of rooms on the façade and in the forward half of the right wing.
He commissioned Francesco Salviati to fresco the room over the central portal, which
was completed by Taddeo Zuccaro under Cardinal Alessandro II (Vasari, VII, pp. 32,
97). His arms appear in the ceilings of the great *sala*, and in the central room over the
right entrance, and his inscription on the entablatures of doorways in the suite (Bourdon
1907, p. 14). He built fireplaces in the two rooms, of which the latter and probably the
former was designed by Vignola (*Regole delle cinque ordini*, Amsterdam, 1617, Pl. XXXV).

Cardinal Ranuccio must have done some building in addition to the decoration of
the interior. We have seen that the sketch of 1554–1560 (Pl. 42b) implies a halt in construction during the early years of his residence; but another draughtsman, who wrote a
frenchified Italian, visited the palace within a few years of his death in 1565 and recorded
substantial progress (Pls. 49a–b; Anonymous drawings from the former Destailleur
Collection, Berlin, Ehemals Staatliche Kunstbibliothek, Hdz. 4151, fols. 97 ff. Tolnay
1930, Fig. 21, published the façade elevation; the remaining drawings were found by
Lotz. The Berlin volumes are not sketchbooks, as they frequently are called, but a collection of French and Italian sixteenth-century drawings by several architects, similar in
character and perhaps in provenance to the group now in the Metropolitan Museum).
He drew measured plans of most of the existing portions of the first and second stories
(Pls. 49a–b), a longitudinal section/elevation through the façade wing and court (Pl. 48b),
the right part of the façade elevation (excluding the central window), and many details.
We cannot clearly distinguish in this survey the portions built for Ranuccio from those
completed before 1550, except at the rear of the court, where the earlier state is recorded
in Pl. 42b. What appear to be nearly identical versions of some of these sketches by the
same hand – with all their inaccuracies in proportion and scale – are preserved in the
Albertina. Berlin fol. 99 corresponds to Albertina, Ital. arch., Rom, No. 1085r; fol. 97r to
No. 1046r; fol. 97v to No. 1046v. I cannot explain why on-the-site sketches of this sort
would have been reproduced without emendation. The following summary of the
sketches includes only those that bear on problems of chronology.

Façade wing. The façade itself appears in its present condition in an elevation (Tolnay, *loc. cit.*) on fol. 98 (the cornice is sketched only in profile) and section, fol. 99 (Pl. 48b). Nothing of the third story appears on the court side, but since the artist shows a roof, the interior walls probably were finished. In plans of the ground floor and second story (Pls. 49a–b; fol. 97r, v), the only major difference from the existing palace is the open second-story court arcade (in Pl. 49b the balustrade has been built only in the central bay).

Side wings. The court elevation of the right wing appears in the section, fol. 99 (Pl. 48b). Again, only two stories are shown; all the second-story windows are drawn, but the brick wall into which they are set is indicated only in the three forward bays; apparently the two rear bays were still under construction. In the plans (Pls. 49a–b), we see only the left wing, in its present state; here all the windows are in place.

Rear wing. On the ground floor the condition of the left corner apparently is unchanged since Sangallo's time (Pls. 47a, 49a). The corner stairway and room and the *tinello* have the form of Pl. 47a. A confusion about the corner window overlooking the garden appears in other plans, where it is sometimes walled up. The *dispensa* to the left of the rear loggia is unclear; while the forward half is inked, the rear is sketched only in chalk without apertures, indicating that at most the foundations were finished. A choice between the corridor scheme (Pl. 47b and Vignola's drawing) and the loggia scheme (Pl. 48a) still had to be made. Nothing is shown of the right half of the rear wing.

In the second story (Pl. 49b), only three arches of the court arcade are complete; their balconies are not built, nor are the windows in the end bays proposed by Michelangelo (Pl. 43b; perhaps the proposal already had been abandoned). The rooms behind have not been started, since the ground floor walls were unfinished; the street façade on the left has not quite reached the rear corner.

The third story. Although the drawings show none of the third-story construction on the court, a sketch (fol. 100v) of Michelangelo's windows is measured so meticulously that one or more of them must have been in place, presumably on the façade wing.

Summary. The garden front remained as it had been since 1546; the second-story court elevation was finished to a height of two stories except for two windows on the right wing, and two arches on the rear wing; the third story was partly or wholly complete on the façade wing.

The date of these drawings cannot be fixed more precisely than in the decade 1558–1568. Comparison with the drawing of 1554–1560 (Pl. 42b) suggests 1558 as a plausible *terminus post quem*. For the *terminus ante* we may turn to an inventory of antiquities in the palace collection made in 1568 for the second Cardinal Alessandro, who occupied the palace in 1565–1585 (*Documenti inediti per servire alla storia dei musei d'Italia*, I, p. 72). Most of the entries concern the suite decorated by Ranuccio on the second story of the right wing: the "Camera grande dell' Ill.mo Cardinale detta la Galleria" must be at the right rear corner of the court, because there are statues "in la loggia à canto la detta camera verso il fiume", which is the rear second-story arcade of the court (the Galleria should not be confused with the Carracci gallery in the centre of the rear wing overlooking the garden; Guglielmo della Porta's letter discussed below shows that the construction of the rear wing was not begun for some time after the arrival of Cardinal Alessandro in

1565). Ranuccio's hall at the centre of the right wing is called the "sala grande nuova" (Bourdon 1909, p. 171n), and the "loggia grande dinanti la sala" is the enclosed passage behind the court windows. There are "statue di marmoro de la banda del Vigniola", a note that is more helpful in identifying the architect than in locating the portions built by him; the reference is either to the right wing or to the rear, which Vignola must have started by 1568, since probably he finished two stories before his death in 1573. The foregoing identifications are speculative, but the fact that sculptures were exhibited in the court loggia "verso il fiume" (to the rear) indicates that it was completed after the visit of the author of Pl. 49b and before 1568.

Further additions by Cardinal Alessandro are documented by decorative insignia; in the small chapel at the right of the façade wing toward the court, and in the central third-story *sala* of the right wing, just above Ranuccio's (Bourdon 1907, p. 15). Alessandro also commissioned Daniele da Volterra to paint friezes in three corner rooms on the right wing in Ranuccio's suite (Vasari, VII, p. 56, Bourdon 1909, p. 176). In 1578, Giacomo della Porta, Vignola's successor, was consulted on the ceiling of the *studiolo* of the family librarian and curator, Fulvio Orsini (Ronchini, *Atti e memorie delle RR. deputazioni di storia patria per le provincie dell' Emilia*, N.S. IV, 2, 1880, p. 58). These records suggest that the third story of the front and right wings was in use before 1578. Other rooms in the rear of the third story were decorated by Duke Alessandro Farnese of Parma, who lived in the palace from 1586 to 1592, and by his successor, Cardinal Odoardo, who also decorated the rear rooms on the right of the second story (Bourdon 1907, *passim*).

Evidence for the construction of the rear wing is found in the draft of an undated letter from the sculptor Guglielmo della Porta to Cardinal Alessandro (from Porta's Düsseldorf sketchbook published by Gronau 1918, pp. 199 f.) To paraphrase his principal points: first, additional lodgings must be provided elsewhere than on the existing roofs where they are now being built; second, a proper, large court with open *loggie* must be built, as Sangallo and Michelangelo knew, though the latter left no design for it (Guglielmo overlooked the 1560 engraving, Pl. 43b); third, when there was a discussion in Cardinal Santo Angelo's time on building the open loggie, the cost was estimated at 60,000 scudi, which is excessive for a project unsuitable to both summer and winter living. At that time I was asked to prepare a design of my own, following the discussion, in which many able men took part, which I did, and which may be seen in the present drawing (none of the architectural projects in the sketchbook seems to be for the palace). Duke Ottavio (of Parma, ruled 1547–1586) saw my drawing and said that unless the court is to be enlarged, no more rooms can be made, nor can the palace be finished properly, and that money spent for any other solution would be thrown away. Here Guglielmo closes, but in a second version of the report (*loc. cit.*) he adds that his project could be carried out for the same price – 25–30,000 scudi – as the proposal currently being considered to "finish it as it had been begun". Probably the alternate proposal was to screen off the rear of the court without providing the additional rooms that Guglielmo and the Duke held to be essential. This suggests that there may have been a controversy between adherents of Michelangelo's project, which eliminated a number of rooms, and proposals similar to the one finally executed.

Guglielmo's letter is undated; it surely was written after 1565, since it refers in the past tense to "Santo Angelo", or Cardinal Ranuccio, who died in that year, and before the resumption of construction. The latter date remains to be fixed.

In 1577 the finished court elevation of the rear wing appeared in Dupérac's plan of Rome (F. Ehrle, *Roma prima di Sisto V*, Rome, 1908; the completed garden façade first appeared in Salvestro Peruzzi's sketch for a Rome plan, Rocchi 1902, p. 113, Pl. XXI, which Rocchi dated 1564–1565, but which now seems to be almost twenty years later as indicated by the state of other contemporary buildings as well). Ferrerio's seventeenth-century elevation of the garden façade (*Palazzi di Roma de' più celebri architetti*, Rome [1655], Pl. 4: a companion plate to Pl. 43a) is inscribed: "Parte del Palazzo de' Farnese verso Strada Giulia con l'aggiunta delle loggie di mezzo architettura di Giacomo Barozio da Vignola fatte l'anno MDLXXV". Ferrerio's date fits the evidence of the Dupérac plan but clashes with an existing inscription on the uppermost loggia that credits Cardinal Alessandro with the completion of the palace in 1589. Furthermore, the attribution of both central loggias to Vignola is not sustained by the more scholarly Baglione, who gives the uppermost to della Porta (*Vite*, Rome, 1642, p. 81): "nella parte di dentro del maravigliosa palagio de' signori Farnesi, l'ultime finestre, e cornicione del Cortile, con la Loggia, che guarda verso strada Giulia".

Only one hypothesis will reconcile the conflicts in our documents: that Vignola designed and started the rear wing after 1565 and before his death in 1573; that by 1575 the court elevation and two stories of the garden façade were finished; and that between 1573 and 1589 della Porta completed the garden façade. But these suggestions are based on seventeenth-century hearsay; Ferrerio made at least one error, and we find another in Baglione: the court windows and cornice which he attributed to della Porta appear in the engraving of Michelangelo's project of 1560 (Pl. 43b), before Porta was practising architecture; at most he might have supervised the execution of those on the rear wing. If both Baroque sources are mistaken in the facts that can be verified, it is unsound to accept those facts that cannot; the best that can be said for the present hypothesis is that it is plausible.

A broad passageway and bridge extending along the right side of the garden across the Via Giulia, and a garden casino between the street and the river which was built shortly before 1600 (Bourdon 1909, pp. 181 ff., Pl. XIX), may have been designed by della Porta to complete the palace in its present form.

The Basilica of St Peter, 1546–1564

I HISTORY

1. CONSTRUCTION PRIOR TO 1540

Julius II (1503–1513) decided to replace the hallowed but decaying Early Christian Basilica of St Peter shortly after his election and, in 1505, together with his architect Donato Bramante, developed a series of studies that promised a monument of unparalleled grandeur. In his capacity as a sculptor, Michelangelo was involved in the preparations from the start. As Tolnay pointed out (1954, pp. 19 f.), Michelangelo aimed to put the monumental tomb of Julius II in the fifteenth-century choir of the Basilica (Condivi, Ch. XXVII); Giuliano da Sangallo suggested a separate chapel (Vasari IV, p. 282). These discussions may have encouraged Julius and Bramante to visualize the Basilica itself as a majestic housing for the tomb; the first plan (Fig. 11a), which immediately followed the initial tomb studies, could be called a grandiose funerary chapel (Tolnay, p. 21), though the central form was so popular at the period that it might have been adopted without this connotation. (For the early history of the new Basilica see H. von Geymüller, *Les projets primitifs pour la basilique de Saint-Pierre de Rome*, Paris–Vienna, 1875; D. Frey, *Bramantes St Peter-Entwurf und seine Apokryphen*, Vienna, 1915; K. Frey 1911, 1913; T. Hofmann, 1928; Schüller-Piroli, *2000 Jahre Sankt Peter*, Olten, 1950, pp. 491–557; O. Förster 1956, pp. 209–274.) For convenience the term "Basilica" will be used for centralized as well as for longitudinal projects.

A bewildering number of preparatory drawings survive from the early period and, after nearly a century of careful study, their chronology – and in many cases their authorship – remains unclear. We know from them only that Bramante first designed a central-plan Basilica: a square penetrated by a Greek cross with hemicyclical apses terminating each arm (Fig. 11a) and dominated by a great dome over the crossing, as in the commemorative medal of 1505 (Pl. 51a), perhaps made from the preliminary model. Alternative schemes for a traditional basilical plan with a long nave to the east (the Basilica is unconventionally oriented with its choir toward the west) probably were drawn as a result of pressure exercised on the Pope by more devout contemporaries. They contended then, as they did with success at the end of the century, that a centralized plan could not properly accommodate hoards of worshippers, that it would cover the sanctified area of the ancient Basilica and further that its pagan character was an affront to ecclesiastical tradition. The final project of 1506 was probably a compromise that extended the eastern arm into a proper nave, but its form is uncertain.

The foundation-stone for the new Basilica was laid in April 1506, and with an army of 2500 labourers, work on the crossing piers proceeded rapidly until the death of the Pope in 1513. The piers were completed within three years and were joined in 1510–1511 by great coffered arches built in the technique of Imperial Roman architecture. At the same time the choir started by Rossellino for Nicholas V half a century earlier was completed after a new design by Bramante (Pls. 52b, 53a, 56b). The decision to retain the old choir at the expense of homogeneity represents the sole concession to historical continuity; it was demolished in 1585 in order to equalize the arms of the cross. Before Bramante's death in 1514, the secondary buttressing piers to the north and south of the crossing (Fig. 11) were raised to the height of one story, and a temporary Doric altar-house incorporating the Early Christian apse was constructed of Peperino in the centre of the crossing (Pl. 56b; on this structure, destroyed in 1592, see Apolloni *et al.* 1951, pp. 205 ff., Figs. 137, 158 f., Pl. LXXXV).

In 1514 Giuliano da Sangallo and Fra Giocondo, both of whom had been Bramante's competitors in 1505, were summoned by Julius' successor, Leo X (1513–1521), to consult with the dying master, and a new series of projects aimed at reducing the cost of the original scheme was developed in a contentious atmosphere. On Bramante's death in 1514, Giocondo continued with foundations for a sacristy alongside the remodelled fifteenth-century choir. A year later, Giocondo's death led to the appointment of Raphael who, in the remaining five years of his life, prepared designs and a model based on Bramante's scheme, and completed some of the surface membering around the crossing. In 1520 the post passed to Antonio da Sangallo the Younger, who had served in the *fabbrica* for more than ten years, first as a carpenter and later as sub-architect. Baldassare Peruzzi was appointed to assist him, and both architects prepared new models. Hampered by the death of Leo X and by the succession of the dour and cautious Hadrian VI, they made little progress until the pontificate of Clement VII (1523–1534) when, after an energetic construction campaign of 1524–1527 (cf. K. Frey 1911, pp. 71–90), they were again frustrated by the Sack of Rome and the consequent impoverishment of the Holy See. During the mid-'twenties, columns were prepared for niche-tabernacles; Bramante's altar-house was completed, and cornices were made around the crossing. The chief progress was in the southern arm of the Basilica, where the crossing piers were joined to the outer buttressing piers by coffered barrel vaults; the side walls of the arm were completed up to the entablature from which the great vault would spring (Pl. 52a), and the terminating hemicycle was built much as it had appeared in Raphael's plan to a height of one story above ground. In this state St Peter's was pictured in the invaluable series of views drawn by or copied after the Netherlandish painter Marten van Heemskerk, who was in Rome from 1532 to 1535 (Berlin, Kupferstichkabinett; see Egger 1911, Pls. 26, 29, 30, 32, 33, 34; Huelsen-Egger 1913, Pls. 9, 13, 16; 1916, Pls. 9, 28, 67, 69, 70, 72, 130; R. Krautheimer, *Art Bulletin*, 1949, p. 211, Fig. 1). These views of the roughly-finished masses of masonry towering above the old Basilica and the Vatican palace give a more impressive sense of the colossal scale of the structure than can be had today. They show the completed crossing piers with their broad arches temporarily protected by gabled roofing. The pendentives are barely begun, so that there is no sign of the ring that will carry the drum. On the west, the Rossellino–Bramante choir with its exterior colossal Order and Doric entablature is shown complete except for the glazing of its large windows; the interior of its half-dome echoes Bramante's favoured shell design (e.g., Sta Maria del Popolo, Rome). The southern arm appears as described above, while the northern one has its niched buttressing piers raised to the level of the first

Order but lacks walls and a terminating hemicycle. Little progress is shown in the façade arm to the east. Remnants of the Early Christian transept are preserved around the crossing.

In the years immediately following Heemskerk's visits to the site, the only major addition was a temporary wall separating the old from the new Basilica, constructed in 1538 (recently excavated; Apolloni *et al.*, 1951, pp. 205 ff., Figs. 163-168, Pl. LXXXVI). But in a few years Pope Paul III, Farnese (1534-1549), had regained sufficiently the financial means and the reckless optimism of Julius II to begin construction on a large scale. So large, in fact, that he first abandoned earlier projects in favour of a more ambitious scheme proposed by Sangallo which required the destruction of some parts of the existing Basilica, and later permitted Michelangelo to remove unwanted features of Sangallo's work in preparation for a completely different approach to the exterior.

2. SANGALLO'S MODEL PROJECT (Fig. 11, Pl. 51c)

In 1539, Sangallo was ordered to prepare a large model from his drawings. This model, which still exists (cf. K. Frey 1913, Figs. 1-4), took seven years to finish and cost as much as a full-scale church (*idem* 1909, pp. 167-170; Vasari, V, pp. 467 f.) The new project was a compromise between the central and longitudinal plans that had been envisaged earlier (Fig. 11). The interior space retained Bramante's Greek-cross form, but at the entrance a huge porch was added, flanked by two *campanili* that rose higher than the lantern of the dome. The porch had the effect of adding a semi-enclosed nave over 50 metres long to the main body of the Basilica. Although the design retained elements of earlier schemes, the only portion that remained entirely unchanged was the crossing, and even there Sangallo filled in the niches of the four principal piers, probably for expressive rather than structural reasons. The secondary buttressing piers that had been built at the base of the great hemicycles on the north and south (cf. Heemskerk's views from the north: Egger 1911, Pls. 33, 34; and south-east: Pl. 29) had to be destroyed partially, since Sangallo wanted to use them as passageways leading to the ambulatories around the hemicycles (Fig. 12). A fundamental departure of the model-plan from the scheme of Bramante and Raphael was the isolation of these ambulatories from the central area; on the interior, the *inner* hemicycle now became the visual terminus of the arms, which must have prompted Michelangelo to dispense with ambulatories altogether (D. Frey 1915, p. 65). The elevation of the model (Pl. 51c) deserved Michelangelo's sarcastic criticism (see below); it was a Tower of Babel that paradoxically produced a Gothic effect by the excessive application of under-scaled classical Orders.

In walling up niches and in closing off the ambulatories, Sangallo aimed to limit Bramante's spatial effects; probably for the same reason he elevated the floor level by $14\frac{1}{2}$ *palmi* (over 3 metres), covering the whole socle-zone of Bramante's pilaster Order (K. Frey 1913, p. 97; D. Frey 1915, pp. 66 ff.; G. Giovannoni, *Istituto di Studi romani; Quaderni di storia dell' Architettura*. II, 1941, p. 11 – where the height appears as 11 *palmi*. It was D. Frey's proposal that the purpose was purely aesthetic). According to the documents of 1543-1544, the new flooring was laid only in the southern arm; the crossing remained at Bramante's level until much later, probably to avoid engulfing the ancient altar and Bramante's housing (cf. Pl. 56b, a drawing of *ca.* 1559–1561). In 1574, T. Alfarani spoke of the cleaning of the Early Christian pavement still visible in the nave and crossing. The documents were confirmed by the recent excavations in the Basilica, which revealed that when Sangallo built the partition wall between the old and the new structures in 1538, the two were on the same level. After the raising of the crossing (in 1592?), a flight of 17 steps was passed through Sangallo's wall to reach the new level (Apolloni *et al.*, pp. 208–216; Fig. 166 shows the two levels to be about 1·75 m. apart, substantially less than the figures given in the documents; I cannot find a convincing explanation for these inconsistencies).

Sangallo's changes hampered the progress of construction until the early 1540's, while the model was being completed; but once his project was accepted, there was a spurt of activity. In 1543–1544 the nave vault was raised from the crossing toward the entrance (K. Frey 1913, pp. 73 ff., 98 f.), and in 1545–1546 the vault of the southern arm from the crossing toward the "Cappella del Re di Francia" (the southern hemicycle, *ibid.*, pp. 78 ff., 116). When the latter was finished in June 1546, a banquet was served to the workmen on the site (*ibid.*, p. 81). Work on the inner hemicycles terminating these arms was continued without interruption during 1544–1546 (*ibid.*, pp. 97 f., 101 f., 106 f., 123 ff., 129 f.), but only the façade (eastern) hemicycle was completed (*ibid.*, pp. 111 ff.) In 1545 Sangallo added a new crown to the medieval campanile by the atrium of the old Basilica (*ibid.*, pp. 86; the correct interpretation of these documents is due to Egger, *Mededeelingen van het nederlandsch historisch Instituut te Rome*, V, 1935, pp. 70–76). By 1546 the niches in the four crossing piers had been filled in (K. Frey 1913, pp. 97 f., 108), and a reference of that year to the "muro della cupola", at that time two-thirds finished (*ibid.*, p. 110), probably accounts for the construction of the pendentives for the central dome, one of which appears in Pl. 52b. In 1546 foundations were started for the north transept arm and hemicycle by the palace (Cappella del Imperatore; *ibid.*, pp. 108, 119), but the documents are not clear on how far this work extended above ground level. A "vault with rosettes" (*ibid.*, pp. 133, 135) on the palace side probably connected the buttressing pier on the north (right) of the façade area to the corresponding pier of the crossing.

Information from the documents is supplemented in a drawing by an anonymous Fleming showing the Basilica and palace from a high vantage point south of the piazza (Pl. 52a; Egger 1911, Pl. 20). Since the vaulting of the eastern (façade) arm, begun in 1543, appears complete, and the vaulting of the southern arm, begun in 1545, had not been started, the drawing must have been made in 1544. The two barrel vaults connecting the southern buttressing piers with the corresponding crossing piers are shown on either side of the southern arm, but nothing had been built in the south-eastern corner where Sangallo planned one of the minor domes (Fig. 12). The side aisles alongside the eastern hemicycle, however, are well advanced. A domed octagon which rises above the left side aisle, abutting the crossing pier, explains a cryptic group of documents of 1544–1545 (K. Frey 1913, pp. 98 ff., 102 f., 116 f., 120, 124) that refer to "una cupoletta dello ottangolo verso le stalle" (and others "verso frate Mori", "verso la cappella de Re", "verso la sagrestia") sopra volta a rosoni . . . fatto tutto tondo sanza alcuna armadura". Eight of these must have been planned to help buttress the piers without increasing the mass of masonry (another appears in Pl. 52b to the left of the unfinished vault); they were placed in an unorthodox fashion on top of the eight barrel vaults connecting the crossing piers to the buttressing piers, so that they do not appear in a plan or elevation and can be mistaken easily for the larger corner domes that were planned but not built by Sangallo and Michelangelo (they appear alongside the corner domes in Fontana's engraving: Schiavo 1953, Figs. 46, 47).

Vasari's fresco in the Palazzo della Cancelleria in Rome (Pl. 52b) gives a clear picture of the condition of St Peter's at the time of Michelangelo's appointment, in which Paul III is shown directing the execution of Sangallo's model project. Although the fresco was painted in the 1550's, a comparison with the documents shows that it was based on a sketch of 1546. The standpoint is at the southwest of the building, so that we see the exterior of Rossellino's choir and the Cappella del Re, and the interior of the southern arm with a pier and pendentive of the crossing behind it. Workmen are putting finishing touches on the great vault of the southern arm, which still has its wood centring in place. The eastern arm apparently has been roofed in the two years since the Flemish artist sketched Pl. 52a (cf. K. Frey 1913, p. 117). The columns, but not the wall of the inner hemicycle of the Cappella del Re are in place. Bricklayers are adding another course to the exterior hemicycle, which is unchanged since Heemskerk's time, except for the walling-in of the central door (cf. Egger 1911, Pls. 29, 32). Comparing Vasari, Heemskerk, and Sangallo's model, we find that the decision was made to continue with minor changes the exterior membering of the lowest Order according to the pre-model design of the 1520's.

From payments and views of this period and later we know that Sangallo had completed only the portions mentioned above before his death in 1546. Nothing had been done west of the crossing, where the small Rossellino-Bramante apse, tied into the crossing-piers, remained unchanged. Some foundations had been begun for the northern arm of the Basilica, but otherwise it probably remained as it appears in Heemskerk's drawings of 1532–1535 (Egger 1911, Pls. 33, 34), where the buttressing piers remained as Bramante had left them, and the vaults and walls had not been started. The following summary indicates what portions of the Basilica had been established so definitely by 1547 that Michelangelo was constrained to accept them with only superficial changes (Fig. 11).

The four piers of the main crossing; the arches connecting them; and the pendentives defining the base of the drum.

The four main arms of the church with their barrel vaults, and the easternmost of their terminal hemicycles (although only two of the arms had been built, there could be no question in a central-plan church of a different design for the remaining two).

The barrel-vaulted transverse aisles between the crossing piers and the buttressing piers (of the eight vaults planned, four were completed: those on either side of the southern and eastern arms).

The side aisles of the eastern arm, up to the narrow doorway alongside the hemicycle (lacking views from the north, we cannot be certain that the right side aisle was as far advanced as the left).

3. MICHELANGELO'S APPOINTMENT

Antonio da Sangallo the Younger died in September 1546, after twenty-six years of service as *capomaestro* of St Peter's. Sometime in the ensuing two months Paul III asked Michelangelo, now 71 years old, to take the position. Protesting that architecture was not his field, Michelangelo remained so reluctant that the Pope was forced to command him to accept (Condivi, Ch. LIII; Vasari, VII, pp. 218 ff.; K. Frey 1909, p. 171; 1913, p. 92; 1916, pp. 31 ff.) The appointment, officially confirmed in a lost document of 1 January 1547, must have been agreed upon several weeks before, since a clay model had been made and a wooden one started by December of 1546 (Pollak 1915, p. 52). In later years, Michelangelo rarely referred to the appointment without emphasizing that it had come against his will, and that he never became reconciled to the burden (*Lettere*, pp. 537 f., 544, 558, etc.) His unique stature allowed him to drive a hard bargain: he was given full authority over not only the design of the Basilica but the administration of the *fabbrica*, which previously had been the responsibility of the deputies and the ecclesiastical chapter; he was given leave to alter or to destroy parts of the existing structure that did not suit his programme; and finally, he stipulated that he should work only for the love of God, without pay (Vasari, VII, p. 220). In view of the fact that he received 50 scudi a month from the papal treasury (K. Frey 1916, p. 34) and the benefice of the port of Parma, this final condition gave him the moral advantage of an act of faith without its material discomforts.

The commission would have been distasteful to any creative architect, because Sangallo had left not only a definitive testament in the form of a model that represented a huge investment, but a throng of well-organized and influential trustees determined to see that his achievement should be respected. The "setta Sangallesca" (Sangallo crew), as Vasari disdainfully called them, retained firm control of the *fabbrica* administration, and after Sangallo's death attempted unsuccessfully to persuade (without papal confirmation?) Giulio Romano to succeed him (Vasari, V, p. 554). Michelangelo's appointment (presumably after Giulio's death on 1 November 1546, as noted by Wittkower 1933, p. 361) stirred up a political battle that continued even after his death. The "setta" was probably not the company of scheming scoundrels pictured in Vasari's biased account, but a group of unimaginative – but irreplaceable – architects and administrators trained in Sangallo's efficient "office", who earnestly attempted to save time and money and to preserve what they believed to be a noble inheritance. Michelangelo made no effort to collaborate with them and on his first official visit to the *fabbrica* took the opportunity to ridicule their master (Vasari, VII, pp. 218 f.) Later he publicly attacked the Sangallo project in detail, saying that it lacked sufficient light, that there were too many Orders of columns on the exterior, that the projections, spires and details made it appear more Gothic than Roman or modern, and finally that a clearer and more grandiose scheme could be carried out at a saving of 300,000 scudi and 50 years of work (Vasari, *loc. cit.*) A letter of 1546/1547 addressed to a certain "Bartolomeo" (K. Frey [1914, pp. 199, 324 f.] proposed Bartolomeo Ferratini, one of the deputies of the Basilica, and showed that Milanesi [*Lettere*, pp. 535 f.] erred both in naming Ammanati as the recipient and in assuming the date to be 1555) gives a first-hand record of Michelangelo's criticisms, the most damaging being that the plan would impinge on the palace site and would demand the demolition of several essential Vatican buildings. An ironic passage prophesies the danger of encouraging criminals to seek cover in a building that would provide so many dark passages. This letter is worth quoting for its comments on Bramante, who had been one of Michelangelo's enemies early in the century: "One cannot deny that Bramante was as worthy an architect as any since ancient times. He laid down the first plan of St Peter's, not full of confusion, but clear and pure, full of light, and did no damage to any part of the palace. And it was regarded as a beautiful thing, and it is obvious now, so [one can say] that whoever departs from this order of Bramante, as Sangallo has done, has departed from the truth. That this is so, anyone with unimpassioned eyes can see in his model." In closing, Michelangelo asks Bartolomeo to intercede with the Pope in favour of removing the outer periphery of Sangallo's apses, pointing out that the loss of the investment made in Sangallo's design would be more than compensated by the economy of a more compact plan.

Once construction was resumed, the tension caused by this controversy over the design was compounded by the fact that Michelangelo's age and infirmities did not allow him to supervise the *fabbrica* with any regularity. He directed the work from his studio near Trajan's Forum, mostly by letters and by messenger, a procedure that accounted for constant misunderstandings and occasionally major catastrophies in construction (cf. his complaints in K. Frey 1914, p. 215; *Lettere*, pp. 334, 534, 537, 546 f., 555, 558 f., and the deputies' reaction to the destruction of existing portions and to their lack of information on Michelangelo's intentions in Vasari, VII, p. 232; K. Frey 1911, p. 93). One of Michelangelo's lieutenants was regularly on the site as a *soprastante* (K. Frey 1916, pp. 34 ff., 47), but being *persona non grata*, and lacking the authority to make important decisions, he must have been regarded more as a spy than as an administrator. A year before his death the master sought to avoid further conflict by retiring in favour of one of his most distinguished disciples, Daniele da Volterra, but the negotiations ended in the appointment of the chief of the "setta Sangallesca", Nanni di Baccio Bigio, as *soprastante*. This affront was so grave that the Pope was forced to dismiss Nanni within a month to keep Michelangelo from resigning (Vasari, VII, p. 264 f.; K. Frey 1916, pp. 45 ff.), and a neutral administrator was given Nanni's post.

4. CHRONOLOGY OF CONSTRUCTION UNDER MICHELANGELO

Michelangelo characteristically made his first study for the design in the form of a clay model, as Tolnay concluded (1930, pp. 3 ff.) from Vasari's account (VII, p. 219) of a model made for 25 scudi in fifteen days to demonstrate proposed alterations. Michelangelo habitually began designing with terracotta sketches; a fortnight would suffice for making such a model, but not for the wooden scale model begun early in December (K. Frey 1909, pp. 170 f.; 1913, pp. 93 ff.; 1916, p. 65. Cascioli, *Roma*, V, 1927, p. 206, mistranscribed payments of July 1547 as being of July 1546). The payments indicate that the model was almost finished by the autumn of 1547, although finishing touches may not have been added until the beginning of the following year. The model is lost, and a painting by Passignani of 1620 (Pl. 58a) is the only surviving document by which we can judge its appearance.

Its rapid construction and moderate cost in comparison to Sangallo's, together with later uncertainties of the deputies concerning Michelangelo's intentions, suggest that it was relatively small and probably incomplete, and could not be used as the ultimate authority in details of construction (K. Frey 1916, p. 32). Yet, aside from what must have been a large-scale model of the interior drum cornice executed in 1548/1549 (*ibid.*, p. 67), and another made in 1556/1557 for the vaulting of the hemicycles (*Nachlass* I, pp. 481–484), it cannot have been supplemented by many detailed studies because no drawings other than those for the dome survive, and only the plan and a window design were recorded in Michelangelo's estate at his death (Gotti 1875, II, p. 151). A great controversy over acceptance of the model may be read into the comments of Vasari (VII, p. 220: "finalmente fu dal papa aprovato il modello") and Condivi (Ch. LIII: "Il quale modello, lodato ed approvato dal pontefice, al presente si seguita con molto sodisfazione di quelle persone che hanno giudizio, sebben son certi che non l'approvino"). In 1547 the deputies complained to the Pope in vigorous language that "sibi non placere modum quem dominus Michel tenet, pracscrtim in destruendo . . .", and objected that they were kept in the dark concerning his intentions (Gotti 1875, I, p. 311; Frey 1911, p. 93). In October 1549, the Pope found it necessary to issue a stern *motuproprio* requiring that the model be respected (Steinmann-Pogatscher 1906, pp. 400 ff.: mistaken by earlier scholars for the original appointment of 1547). The order, confirmed by Julius III in 1552 (*ibid.*, pp. 403 ff.), apparently was obeyed, and we assume that construction of the Basilica up to the base of the drum essentially followed the design of the model, although Michelangelo introduced certain changes (as suggested by the conference recorded in Vasari, VII, p. 232).

The chronology of the construction of the Basilica under Michelangelo can be established fairly accurately by analysing three kinds of sources: the documents of the papal treasury, extensively published by Karl Frey, the views and perspective plans of the Vatican area drawn during this period, and Vasari's *Lives*, the only published literary account that bears on the subject.

Vasari (VII, p. 221) explains the principal departures of Michelangelo's model from that of Sangallo in an account which is open to misinterpretation, but which can be interpreted with the assistance of the sixteenth-century views and engravings (Figs. 11 and 12):

1. "The four principal pilasters [piers] made by Bramante and left by Sangallo, intended to support the weight of the cupola, he filled in and made two spiral stairs on each side."

The four piers referred to are not the crossing piers (which could not have been opened up for new stairwells without vast demolitions), but the secondary ones at the entrances to the northern and southern hemicycles, which Bramante had founded as solid masses, but which Sangallo had penetrated with passages giving access to his outer aisle around the hemicycles. Since they had been pierced through, Michelangelo could insert the stairwells with only minimal destruction. The new spiral stairs appear clearly in Michelangelo's plan (Pl. 59b).

2. "He made the first cornice above the travertine arches, that circles about, a wonderful and graceful thing, quite different from the others."

The cornice referred to is a ring 6·1 m. high placed upon the pendentives as a base for the great drum. Vasari refers to the elegant interior entablature, not to the stern moulding applied outside.

3. "He began the two great niches [hemicycles] of the crossing, and whereas previously, by order of Bramante, Baldassare [Peruzzi] and Raphael, they had made eight taber- nacles [in the southern one] toward the cemetery, and Sangallo continued this, Michelangelo reduced them to three, and behind them [put] three chapels, and above them a travertine vault and an order of amply lit windows of varied form and awesome grandeur."

This is the most important change for the future of the Basilica: Michelangelo lopped off the entire perimeter of Sangallo's plan, eliminating the aisle (ambulatory) around the hemicycle by removing the outer ring of masonry and by transforming the inner hemicycle into an exterior wall. By this means the hemicycles of the four arms could be lit directly from the exterior, and a great confusion of passages and arches was elimi- nated. Vasari's wording does not make clear that Sangallo's outer hemicycles had the eight tabernacles (plus a central doorway), while his inner hemicycles had the three niched passageways; these Michelangelo preserved, changing them into chapels by adding the heavy outer wall of the new perimeter. The elimination of the outer rings explains item 1: Michelangelo could block the now useless passageways with stairwells that helped to strengthen the piers.

Vasari's account is incomplete because he speaks only of the innovations that were immediately put into effect in construction. Other important changes in plan were:

4. The reduction of the four corners to give the minor domed areas direct access to exterior light. This change sacrificed the idea of small, Greek-cross replicas of the main body of the Basilica, which Sangallo had inherited from Bramante. In Michelangelo's plan the domed corners cease to be independent spaces and become accents for the angles of a square that is superimposed upon, and equal in significance to, the main cross.

5. The elimination of Sangallo's twin-towered porch and forenave in order to restore a central-plan scheme. Michelangelo's façade was placed directly against the eastern arm that Sangallo had completed, with only minor alterations to the existing side aisles.

These innovations, by greatly reducing the dimensions of the Basilica, avoided the problem of encroachment on existing palace structures, brought direct light into all parts of the interior, and saved incalculable time and expense in construction. Since they altered the entire exterior form of St Peter's, they enabled Michelangelo to abandon all dependence on the character of the earlier outer elevations. But the previously executed interior elevations of the four arms and of the crossing up to the top of the pendentives could be altered only by changing details of the facing and the membering of portals and tabernacles. Since most of these details were carried out after Michelangelo's death, there are few traces of his design on the interior. A comparison of his model section

(Pl. 61) to that of Sangallo (Pl. 51c) shows that he intended only to simplify the vault coffering and a portion of the membering of the crossing piers. He surely intended to use far more sober facing materials than either Sangallo or the seventeenth-century architects who chose the marbles we see today.

The new plan, so vigorously attacked for its drastic innovations, actually demanded no more destruction of existing portions than had Sangallo's project. Of the three outer hemicycles eliminated by Michelangelo, only one – the southern Cappella del Re (Pl. 52b) – had been raised above ground level, but to the height of only one story. Hofmann's assumption (1928, p. 217) that Michelangelo intended to destroy everything but the crossing piers was based on insufficient knowledge of contemporary views.

The following schedule traces the chronology of the construction during the seventeen years from Michelangelo's appointment to his death (entries that appear in brackets are not precisely dated in documents, but are deduced from a comparison of sources).

1547 *March to August.* Granite columns are ordered, probably to complete tabernacles started by Sangallo near the crossing (K. Frey 1916, pp. 103 ff. Further work in the mid-1550's).

December. Payments begin for the carving of pilaster capitals in the chapels of the northern arm. They continue into the 1550's (*ibid.*, pp. 106 ff.)

August. A windlass is erected for construction of the circular cornice at the base of the drum. A wood model of this cornice is paid for in 1549. In February 1552 a banquet is given to celebrate the completion of the cornice (*ibid.*, pp. 66 ff.)

1547/1548 [Construction of the unfinished walls of the northern arm towards the Cappella del Imperatore. Dating based on initiation of the vault of this arm in 1549.]

1548 Demolition of portions of the Early Christian Basilica remaining in the northern arm (*ibid.*, p. 134).

1548/1549 [Demolition of Sangallo's outer hemicycle to the south. An anonymous drawing added to Heemskerk's sketchbook (Egger 1911, Pl. 35; Huelsen-Egger 1916, Pl. I, p. 3: dated 1547/1548) shows this demolition in progress. Centring for the vault of the southern arm (cf. Pl. 52b) has been removed, and a portion of Michelangelo's new cornice appears over the crossing, establishing 1548 as *terminus post*.]

1549 *April to August.* Centring built for vault of the northern arm (K. Frey 1916, pp. 67 f.) [Construction of the vault in 1549/1550?] Pilaster capitals for this arm are paid for in 1555/1562 (*ibid.*, pp. 88 ff.)

June. Gateways built in the entrance to the first of the new spiral staircases in the outer piers at the base of the Cappella del Re (*ibid.*, p. 68). Payments for the construction of these in 1550/1552 (pp. 69 ff.) Pilasters on their exterior being finished in 1556 (p. 116).

1549/1550 Construction of the first and second Orders of the Cappella del Re hemicycle (Vasari, VII, p. 232: "innanzi che fussi il principio dell'anno 1551 . . . avendo egli [Michelangelo] già murato la cappella del re dove sono le tre cappelle, e condottole con le tre finestre sopra . . .")

[Construction of the lowest story of the northern Cappella del Imperatore hemicycle? (see entries of 1554 and 1555; Pl. 53a).]

[An anonymous drawing can be dated securely early in this period (Uffizi 4345, Egger 1911, Pl. 36). It shows the partly-constructed lower Order of the hemicycle with one window frame completed; the western spiral staircase finished; the eastern staircase not begun; the socle of the drum (see following entry) completed.]

1551 Bufalini's plan of Rome (Frutaz 1956, Pl. XX). The groundplan of St Peter's shows the new hemicycles on the north and south; the remainder as left by Sangallo.

1552 Payment for the construction of a doorway in the socle of the drum "sopra il primo cornicione" (K. Frey 1916, p. 70).

1552/1554 [Standstill in construction], continued carving of granite columns, travertine capitals (*ibid., passim*).

1554 January. Columns prepared for buttresses of the drum (*ibid.*, pp. 121 f., 72 f.) Payments continue for a decade.

1554/1555 [Several drawings and prints document the work of this period, following the initiation of the drum-columns and prior to the initiation of the inner drum wall:

a. Anonymous addition to Heemskerk sketchbook (Egger 1911, Pl. 37; Huelsen-Egger 1916, Pl. 83, p. 37) showing the Basilica from the south-west. The drum buttresses are just being begun on the façade side: the Cappella del Re hemicycle is complete to two stories with its window frames and pilasters but without entablature; the spiral staircases are both completed; no other new construction.

b. Pl. 53a: Anonymous addition to Heemskerk (Egger 1911, Pl. 38; Huelsen-Egger 1916, Pl. 82, p. 37) showing the Basilica from the north. The drum buttresses appear as in *a*. The Cappella del Imperatore hemicycle is only one story high; its western spiral staircase is complete, the eastern half-finished. The construction may be assigned to 1549/1550 in view of the intervening inactivity. Through the crossing, beyond Bramante's sanctuary, appears the southern hemicycle as in *a* (the entablature is finished on the interior due to the difference in height of the interior and exterior pilasters).

c. Perspective plan of Rome by Paciotto published in 1557 (Frutaz 1956, Pl. XXII) showing the same condition as *a*.

d. Perspective plan of Rome by G. A. Dosio published in 1561 (*ibid.*, Pl. XXIII, 2), showing the same condition as *b*.

e. Perspective plan of Rome by Dosio, pen and ink (London, R.I.B.A., *ibid.*, Pl. XXVI) showing buttresses in construction; remainder unclear (Wachler 1940, pp. 233 f. and Ackerman 1954, pp. 217 f. have noted that *d* and *e* are based on a survey of the mid-1550's).]

1555 April. First payments for carving capitals for the interior drum pilasters. Payments continue after Michelangelo's death (K. Frey 1916, pp. 87 ff.)

Carving of capitals for the exterior of the northern and southern hemicycles, continuing until 1565 (*ibid.*, pp. 112–125).

1555/1557 Partial construction of the drum (Vasari, VII, p. 248, on events of 1557 leading to the initiation of the second dome model: "[Michelangelo], vedendo che in

San Pietro si trattava poco, ed avendo già tirato innanzi gran parte del fregio delle finestre di dentro, e delle colonne doppie di fuora, che girano sopra il cornicione tondo, dove s'ha poi a posare la cupola . . .")

[A drawing by Dosio (Uffizi 91, Egger 1911, Pl. 27) shows the drum in construction in a view northward through the crossing. The western part is complete up to the entablature base (we see one window-frame with a segmental pediment), the eastern, half as far. The view may be dated *ca.* 1557/1561 (the entry of 1561 below suggests that the entablature, which Dosio does not show, was started in that year).

Pl. 56b: An anonymous drawing (by Ammanati?) of the crossing looking westward (Hamburg, 21311; Egger 1911, Pl. 28). The drum is finished nearly to the base of the entablature, with all the existing window frames in place. As the portion of the drum visible here was built before the portion shown by Dosio, we cannot be sure that the drawing is later than Dosio's. But the appearance of alternating window-pediments helps to date it more accurately: the dome model of 1558/1561 (Pl. 57b) has only segmental pediments on the drum interior. Michelangelo apparently changed his mind during the construction of the model-drum, so that this sketch must have been done in *ca.* 1559/1561 (the attribution to Ammanati is based on similarities to other drawings of the 1550's: Egger 1932, Pl. 1; Mongan-Sachs, *Drawings in the Fogg Museum of Art*, Cambridge, Mass., 1946, pp. 44 f., Fig. 45; Ackerman 1954, pp. 216 f.)]

The Beatrizet plan of Rome, published in 1557 (Frutaz 1956, Pl. XXIII, 1) shows the drum complete, an inaccuracy that is surely due to the small scale of the building.

[Construction of the entablature of the Cappella del Re, preparatory to vaulting in 1557.]

1557 *April.* Construction of the hemispherical vault over the Cappella del Re on the basis of a new model. Described in detail in two letters from Michelangelo to Vasari of July 1557 (Vasari, VII, pp. 247 f.; *Lettere*, pp. 334, 543, 546, 547: more accurate versions with correct date and extensive commentary by Frey in Vasari, *Nachlass*, I, 1923, pp. 479, 481 ff.) Due to Michelangelo's absence from the *fabbrica*, the *soprastante* Malenotti erected the wrong kind of centring, laying his boards in concentric arcs across the entire span instead of making separate vaults over each of the three windows (cf. Pl. 56a). These were to have a complex curve that could not be established by a concentric system, as Michelangelo explains in his letters and in two explanatory drawings (*Nachlass*, Pls. facing pp. 482 [our Pl. 56a], 484). The vault had to be dismantled and remade entirely in 1558 (the new centring was removed by June 1558, K. Frey 1916, p. 75); a costly procedure, since it was made in travertine rather than the customary brick. Michelangelo remarked, "if one could die of shame and suffering I should not be alive".

[A drawing by Dosio (Uffizi 2535; Egger 1911, Pl. 39) shows the completed vault from the exterior prior to the addition of the attic facing above the second story entablature of the hemicycle. It may have been drawn any time between

1557/1558 and della Porta's administration, since Michelangelo did not finish the attic exterior on the south. Thode's misinterpretation of this drawing (1908, II, pp. 171, 175 f.) led him to date it before the erection of the vault. Not realizing that it showed the attic and that the attic would not have been built independently of the vault, he concluded not only that the hemicycle vault was not represented, but that the contiguous barrel vault over the southern arm had been torn down.]

July. Payment for a clay model of the dome, a study for the large-scale wood model of 1558/1561 (K. Frey 1916, p. 81).

1558 *June–July*. Construction in progress on the northern hemicycle and its unfinished eastern staircase (*ibid.*, pp. 75 ff., 112 ff.), reaching the entablature early in 1560 and continuing until Michelangelo's death. The hemicycle vault and attic-facing appear half-finished in an engraving of 1565 (Pl. 53b).

November. Beginning of the wood model of the dome, completed in November 1561 (K. Frey 1909, pp. 177 ff.; 1916, pp. 81 ff., 87). Vasari (VII, pp. 249 ff.) explains how it came to be made and describes it in meticulous detail.

1560 *September*. Michelangelo denies the rumour that the construction is going badly (*Lettere*, p. 558).

1561 *April*. Excavations for new foundations "verso il palazzo" (K. Frey 1916, p. 76): for the future Cappella Gregoriana, the domed chapel on the north-east?

August. First payments for the capitals and imposts of the drum buttresses (*ibid.*, pp. 91 ff.), unfinished at Michelangelo's death.

1563 *May*. Window-frames and sculptural relief for the Cappella del Imperatore (*ibid.*, pp. 78, 120 f.)

1564 *February*. Michelangelo's death.

Summary of the condition of St Peter's at Michelangelo's death:

Façade arm and crossing: apparently left as finished by Sangallo.

Southern arm and Cappella del Re: complete on the interior (except for decoration); exterior membering executed on the hemicycle only, not including its attic-facing.

Western arm: the Rossellino–Bramante apse still untouched.

Northern arm and Cappella del Imperatore: completed as the southern arm except that the hemicycle vault was only half constructed. The attic-facing, however, was begun on this side either just before or just after Michelangelo's death (Pl. 53b).

Drum: largely completed up to the level of pilaster-and-buttress capitals; imposts and entablatures executed on the eastern but not the western half (Pls. 53b, 56b).

Corner chapels: foundations begun on the north side.

5. CONSTRUCTION AFTER MICHELANGELO'S DEATH

Although we are not concerned here with the history of the Basilica in itself, the following survey, less detailed than the preceding, will show what departures Michelangelo's successors made from his designs.

1564/1565 Pirro Ligorio appointed as chief architect, but initiates no new construction (K. Frey 1916, pp. 48 ff.)

1567/1573 The post is held by Vignola, formerly assistant to Michelangelo, and sub-architect under Ligorio. Completion of the vaulting of the Cappella del Imperatore and the drum entablature; construction of the chapel on the north-east corner (later, Cappella Gregoriana); no departure from Michelangelo's designs (Coolidge 1942, pp. 63 ff.) A view of the Basilica from the north-west (Netherlandish "Anonymous Fabriczy", Stuttgart, Kupferstichkabinett; Egger 1911, Pl. 40) executed around 1570, shows the completed vaulting and attic of the Cappella del Imperatore but the drum still unfinished. An engraved panorama of the Vatican in 1574 by Mario Cartaro (Coolidge 1942, Fig. 2; Ackerman 1954, pp. 227 f. and Fig. 34) shows the main drum and the Cappella Gregoriana finished, but without domes.

1573/1574 Appointment of Giacomo della Porta as chief architect.

1575/1576 Cappella Gregoriana given exterior decoration (K. Frey 1916, pp. 130 f.) [probably for della Porta's newly-designed drum and dome].

1578 A new model in progress [probably for the main dome; *ibid.*, p. 132].

Construction of the lantern for the first dome (later rebuilt with a higher profile) over the Cappella Gregoriana (*loc. cit.*; the rich documentation in the Roman Archivio di Stato [*Tesoreria Segreta*, Vols. 1305 ff.] remains unpublished). [An anonymous drawing, possibly from 1577 (Frankfurt, Städelsches Kunstinstitut; Egger 1911, Pl. 41), shows the drum nearing completion, and a windlass erected for construction of the lowest Order of the opposite (south-east) Cappella Clementina. The attic-facing on the hemicycle of the Cappella del Re is still not finished (see also the view in a fresco of 1580 in the Vatican Loggia of Gregory XIII, in Frutaz 1956, Pl. XXXVI).]

1579 Work in progress on the Cappella Clementina (K. Frey 1916, p. 133). Its dome under construction in 1585 (*idem* 1911, p. 95, see following entry).

1580?/1585 The new apse (western arm) constructed from foundations up in place of the Rossellino–Bramante choir. Its vaulting under way in 1585. Vestiges of the Early Christian Basilica removed from the crossing (Frey, *loc. cit.*) [Although this impressive progress is reported in an estimate of work executed in 1585, it must have been initiated several years before.]

1586 Approval of della Porta's new design for the main dome. A major departure from Michelangelo.

1588/1590 Construction of the dome (Orbaan 1917, pp. 189 ff.) Mass celebrating its completion in May 1590 (*idem, Archivio Soc. rom. di storia patr.*, XXXIII, 1910, p. 312). Della Porta assisted by Domenico Fontana.

1590/1593 Construction of the lantern.

1592 Demolition of Bramante's altar-house and the Constantinian apse and baldachin (Apolloni *et al.* 1951, p. 207).

1598/1612 Decoration of the interior of the dome.

1607 Competition for the design of a long nave to replace Michelangelo's eastern arm and façade; won by Carlo Maderno. A model is prepared.

1608 Foundation of the new façade; the inscription indicates completion in 1612. Porch behind is completed in 1619. Several unsuccessful attempts made in subsequent years to support façade towers on the unstable foundations.

1614 Vaulting of nave begun; completed in one year. The vault is somewhat higher than that of Sangallo to which it is attached. The elements of Michelangelo's design are continued on both the interior and exterior of the nave.

The energy of Paul V (1605–1621) is largely responsible for the completion of the Basilica after more than a century of construction. At his death only portions of the interior decoration remained unfinished. With the construction of the piazza in the seventeenth and the Sacristy in the eighteenth century, the colossal enterprise was finally finished.

The Basilica of today owes more to Michelangelo than to any other architect (Pls. 50, 63, 64) and yet its design is far from what he intended. The exterior articulation faithfully follows Michelangelo except for the façade, the main dome and lantern, and the minor domes and drums. But the basic form of the building was so altered by the addition of the nave that the observer in the piazza (the only readily accessible point of view) sees only a single feature of his design: the main drum. The power of Michelangelo's conception can be appreciated properly only from the Vatican gardens to the west (Pl. 63); the portions visible from there follow his designs from the foundations to the top of the drum. Inside, the visitor standing in the crossing can sense something of Michelangelo's handling of space (considerably altered by della Porta's changes in the elevation and, equally important, the lighting, of the dome) but nothing of his intended treatment of the surfaces, which, enframed by pilasters and entablatures designed by Bramante, Raphael and Sangallo, are transformed by the mosaics, marble veneers, and sculptures of the Baroque period.

II MICHELANGELO'S DESIGN

I. THE SOURCES

A wealth of archival, graphic, and literary sources is available for the reconstruction of Michelangelo's design, but the sources are so frequently contradictory that their interpretation has become the most controversial problem in the study of the Basilica. In part, the problem arises from customary gaps in documentation which have left insufficient records of alterations by Michelangelo's successors; the chief source of confusion, however, is the fluid nature of Michelangelo's own approach to the design: his scheme was not definitively formulated at the outset but evolved gradually in the course of seventeen years of construction.

From the documents cited in section I we know that Michelangelo prepared four models for the Basilica:

 i. A clay sketch-model of the whole structure (November/December 1546)
 ii. A wooden model based on No. *i*. (December 1546 to autumn 1547)
 iii. A clay sketch-model for the main drum and dome (July 1557)
 iv. A large wooden model based on *iii* (Pl. 57b; November 1558 to November 1561).

All the models are lost except for *iv*, which was altered drastically by Michelangelo's successors. A painting by Passignani of *ca.* 1620 (Pl. 58a; Steinmann 1913, p. 89, Pl. 91) shows Michelangelo presenting to a Pope (the portrait is of Pius IV but the inscription refers to Paul IV) his model of the whole Basilica, lacking the façade and attic-facing. Coolidge has argued persuasively (1942, pp. 77, 117) that this is model *ii*, altered by the addition of post-Michelangelo domes. This scanty evidence is supplemented by the following records.

I. The letters of Michelangelo and Vasari's *Life*, which includes a lengthy and detailed description of model *iv* (VII, pp. 250–257).

II. Drawings executed by Michelangelo or under his direction:

    a. Haarlem, Teyler Museum, No. 29r; F.326; D.148. Lantern elevations; dome section (Pl. 54). *Verso:* plan of a podium for the lanterns on the left side of the *recto*. Here dated 1546/1547.

    b. Casa Buonarroti, No. 118v; D.140. Lantern elevations (Tolnay 1930, Fig. 4; 1951, Pl. 358). Here dated 1546/1547, immediately following "a".

    c. Casa Buonarroti, No. 117v; D.139. Dome section and lantern elevation; drum plan (?two concentric semicircles with a pair of columns tangent to and inside the outer ring; notation in Michelangelo's hand: "la laterna". The drawing is so rubbed that it cannot be reproduced satisfactorily (cf. Florence, Gab. Fot., No. 21958), and was not noticed before Dussler. Here dated 1546/1547, contemporaneous with "b".

    d. Lille, Musée des Beaux-Arts, Coll. Wicar, No. 93; F.170; D.301. Elevation of the drum and the lantern; dome section (Pl. 55a). Here dated 1546/1547, following "c".

    e. Casa Buonarroti, No. 31; F.208; D.457. Partial plan of the drum and buttresses by an assistant with notes by Michelangelo. Here dated 1546/1547, contemporaneous with "d".

    f. Oxford, Ashmolean Museum, No. 344r; F.168; D.207. Rapid sketch of the crown of the dome, and lantern section, tentatively dated 1557 by the fragment of a letter (Pl. 55b). *Verso:* studies for central plan churches, not related to St Peter's (see p. 124).

    g. Arezzo, Casa Vasari; D.1. Letters from Michelangelo of the summer of 1557 illustrated by two sketches of the vaulting system of the Cappella del Re (Pl. 56a; Vasari, *Nachlass*, pp. 481, 484).

    h. Codex Vaticanus 3211, fol. 92; D.228. Quick sketch, showing a Greek-cross plan church with a 5-column porch abutted by a number of structures on the right. The resemblance of the latter to old portions of the Vatican palace (see IV f.) suggests that the church may be St Peter's in spite of the dissimilarity in plan and the fact that at the requisite scale the porch columns would be 30-plus feet on centre and could not carry a stone lintel (published by Tolnay 1927, pp. 158 ff., Fig. 2; 1951, Pl. 357). No firm grounds for dating.

III. Contemporary copies of Michelangelo's drawings and models.

    a. Uffizi, *Arch.* 96r, attributed to Vignola. Exterior elevation of one of the hemicycles, without the attic (identified by Tolnay; Coolidge 1942, Fig. 11). Here dated 1546.

b. Uffizi, *Arch.* 92, by G.-A. Dosio. Half-section of the dome and lantern with the upper portion of the drum (Tolnay 1930, Fig. 6).

c. Uffizi, *Arch.* 94, by Dosio. Section of the dome with interior perspective; profile (Pl. 57a; Tolnay 1930, Fig. 7). *Verso:* a detail of the drum.

d. Uffizi, *Arch.* 2031, by Dosio. Section of the dome and lantern; plan of the stairway between the shells (Körte 1932, Fig. 8). *Verso:* a version of "e" below.

e. Uffizi, *Arch.* 2032, by Dosio. Drum plan at four levels (Wittkower 1933, Fig. 1).

f. Uffizi, *Arch.* 2033, by Dosio. Detail of the drum-section; drum-column, with measurements of entasis (*ibid.*, Fig. 2).

g. Casa Buonarroti, No. 35; D.460, anonymous. Measured half-section of the dome model. *Verso:* rapid sketch of the same (Tolnay 1932, Fig. 1; 1951, Pls. 363–364).

IV. Records which combine information from the models, drawings, and the Basilica itself.

a. British Museum, album attributed to Dupérac, formerly in the Dyson Perrins collection. Sketch of the eastern (façade) elevation of the Basilica in perspective (Pl. 62a). Here dated 1558–1564.

b. V. Luchinus, engraved elevation of the exterior of the hemicycles, inscribed MICHAEL ANGELUS BONAROTUS INVENTOR, dated 1564 (Pl. 59a).

c. E. Dupérac, engraved plan of the Basilica, inscribed EX ESEMPLARI MICHAELIS ANGELI, dated 1569 (Pl. 59b). A seventeenth-century copy of this plan by van Schoel was mistakenly dated 1559 by Bonanni.

d. E. Dupérac, engraved southern elevation of the Basilica, inscribed MICHAEL ANGELUS BONAROTA INVENIT (1569? Pl. 60). Later copied by Brambilla (Alker 1920, Pl. 3a).

e. E. Dupérac, engraved longitudinal section of the Basilica, companion to "c" (1569? Pl. 61).

f. New York, Metropolitan Museum, No. 49.92.1 ff.; loose-leaf sketchbook of an anonymous French architect with drawings after the dome model and the Basilica. As Dr de Tolnay first identified the group and anticipates publication, I mention here only the more notable sheets; No. 71, a copy (?) of "c" above; No. 1, a perspective, and No. 92, a section, of the dome model. In a hasty examination of the sketches I found no data that had not been known previously from other sources.

g. T. Alfarani, plan of the Basilica superimposed upon the plan of old St Peter's, similar to "c" (*ca.* 1580? Vatican library? Schiavo 1953, Fig. 48). In the engraving of 1590 based on this drawing, the Michelangelo façade does not appear.

h. Uffizi, *Santarelli* 174, anonymous. Plan of the Basilica, a variant of "c" with a different plan for the entrance stairs and columns placed before the pilasters at the left corner (unpublished).

i. Uffizi, *Arch.* 103661, anonymous. Plan of the Basilica, inscribed "di Bramante". Probably a copy of "c" at second hand (G. Marchini, *Boll. d'Arte*, XLI, 1956, p. 316, Fig. 6).

    j. Windsor Castle Library, No. 10448. An anonymous plan drawn to show the then existing location (by the SE pier of the crossing) and the one proposed (in the NE corner chapel) for the tomb of Paul III. The author misrepresented those portions of Michelangelo's plan that were not actually built: the façade arm appears the same as the other three; an unbuildable porch is extended across the whole width of the Basilica, etc. After 1560 (A. Noach, *Burlington Magazine*, XCVIII, 1956, pp. 376 f., Fig. 40; Noach's proposal that the plan might be as early as 1550 is unlikely. In our Pl. 56b, of 1559–1561, the tomb does not yet appear in the spot indicated on the plan; the pier is still encumbered by rubble).

V. Later variants of Michelangelo's design, interpolating the work of other architects.

    a. Medal of Gregory XIII with the east elevation of the Basilica on the reverse, *ca.* 1580 (D. Frey 1920, Fig. 42; reproduced in a medal of Sixtus V, *ca.* 1585, Alker 1920, Fig. 11; in another medal of Sixtus V [Frey, Fig. 43], the façade is obscured by the obelisk in the piazza).

    b. Vatican, Gallery of Pius IV, fresco by Paris Nogari (?) showing the Basilica from the east surrounded by a huge piazza, *ca.* 1587 (?) (Pl. 58b).

    c. Giovanni Guerra, engraved vignette, based on the same source as "b", 1587 (Rose 1925, Fig. 160).

    d. Domenico Fontana, engraved plate showing the Basilica from the east, with the actual building supplemented by the presumed Michelangelo façade (*Del modo tenuto nel trasportare l'obelisco vaticano . . .*, *Libro primo*, Rome, 1589, fol. 35r. Orbaan 1917, Fig. 6 [1590 ed.]). Reproduced by N. van Aelst in an engraving of *ca.* 1595 (Frutaz 1956, Pl. XLII).

    e. New York, L. G. White coll., anonymous plan of the Basilica proposing the extension of the nave but retaining Michelangelo's façade plan, late sixteenth century (W. W. Kent, *The Life and Works of Baldassare Peruzzi*, New York, 1925. Pl. 43, 1).

In the following pages these documents will be used in reconstructing Michelangelo's intended design for the body of the Basilica (section 2), the façade (section 3), and the major and minor domes (sections 4 and 5). The analyses required for a full justification of these conclusions, many of which are too complex and technical to be repeated here, may be found in the specialized studies cited in each section.

2. THE SIDE ELEVATIONS

In 1547 construction began on the exterior of the southern hemicycle; it must have followed the design of Michelangelo's model *ii*, completed in that year. But the design was altered in the course of construction, and several versions of the elevation appear in contemporary documents.

A change in design is documented by Vasari's report of a conference held on the site early in 1551 (VII, p. 232). At this time, the hemicycle was completed up to the entablature, and the deputies "not knowing what was to be done with the vault", complained that it would be poorly lit. Michelangelo answered: "above these windows in the vault, which is to be built in travertine, go three others". The Cardinal deputy replied: "you never told us that", with which Michelangelo closed the discussion, saying that he had no responsibility to announce his intentions since it was his job to design and the deputies' job to provide money and to keep away thieves. Since we know from Vasari that the deputies had seen – and disapproved of – the 1547 model, this argument must have arisen over changes made by Michelangelo in 1547–1551, and not communicated to them.

The altered project affected the vault and attic design; we may assume that portions below the entablature followed the 1547 model since, with one exception, the documents differ from the existing building only in the portions above. The exception, a drawing attributed to Vignola (IIIa; Coolidge 1942, p. 64, n. 13, Fig. 11), is probably a copy of 1546 from a preparatory study for models *i* or *ii*, since it shows a different design for the windows below the entablature (Vignola was not in Rome in 1546–1549, so the attribution is suspect; at the time of his employment at St Peter's in 1551 the windows in question had been built, and he would have had no reason to copy a rejected design).

The model of 1547 may be identified with the one represented by Passignani (Pl. 58a), who saw it in 1620, after della Porta's major and minor domes had been added to it (Coolidge 1942, p. 77; Schiavo 1953, p. 185). The same model was also a source for the side elevations in the "Dupérac" sketch (IVa; Pl. 62a), where again later domes were added: the major dome shows Michelangelo's design as described by Vasari (Tolnay 1930, p. 4, identified IVa with model *i* of 1546; Coolidge's analysis, pp. 120 ff., revealed that it is a pastiche of several phases in the design. Reasons for dating it in the period 1558–1564 are given in section 3 below). In the 1547 model, then, the attic remained without any facing.

The new attic-and-vault design discussed in the conference of 1551 recorded by Vasari put two orders of three windows in the vault in place of the single windows shown in the model. This change appears in Michelangelo's drawings of 1557 (IIg; Pl. 56a) which, he said, were after a model of the vault. We gather from the letters accompanying these sketches that both the arched rectangles at the base of the vault and the three *tondi* near the centre were to be windows (in *Nachlass*, I, p. 484, Michelangelo says that the semi-dome is divided "in tre volte in luogo delle finestre da basso, divise da pilastri". He does not say that the *tondi* are windows, but since he calls the rectangles "lower windows" there must have been windows above them). Accordingly, the exterior of the attic must have been redesigned to allow fenestration at two levels: one higher and one lower than the model-windows. But the two-level scheme was abandoned; in 1557/1558 the attic was built on the southern hemicycle according to the model (see views of the Basilica in construction: Egger 1911, Pls. 39, 41). Consequently the Luchinus engraving (IVb, Pl. 59a) may be interpreted as a copy either of the model or of the incomplete southern elevation of the building itself (discrepancies between the engraving and the building are slight enough to be attributed to faulty recording).

The attic remained bare until the end of Michelangelo's life (the façade attic-facing in Pl. 62a, of 1558–1564, shows what may have been Michelangelo's *concetto* of that period;

it is borrowed from the attic of Bramante's altar-house, Pl. 56b). The existing facing was built on the northern hemicycle simultaneously with the vault, and appears, half finished, in an engraving of 1565 illustrating a tournament held in the Cortile del Belvedere (Pl. 53b). It must have been started just before Michelangelo's death in 1564 (Luchinus did not show it in his engraving of that year, Pl. 59a), or immediately after, by Ligorio and Vignola. In either case, Michelangelo must have designed it: the window-frames are close to the Porta Pia cartouches (Pl. 79a) and the overall style is unrelated to that of the younger men.

The attic in Dupérac's southern elevation (Pl. 60) probably was based on the portion built around the northern hemicycle in the 1560's; on the remainder of the Basilica, later architects replaced the oval light over the windows with a shell-ornament surmounted by a recessed panel (Pl. 63; the difference was observed by Tolnay 1930, p. 6n). The restricting effect of the change on interior illumination may be deduced from Pl. 61.

In the reconstructions of Michelangelo's project by Nogari (?) (Vb; Pl. 58b) and Guerra (Vc), a balustrade surmounts the attic all around the Basilica. It never was built, and does not appear in Dupérac's plates, but a similarity in form and purpose to the Campidoglio balustrades (Pl. 37) suggests that Michelangelo designed it; the Campidoglio analogy also recommends acceptance of the balustrade statues as authentic (Alker 1920, pp. 31, 115). Another feature of these reconstructions, the spire-like baldachins stuck on to the crown of the northern and southern hemicycle vaults, on stylistic grounds seem to be interpolations by one of Michelangelo's successors (cf. Alker 1920, pp. 35 f.)

The attic facing of 1564/1565 differs both from the 1547 model and from Michelangelo's revisions of 1551–1557 in screening the high, arched windows (Pl. 59a) by a combination of rectangular frames and oval *oculi*, so that the dominant accent was shifted from vertical to horizontal. It must have been designed after the construction of the dome model of 1558–1561, in accordance with the latest decisions on the form of the drum and the dome. Michelangelo cannot have intended to leave the attic without architectural membering as it appears in views of the 1547 model. As the key to the transition from the body of the Basilica to the central drum, the attic could not be satisfactorily designed before the character of the dome had been fixed. For this reason, the 1547 model, which apparently had no dome, was given a simple framework to which an attic facing could be added later, and the same was done in building the southern hemicycle. Views of this hemicycle made before the facing was added (*e.g.*, Egger 1911, Pl. 41), show a rough and obviously temporary masonry surface set back some distance from the plane of the entablature to leave room for an eventual facing.

3. THE FAÇADE

Michelangelo did not start building the façade before he died. Our knowledge of his design is based on graphic documents that are so inconsistent and inaccurate that it is impossible to make a convincing reconstruction.

The one original drawing that may be related to the façade (IIh; the identification with St Peter's is tentative) was rapidly sketched to show the relationship of the portico to the neighbouring buildings. The portico columns are too far apart and too distant from the Basilica to support lintels or beams and, as there are only five of them, the central one would block the axis of the entrance portal. Probably six columns were intended and were to be arranged like the central ones in the rear row of Pl. 59b, but placed three column-bays out from the portal. K. Frey (*Dichtungen*, p. 485) dated a poem which appears on the same sheet *ca.* 1550; Tolnay (1927, pp. 158 ff., followed by Dussler, No. 228) believed that the plan must be a preliminary study of 1546 for model *i*; but since we know nothing of the façades intended for models *i* and *ii* – and we shall see that Michelangelo's contemporaries were equally uninformed – we can place it only at some undetermined time prior to the more plausible plan used by Dupérac (Pl. 59b).

All other records of the façade are posthumous, with the exception of the drawing (IVa, Pl. 62a) from a sketchbook that Ashby dated 1581 and attributed to Dupérac (1916, pp. 19–27). It is by an unknown draughtsman and certainly earlier (Coolidge, pp. 120 ff.), since it shows the dome project as described by Vasari, including emendations made after the construction of the model of 1558–1561 (*e.g.*, the drum has segmental as well as triangular pediments) but not including emendations that appear in the Dupérac engravings of 1569 or after (*e.g.*, the podium at the base of the lantern). Since the latter change must have been made by Michelangelo before his death in 1564 (see section 4 below), and since the attic of the transept arms is shown without the facing added in 1564/1565, the drawing may be dated 1558–1564 (Tolnay 1930, p. 4 identified it with model *i* of 1546). Here the portico is six columns wide – the depth is uncertain – and carries a pediment so broad that its apex rises far above the attic; the central part of the attic had to be boosted up to enframe it. The relationship of the columns to the wall and pilasters behind is equally unfortunate; in fact, the draughtsman completely misunderstood the form of the Basilica, and put two doors on either side of the central portal which could not have been cut through the heavy masses of masonry – already built by Sangallo – that support the hemicycle vault. Having drawn doors that could not be opened, he suppressed the side aisle doors which, in the logic of the plan, had to be open. The amateurishness of his façade proves that it was not based on any serious proposal by Michelangelo; it can have derived only from a scribbled fantasy like the Vatican plan (IIh). If Michelangelo had not arrived at a more plausible solution than this by 1558, his study of the façade must have begun at the end of his life and must have ceased, as we shall see, at a point where the plan still did not fit the elevation.

If this is true, what of the façade of the model of 1546–1547? The only record of the second model is Passignani's painting, where the façade is lacking (Pl. 58a). It might have been built separately and have been removed or lost by Passignani's time (Coolidge 1942, p. 117), but perhaps it was never made. Not one major feature of the Basilica was designed by Michelangelo before the moment came to build it; furthermore, the attic cornice in Passignani's model runs right across the front of the truncated nave, as if the addition of a façade block had not even been contemplated. That the model was incomplete in other respects is revealed by its flat roof. If there had been a façade, the author of Pl. 62a would not have made such unaccountable blunders.

These observations suggest that it was only shortly before his death that Michelangelo designed the more plausible but still problematical façade illustrated in Dupérac's engravings (Pls. 59b, 60, 61) and Alfarani's drawing (IVg). The plan of 1569 (Pl. 59b), inscribed "ex esemplari Michaelis Angeli", may have been based on the 1546 model and a drawing recorded in the inventory of Michelangelo's estate at his death: "Item un cartone, di più pezzi incollati insieme, dove è designato la pianta della fabrica di San Pietro" (Gotti 1875, II, p. 151).

The other engravings (Pls. 60, 61) do not claim to be from *esemplari* of Michelangelo, and a close inspection of the façade proves that Dupérac had only a vague idea what Michelangelo intended. In his section (Pl. 61) the entrance portal and the window above it are walled over; in the elevation (Pl. 60) his confusion is still greater, though difficult to detect without projecting the façade in perspective: the foremost attic pilasters are not centred on the columns beneath them, and their bases would have been lopped off by the slope of the pediment; there is no attic at all over the rear row of columns, which apparently carry an absurd platform extending back to the body of the Basilica. Whereas the plan (Pl. 59b) shows the outermost columns of the rear row to be in line with the lateral walls of the nave, the elevation (Pl. 60) shows a setback in the entablature between the lateral wall and the end column, indicating that the latter should be moved in several feet toward the centre, which would upset the entire proportion system of the plan (for a detailed analysis of these inconsistencies, see Alker 1920, pp. 12, 30 ff., 101–128; Rose, pp. 283 ff.; Coolidge 1942, pp. 112 ff.) A further sign of Dupérac's uncertainty is that he first intended to show the plan without the façade, as in the 1547 model; he centred the façade-less building exactly on the plate so that when he changed his mind, he had room only for the columns at the bottom of the plate, and had to add the front steps at the top, expecting the owners to cut them off and paste them on below, as in Pl. 59b (Coolidge, p. 116, used this ingenious observation to prove that the elevation and section, which included the façade and steps from the start, were engraved later than the plan).

In short, the one authentic façade design left by Michelangelo was in such an early stage of development that Dupérac could not graft it properly on to the Basilica. It must have been sketchy, because later versions of it are not identical to Dupérac's (the Uffizi drawing, IVi, may be discounted as a second-hand copy after Dupérac). Uffizi, S.174 (IVh) has pairs of columns before the pilasters at the corners of the main body of the Basilica where the stairway begins in Pl. 59b, and the stairway is therefore changed to leave a platform before the columns. In the Vatican fresco and in Guerra's vignette (Vb, c; Pl. 58b) the attic is brought forward over the rear row of columns, and the main portal is raised to a height of two stories and correspondingly broadened (Alker, pp. 39 ff. and Pl. 17; Rose 1925, pp. 285 f.) The Gregory XIII medal (Va) has the smaller portal and a unique stairway plan with three successive setbacks. Engravings by Van Aelst and Fontana (Vd) follow the fresco except that they neglect to bring the attic forward over the pediment. These artists cannot have had access to more information on Michelangelo's project than did Dupérac; their variations must have originated in the vagueness of Michelangelo's sketch.

Carefully studied reconstructions of Michelangelo's façade were drawn by Alker (1920, Fig. 23; cf. his reproductions of earlier attempts by Letarouilly, Fig. 16; Canina and Cockerell, Fig. 16a; Jovanovitz, Fig. 21) and Coolidge (1942, Fig. 2; drawn by Conant;

the reconstructions of Rose 1925, Fig. 158, Mariani 1943, Pls. 15, 16, 18, 20, 23, 28; Schiavo 1949, Pls. 99, 121; are less convincing. The last two failed to account for most of the problems raised in earlier literature). Their conclusions give us a clear idea of the façade Michelangelo might have envisaged had his studies continued along the path on which they started. But, as the design of every feature of the St Peter project remained in flux until the moment construction began, and as even the meticulously finished models did not stem the flood of Michelangelo's fresh ideas, no reconstruction of the façade can do more than to capture a moment in a process that might have culminated in an entirely different solution.

4. THE MAIN DOME

Michelangelo's design of the central dome of St Peter's has been the subject of more study and controversy than any other aspect of his architectural work. Because of the great influence of this design on the whole future of domed structures, historians have realized the importance of clearly distinguishing the form determined by Michelangelo from that executed by della Porta. The key to this study is the wooden model preserved in the Basilica (Pl. 57b). Long believed to be basically identical to Michelangelo's model *iv* of 1558–1561, the surviving model was first subjected to careful analysis by D. Frey (1920, pp. 91 ff.), who demonstrated that the elevated outer shell corresponds to the building as executed, while the hemispherical inner shell represents a variant version of Michelangelo's final project as described by Vasari and engraved by Dupérac. This conclusion supports the evidence of della Porta's contemporary, Grimaldi, the late-sixteenth-century archivist of St Peter's (Orbaan 1917, p. 196; from ms. *Barb. Lat.* 2733, c. 486b) to the effect that: "Sub Sixto V erant ibi [in the workshop of the stonecutter's yard] exempla aliqua gypsea et lignea templi Buonarotae et testudinis eius tholi, quam testudinem aliquantulum depressiorem tenebat. Sed Jabobus (*sic*) Porta architectus, Bonarotae alumnus, tholum ipsum altiorem surgere fecit, quia consideravit venustiorem fore et etiam validiorum". Frey, however (pp. 99–104), made the error of attributing the entire model to the eighteenth-century engineers assigned to the restoration of the dome, which left no valid reason for the appearance of part of Michelangelo's abandoned scheme (but see Frey's emendations, *Kunstchronik*, 1922). This led Alker and Brinckmann (1921, pp. 96 ff.) to more careful studies that resulted in the identification of the inner shell with Michelangelo's model *iv*, and the outer shell with della Porta's model; they dated the latter 1585–1590 from the arms of Sixtus V carved on it (documents for a model in 1578 suggest an earlier start). Tolnay (1930, p. 15n, with modifications in 1932, pp. 238 f.) hoped to explain differences between the purportedly original portions and Vasari's description by assigning the entire model to della Porta (he abandoned this theory in 1951, Pl. 256); but Körte (1932, p. 111) noted differences in workmanship between the upper and lower portions that confirm Alker's hypothesis, and he attributed departures from Vasari to changes made by Michelangelo himself in the period (1561–1564) between the completion of the model and his death. The attempt by Beltrami (1929, *passim*) to restore the whole to Michelangelo was a brave but unscientific gesture of respect for the master (see Körte's review, *Münchner Jhb.*, 1932, p. 162).

This solution of the model problem, however, does not tell us whether Porta's dome, with its elevated curve, or the hemisphere shown by Dupérac (Pls. 60, 61) actually represents Michelangelo's last testament. To answer this question we must reconstruct the final design by comparing the surviving portions of the model with Vasari's description (VII, pp. 248–257), the drawings of Dosio (IIIb–f), and Dupérac's engravings. This comparison is complicated by the fact that all of these witnesses knew of and interpolated the changes made by Michelangelo after the completion of his model in 1561. The following summary is much indebted to Wittkower's definitive analysis of these sources (1933, pp. 348–356).

Vasari follows the original portion of the model and proves its authenticity in his description of: (1) the partly cruciform and partly circular stairways on the exterior of the inner shell and (2) the balustrade (now broken off) around the entablature of the drum, which is mentioned in documents on the construction of the model. He departs from the model in describing: (1) alternating pediments over the drum windows (in the model the exterior pediments are all triangular, the interior all segmental); (2) oval rather than round decorative frames on the interior webbing between the ribs; (3) a uniform thickness for the inner shell (measurements of the model and those inscribed on the anonymous drawing [IIIg] indicate a diminishing thickness towards the top).

These differences are significant for the evaluation of the model and other sources and deserve analysis:

1. Vasari's alternating window pediments are explained by the fact that the actual drum was finished by the time he wrote. It was started in 1555, and had reached the level of the entablature by 1561. Drawings done during the construction by Dosio and Ammanati (?) (Pl. 56b) show that the window frames were contemporaneous, and that they had alternating pediments. Vasari himself reported (VII, p. 248) that the model of 1558–1561 was started *after* the workmen had "già tirato innanzi gran' parte del fregio delle finestre di dentro e delle colonne doppie di fuora . . ." It is difficult to find a convincing explanation for the fact that Michelangelo put uniform pediments on the model while building alternating ones on the actual drum. He cannot have thought of dismantling half of the new pediments; we must assume either that the drum of the model was superseded as soon as it was started or that it was made two or three years before the dome portion (Dosio's view of the exterior [Egger 1911, Pl. 24], used by Cavalieri as the basis for an engraving of 1575 [Frutaz 1956, Pl. XXXI], shows uniform triangular pediments on the drum; since it was drawn after the completion of the attic of the northern hemicycle in 1565 ff., this reversion to the model must be regarded as a slip of the pen).

2. The substitution of oval for round decorative frames between the interior dome ribs is also documented by Dosio, who drew the round frames in IIIc (Pl. 57a) and IIIb, but revised the latter sketch to show ovals. Michelangelo must have been undecided on this point, as he had been in the models for San Giovanni de' Fiorentini (Pls. 70b, 71a–b).

3. The crucial feature of Vasari's account is his description of Michelangelo's method of constructing the profiles of the two shells (VII, pp. 253 ff.) These were drawn in

cross-section with a compass from three points arranged in the centre of the sheet in triangular form thus: $\begin{smallmatrix} A & B \\ & C \end{smallmatrix}$. From C, placed on the central axis of the dome, the

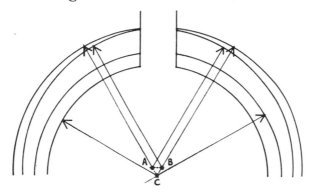

interior and exterior profiles of the inner shell were drawn, so that the shell was uniformly thick. The outer shell, which diminished toward the top, required two compass points; point A was used for its exterior and point B for its interior profile. Vasari (as Panofsky showed, 1927, pp. 44 f.), thought it unnecessary to mention the fact that he was speaking only of the portion to the left of the central axis; on the right, the function of the points was reversed, A being used for the interior, B for the exterior profile. This reveals the startling fact that the exterior of the dome would have been slightly *less* than a hemisphere, though so slightly as to be invisible (this interpretation by Wittkower 1933, pp. 355 f. and Fig. 5, corrects earlier errors by Frey 1920, p. 114; Alker 1920, pp. 23 ff.; Tolnay 1930, p. 11; Rose 1925, pp. 296 ff.)

Dosio's drawings are inconsistent. Like Vasari, he follows the original part of the model with respect to the stairways (IIIb, c [Pl. 57a], d) and the balustrade (IIIb, c), and departs from it by showing the existing window-pediments in the drum. Pl. 57a has decorative roundels between the dome ribs, like the model, while IIIb has ovals, like Vasari. In Pl. 57a, as in the model, it is the inner rather than the outer shell that diminishes in thickness, since Dosio turned Vasari's triangle of compass-points upside down and added a fourth point; in IIId, both shells diminish, and there are seven compass points. IIIb, which has the three-point construction, is close, but not identical to Vasari's description (Wittkower, pp. 350 f.) The inner shell of the model does diminish, so Dosio must have tried to reconcile the theoretical three-point system with measurements from the model. The anonymous drawing in the Casa Buonarroti (IIIg; Tolnay 1932, p. 231; cf. Wittkower, p. 351) seems to be the only record based solely on the model; the slight differences in measurements from those which Dosio took from the model can be attributed to the fact that the author – as is obvious from the carelessness of the sketch – was in a hurry. Apparently both Vasari and Dosio knew the theoretical system determining the form of the shells and other changes made by Michelangelo after the construction of the model (*e.g.*, oval decorative frames) but Dosio was familiar with the actual model measurements, while Vasari ignored them (Wittkower, p. 354).

Dupérac's engravings (Pls. 60, 61), on the other hand, apparently were made without knowledge of Michelangelo's drawings, by combining the dome of the model with the drum as executed by Michelangelo (not only the alternating pediments but the stairways in the base of the drum follow the building rather than the model: Wittkower, pp. 354 ff.) In general, the engraved dome conforms to the data of Vasari and Dosio, but the size of the engravings made it impossible for Dupérac to adhere to the three-point construction, presuming he knew of it, because at this scale the points would fuse into one. Dupérac's lantern, however, differs from that of Vasari and Dosio in being raised on a high podium and in eliminating a proposed corridor between the columns and the windows (Wittkower, pp. 359 ff.) The design of the lantern added to the model in 1561 (K. Frey 1916, pp. 85, 87) may have been changed in the ensuing years. Dupérac's version must represent a late revision. The evidence against Tolnay's identification of Dupérac's engravings with the model of 1546/1547 (1930, pp. 6, 11; 1932, p. 35; *etc.*) is decisive and need not be repeated here (cf. Körte 1932, p. 106n; Wittkower, pp. 354 ff.; Coolidge 1942, pp. 112 ff.; section 5 below).

While the posthumous documents indicate that Michelangelo planned a hemispherical dome, the surviving drawings show an elevated profile. An understanding of the development of the design therefore depends on determining which was the definitive solution.

In the Haarlem sketches (IIa, Pl. 54), the elevated outer shell is uniformly thick and diverges from the spherical inner shell more at the base than at the centre; this proposal is structurally unsound (D. Frey 1920, p. 106), and must represent an early stage in the design. The lantern, which is octagonal, suggests that the dome was to have eight ribs. The 8-rib design must precede the construction of the 16 rib-buttresses in 1554 ff. and therefore cannot be associated (as Tolnay proposed: 1930, p. 8), with the dome model of 1558/1561. The profile and the lantern both reflect the influence of the cathedral of Florence. In July 1547, Michelangelo wrote to his nephew Lionardo (*Lettere*, p. 211): "I should like to have you get from Mr. Giovanni Francesco the height of the cupola of Santa Maria del Fiore, from the base of the lantern to the ground, and also the overall height of the lantern, and send it to me; and mark off on your letter one-third of the Florentine *braccia*". Wittkower (p. 358) noted that the purpose of these measurements was exclusively to determine the proportions of the lantern, a problem that is unsolved in Pl. 54, where the central sketch is close to Florence and the *pentimento* on the upper left is taller. On this account the drawing might be dated immediately before or after the letter (Frey 1920, p. 108; Körte 1932, p. 102; Tolnay, in a revised opinion, 1960, p. 203). Drawings on the lower part of the *recto* and on the *verso* for the *Crucifixion of St Peter* in the Cappella Paolina, begun in March 1546 (Dussler, No. 148, with a review of earlier literature. Tolnay, *loc. cit* believes with Thode that they were early studies for the interior decoration of the dome itself.) support a date in the period of the early models. Wittkower's suggestion that it was drawn even before the construction of the wood model, started in December 1546, is based on a persuasive thesis that the lower part of the Basilica as determined in that model, with its powerful paired pilasters, could no longer be crowned by an 8-sided dome with single columns. The letter of July 1547 was written six months after the initiation of the model, leaving, according to the usual explanation, three months for the design and construction of its dome. But this explanation does not account for evidence – cited in section 5 – that the model had no dome at all. The problem is not, however, relevant to the dating of the drawings, which would have been produced even if they were not to have been used for the model.

The Lille drawing (IId; Pl. 55a) has the 16 buttresses and paired columns of the final project, but since the Tuscan columns on high socles were changed in the 1554 campaign to Corinthian columns without socles, it cannot be associated with models of 1557/1561. Its authenticity has been questioned (Tolnay 1930, p. 8n; Dussler, No. 301, saw it as an assistant's drawing corrected by the master), but it was produced in Michelangelo's studio as indicated by an autograph *ricordo* of 1556/1561 on the *verso*. Furthermore, the (Florentine) round windows of the drum were at one time projected by Michelangelo, who wrote on the Casa Buonarroti drum-plan (IIe): "questa parte che resta bianca è la faccia dove anno a esser gli occhi" (D.457; F.208). That the Lille elevation is closely related to this plan is also indicated by the use of the Tuscan Order in both. Since the low lantern has 8 divisions and the drum 16, the dome was probably planned without ribs, like Bramante's; its form, however, is entirely unclear: various profiles are drawn, one of them close to the impractical solution of Pl. 54. Though the drum is closer to the final solution, the indecisive dome and the single columns of the lantern recommend a date immediately after Pl. 54 and No. IIc, and before the model of 1546/1547; *pentimenti*, such as the garlands in the attic, may have been added later. The drawings on the *verso* are of the 1550's (Tolnay 1960, pp. 220 f., Pl. 219).

The Casa Buonarroti dome project (IIc) is so poorly preserved that we can see only that it is close to the central sketch of Pl. 54, with a hemispherical interior shell and a squat lantern which differs in having a convex moulding (or brackets like IIb?) just below the cone. The dome shells are thicker than in Pl. 54, but the profile of the outer one is, as far as can be seen, nearly the same. If it is true that the additional sketches show the drum-plan with a buttress of paired columns, this drawing, which has been over-looked in the literature on St Peter's, provides the missing link between Pls. 54 and 55a and supports the hypothesis that they were contemporaneous.

The Casa Buonarroti lantern sketches (IIb) are variants of those in the three drawings discussed above (Tolnay 1930, p. 8). In the one sketched at the bottom, the lower volutes that appear in Pl. 54 are placed upon, rather than around the podium. The drawing may be contemporaneous with IIc, its companion in the Casa Buonarroti, because both were drawn on the back of sketches for the Casa Altopascio in Florence. Wittkower noted (p. 359) that similarities in the lantern projects (IIa–e) to motifs used by Sangallo (Pl. 51c) also supports an early dating.

The Oxford lantern sketch (IIf; Pl. 55b) is accompanied by the note: "messer francesco [Bandini] signior mio caro circa al modello ch s'a a fare e mi pare che col Cardinale si sia facto una figura senza capo". The model referred to must be the wooden dome model of 1558–1561 (or the preparatory sketch; Tolnay 1930, p. 8), which Bandini and Cardinal Rodolfo Pio of Carpi had urged Michelangelo to make, since the "figure" of the church remained "without a head" (Tolnay suggests rather a colloquialism equivalent to "una cattiva figura"). The sketch barely outlines a lantern of the type studied a decade before. It is astonishing to find that as Michelangelo started to plan the model, he had not determined the dome profile; various solutions are still proposed here.

Pl. 55b shows a break in the inner shell to admit light from the lantern. Michelangelo also wavered in his decision on this problem (Körte 1932, pp. 95 ff.) Vasari (VII, p. 256) spoke of a passageway around the lantern from which one could peer into the interior of the church, while Pl. 54, Dupérac and Dosio (Pls. 57a, 61) show a slightly conical canopy at the base of the lantern. Beneath the canopy is a band of small apertures that could transmit light only from the uppermost row of dormers in the dome. That the closed canopy was the definitive solution is proven by the minutes of a conference of 1564/1565 in which the absence of direct lighting is criticized as contrary to ancient and modern practice (Körte 1932, pp. 100 f., from K. Frey 1913, p. 152). Michelangelo's purpose was to bring a diffused light into the dome from invisible sources to create a mysterious effect; his remarkable device was rejected by della Porta, but influenced seventeenth-century experiments in lighting (Körte, *loc. cit.*) While Dupérac agrees with Dosio (IIIc, d; Pl. 57a) on this point, he differs in raising the lantern on a high base and in interposing the volutes of Pl. 54 between the entablature and the cone. Both differ from Vasari in eliminating the corridor around the windows – Dupérac puts it outside the lantern, on the crown of the dome. The many disparities suggest that the model lantern proved to be unsatisfactory. Michelangelo's final solution must have come later, and was probably closest to Dupérac's, whose reliability is affirmed by the strength of the design and by the restatement of motifs from the original drawings (Wittkower 1933, pp. 359 ff.) In execution, della Porta followed the essentials of the Dupérac lantern design, though he added Vasari's inner corridor and cancelled the high base and the interior canopy.

Della Porta also made significant changes in the design of the dome itself, in addition to altering the hemispherical profile (Tolnay 1930, pp. 14 f.; Körte 1932, pp. 103 ff.; Wittkower, p. 363. Compare Pls. 60, 63). In the attic, he narrowed the projections at the base of the ribs, made the cornice profiles more complex, and added the decorative insignia of Sixtus V. He inserted a moulding at the base of the dome, and entirely changed the ribs, which he made narrower, uniform in width, and softer, eliminating the central steps (Körte, p. 109). He changed the design of the two upper rows of dormer windows, accentuating the middle one by fancy frames. On the interior, where he also raised the profile above the hemisphere, he increased the attic by 1 m., eliminated the balustrade, and put socles surmounted by lion heads at the base of the ribs. Arches between the ribs (inspired by Michelangelo's hemicycle volutes, Pl. 61, where they make more sense as relieving arches over the windows) spring from these socles and have the effect of narrowing the ribs so that only their central band appears to function structurally.

Della Porta's decision to elevate the dome and to lower the lantern calls attention to the fact that the relationship between the two had been Michelangelo's chief concern from the start. He did not decide until the last moment which should play the chief role in accentuating the aspiring forces.

5. THE MINOR DOMES

It is curious that Vasari, who was so anxious to preserve Michelangelo's design that he devoted over 2000 words to describing the cupola alone, should have overlooked entirely the minor domes. Dosio ignored them, too, and they appear first in the anonymous drawing of 1558–1564 (IVa, Pl. 62a) and in Dupérac's engravings (Pls. 60, 61). These two versions are different, but they are alike in one respect: neither is in any way related to Michelangelo in style.

Coolidge (1942, pp. 63–86) suggested that the small domes in the Dupérac engravings might have been designed by Vignola. His attribution is supported by a tradition accepted generally before the present century that assigned the existing domes of della Porta to Vignola, who was second in command at the Basilica after Michelangelo's death and chief architect from 1565 to 1573. If Michelangelo had failed to leave designs for the domes, Vasari, whose purpose was to preserve the master's last testament, would have had no need to mention them; but Dupérac, whose purpose was to anticipate the finished Basilica, would have had to find a project for them whether or not it was Michelangelo's. The fact that there are small domes in Passignani's painting after the model of 1546/1547 (Pl. 58a) tells us nothing of Michelangelo's intentions, for we find on close inspection that both the major and minor domes are della Porta's, which were either added to Michelangelo's model in the third quarter of the sixteenth century (Coolidge 1942, p. 88), or simply stuck on by the painter to clarify his message. The top of the model, on which they rest, is quite flat, indicating that its uppermost portions never were finished. This cannot have been Passignani's mistake; earlier artists who knew the model were unable to discover from it how to join the Basilica to its cupola. Dupérac (Pl. 60) made a gross error in extending the nave vault from the façade to the apse without interrupting it at the drum, thereby thrusting the entire cupola off-centre beyond the nave (Coolidge 1942, pp. 112 f.) The anonymous draughtsman of 1558–1564 (Pl. 62a) invented a colossal nave-vault that spans the entire width of the eastern arm, side aisles included. Granting that the 1546/1547 model had no vaults, it probably had no domes, either; the builders cannot have expended great effort on carving the intricate domes while avoiding the comparatively simple task of making vaults. Domes set on a flat roof would have been useless – confusing to both the architect and the builders. If we can accept a façade-less model *ii*, we should find a domeless one more digestible. It would explain the urgency with which Michelangelo's friends pressed him to construct the large dome model of 1557: they can hardly have been dissatisfied with the earlier model unless it were, to use Michelangelo's own words (Pl. 55b), "una figura senza capo".

If we are correct in dating Pl. 62a in 1558–1564, it would appear to prove that the small domes were designed before Michelangelo's death. But these underscaled structures, retrogressive in style, might have been drawn by anyone. They serve only to support the assumption that Michelangelo intended to build the minor domes.

Coolidge's attribution of Dupérac's domes to Vignola is convincing: they are more Vitruvian than any other feature of the Basilica; they avoid the ubiquitous doubled Order; they revert to the dome and lantern-volutes of Bramante's Torre Borgia cupola (Pl. 51b); and they reveal the thin wall-layers that are the hallmark of Vignola's style. The only architect other than Vignola who worked at St Peter's before the publication of the engravings was Ligorio, whose style was far less reserved.

Support for the Vignola attribution may be found in a design for the lanterns of the minor domes copied by Oreste Vannocci Biringucci (Pl. 62b; *ca.* 1580. Siena, Bibl. Comunale, S. IVᵢ, fols. 44v, 45. Fol. 45 has drawings from the inner shell of the dome model and plans of the Rossellino–Bramante and Michelangelo hemicycles). This lantern is close to Dupérac's; its dome borrows from Michelangelo the rib-type of the main dome, with steps along the spine; the volutes are the same type as Dupérac's but are now gathered together to form four pairs to support the four broad ribs; pedestals at their base carry tall obelisks, and one bears a sphere as an alternative. There are three reasons for attributing the design to Vignola: first, Vannocci's sketchbook is full of copies after lost Vignola drawings (*e.g.*, for the Gesù [Lotz, Röm. Jbh., VII, 1955, Figs. 26–27], and for Santa Maria in Traspontina, which has the same ornamental obelisks as Pl. 62b); second, the elevation is divided down the centre so as to show the interior on the left and the exterior on the right – a device characteristic of Vignola's drawings and rarely used by his contemporaries; and third, a lantern design – for a tabernacle of 1563 in the church of San Antonio Martire in Fara Sabina – with similar motifs has been proved recently to be Vignola's (A. Sacchetti Sassetti, "Opere sconosciute del Vignola", *Archivi*, Quaderno 1, Rome, 1956, p. 27 and Fig. 1; I believe that Vignola's project for this tabernacle is also recorded in Vannocci's sketchbook, *op. cit.*, fol. 42v).

The existing domes were built by della Porta, who was somewhat more sympathetic to Michelangelo. But, having no original drawings to guide him, he turned to the Medici chapel as a source for his lanterns (Pl. 14a, the only lantern built by Michelangelo), and to Bramante for his drum and dome (Pl. 51b). Grimaldi, in the passage describing Porta's revision of the Michelangelo model, states that Porta rebuilt the finished cupola of the first minor dome after deciding on the elevated profile (Orbaan 1917, p. 196: "immo minoris tholi testudinem quam depressiorem super sacello Gregoriano construxerat, reformavit ed ad maximi tholi imitationem altiorem extulit"). The change is shown in two frescoes, possibly both by Nebbia and Guerra, in the Vatican library: in one, showing the obelisk raised in the Piazza by Sixtus V in 1586, the Cappella Gregoriana has a hemispherical dome (Frutaz 1956, Pl. XL); in the other, showing the coronation of Sixtus in 1585, it has the existing dome (*ibid.*, Pl. XXXVIII). Documents of August 1578, recording the completion of the lantern (K. Frey 1916, p. 132), probably refer to the first cupola, since a fresco of 1580 in the loggie of Gregory XIII (Frutaz, Pl. XXXVI) shows the drum without a dome, as it might have looked in the interim between the two phases of construction. This suggests that Porta's decision to alter Michelangelo's model project was not made before 1578, the year in which his new model was started.

It is hard to accept Coolidge's conclusion that Michelangelo never planned to build minor domes (1942, p. 78; reconstruction by Conant, Fig. 12). Granting that they are useless appendages, and that in the course of 400 years we have become biased in their favour, it would seem incongruous that Dupérac, who did the best he could to adhere to Michelangelo's definitive design, should have interpolated the tentative studies of a successor if they were contrary to the master's intentions. It is more likely that Michelangelo wanted the domes but, as usual, was waiting until the progress of construction should make it imperative to design them.

Vatican Fortifications, 1547–1548

The obsolescence of the ancient and medieval fortifications of Rome was cruelly emphasized by the sack of the city in 1527. Clement VII called Niccolo Machiavelli from Florence to study the requirements for improving the defences, but lack of funds delayed the scheme. A vast and costly programme was initiated by Paul III, beginning with defences on the left bank of the Tiber in 1537–1542, and shifting in 1543 to the walls surrounding the Borgo (Vatican quarter). From the outset until his death in 1546, Antonio da Sangallo the Younger was in charge of the design and execution of the enceinte (on the history of the fortifications, see Guglielmotti 1887, V pp. 334–353; Rocchi 1902, pp. 277–281; *idem* 1908, p. 293; Pastor, *Geschichte*, V, pp. 744–750; Schiavo 1953, pp. 254 ff.)

The Vatican defences were started in 1543 in the section behind the church of Santo Spirito. In 1545 another section was begun behind the Cortile del Belvedere (Rocchi, *loc. cit.*) At this point a controversy started between Sangallo, who wanted an extended system embracing the hills, and Gianfrancesco de Montemellino, who advised restricting it to the nearer valley (Guglielmotti 1887, V, pp. 329 ff.; Gotti 1875, II, pp. 126 ff.) A drawing by Sangallo showing an extended and restricted enceinte is reproduced by Rocchi (1908, p. 281; cf. other sketches reproduced by Rocchi 1902, Pl. 39; Guglielmotti, X, Pls. 72–74). The argument reached such proportions that the Pope called a large conference early in 1545 which, however, ended inconclusively. Michelangelo was present (see the eye-witness account of Guglielmo della Porta, G. Gronau, *Jhb. d. preuss. Kunstsammlungen*, XXXIX, 1918, p. 195) and, according to Vasari (VII, p. 217), opposed Sangallo, who told him that sculpture and painting were his arts, not fortification. He replied that "he knew little of those, but of fortification, considering the thought he had devoted to it over so long a time, and his practical experience, he believed he knew more than Sangallo and his whole family together". In view of the pre-eminence of the Sangallos in the development of military architecture, this was an offensive boast, but Michelangelo probably had more experience in the field than is usually credited to him. As early as 1516 he was recommended to a provincial lord as a military expert (*Briefe*, p. 28); in 1527, he was appointed by a papal Breve as "revisor arcium et fortilitiorum" at Bologna (H. Sauer, *Quellen u. Forschungen aus italienischen Archiven u. Bibliotheken*, XIII, 1910, pp. 224 ff.); he was in charge of the defence of Florence, and he was again appointed by Pope Paul IV as an adviser on fortifications (Vasari, VII, p. 241).

In a letter of 26 February 1545 (*Lettere*, p. 499) to the Castellan of Castel Sant'Angelo, Michelangelo proposed that the Vatican defences should be continued as they were begun but recommended that Montemellino be put in Sangallo's place, in which event he agreed to collaborate in the programme. In spite of the controversy, construction continued speedily under Sangallo for a year, but in 1546 new disagreements halted all work except on the Santo Spirito sector to the west (Guglielmotti, V, p. 338; Rocchi 1902, pp. 278 f.) After Sangallo's death in the autumn of this year, Jacopo Meleghino, a favourite of the Pope's, but a poor architect, was appointed in his place. A letter of March 1547 from a Farnese agent, Prospero Mochi, to Pierluigi Farnese (Rocchi, *loc. cit.*) indicates that Meleghino required Michelangelo's assistance in problems of design:

"Concerning the fortification of the Borgo, the Porta Santo Spirito [started by Sangallo but left unfinished to the present day] is closed off, but they expect to complete the upper part. By the Spinelli palace they intend to erect the curtain wall toward the tower of Nicholas V. We have reached the flanks, and since Master Michelangelo has taken Sangallo's place together with Meleghino – whose orders Master Michelangelo is following (*sic*) for the moment – His Holiness has ordered us to obey Master Michelangelo and none other in matters relating to the design. And as Master Michelangelo is in disagreement with what has already been decided, they are awaiting the arrival of Sig. Alessandro Vitelli as His Holiness has ordered."

The letter continues to explain Michelangelo's point, that an additional bastion of two flanks was required to cover the curtains between the tower of Nicholas V, and the Spinelli Palace (these are the defences along the eastern corridors of the Cortile del Belvedere facing the Tiber, and the proposed bastion would be just north of the Porta S. Anna).

Less than a year later, the famous military engineer, Jacopo Castriotto, arrived in Rome to take charge of the fortifications, and Michelangelo's name disappeared from the documents (Rocchi 1902, p. 281). A letter from Gianfrancesco de Montemellino to Ottavio Farnese of 20 February 1548, refers to the "fortezza cominciata a Belvedere" (Guglielmotti, V, p. 351) and proposes that the plan be changed, which suggests that the construction had only started during the period of Michelangelo's activity.

The attribution of the eastern Belvedere fortifications to Michelangelo is generally accepted; yet the evidence cited gives it equivocal support. We do not know how much was done in the months of his active participation, and the bastion he proposed was not built (Guglielmotti, p. 345, identified the bastion with the angle salient beneath the Villa of Innocent VIII, which conforms neither with Mochi's letter nor with the papal inscription, "Paolo III, Pont. Max. Anno VIII"). The vigorous and monumental style of the defences distinguishes them from Sangallo's and suggests Michelangelo's influence but does not serve (as claimed by Guglielmotti, *loc. cit.*, Rocchi 1908, p. 293, and Schiavo 1953, p. 256) as proof of his authorship.

Vatican, Stairway in the Upper Garden of the Cortile del Belvedere, 1550–1551

The only certain evidence for Michelangelo's authorship of the Belvedere stairway (Pls. 65a, 65c) is Vasari's (VII, p. 228): "Neither at the Villa Giulia did [Julius III] do anything without his advice, nor in the Belvedere, where they remade the present stair in place of the one originally built by Bramante which had a convex half circle of eight steps [followed by] a concave flight with eight more, which was placed in the principal niche in the centre of the Belvedere. Michelangelo designed and had made that rectangular (quadra) one with peperino balusters which is there now: very beautiful. And Vasari, having in that year finished printing the work on the lives of the painters . . ." The closing sentence fixes the date of the design in 1550–1551, which is borne out by other documents. In September 1551, a payment was made by the papal treasury for transporting peperino "per far la scala di Belvedere" (Ackerman 1954, pp. 75, 165). In Bufalini's plan of Rome of 1551, the convex half of Bramante's circle is not shown, perhaps because it had been dismantled. Michelangelo's stairway is a smaller version of the earlier one before the Palazzo dei Senatori on the Capitoline Hill. Sketches for a double-ramped stairway of this type on Casa Buonarroti No. 19F (D.50; F.236) are related to the Belvedere project by Wilde (1953, p. 109) and to the Senatori by other critics who associate tomb sketches on the same sheet with the Bracci monument of 1544 (K. Frey; Steinmann, *Monatshefte für Kunstwiss.*, I, 1908, pp. 963 ff., Fig. 3; Tolnay 1948, p. 208, Pl. 124; Dussler).

The original circular stairway by Bramante was built in 1512 to connect the upper level of the Cortile with a semicircular exedra at the centre of the one-story wall at the short end of the huge theatre-garden (D. Frey 1920, pp. 17 ff., Figs. 2–10; Ackerman 1954, pp. 27 ff., 42, 154; Pl. 2; Figs. 16–20). The substitution of Michelangelo's stairway under Julius III was the first step in the transformation of Bramante's structure into a two-story villa. The suppression of the original stairway was necessary on both practical and structural grounds. Bramante had built only a semicircular wall at the rear of the exedra platform, and with the decision to put suites of rooms on either side the platform had to be remodelled as an internal passageway by the construction of a second semicircular wall on the court side. The second wall was also a prerequisite for roofing the exedra. Since it had to be raised on the uppermost of Bramante's concave steps, the whole stairway was rendered useless. Michelangelo, by designing new stairs in front of the building, provided a platform giving access to the new corridor through a central door and spacious enough to allow dining and relaxation in the open air. As at the Palazzo dei Senatori, the triangular, double-flight form was calculated to minimize the amount of open space occupied by the stairs; in the Belvedere it had the added advantage of masking the awkward junction of the new platform and the Corinthian pilaster Order of the court, and finally, it echoed Bramante's system of ramps in the lower court.

Only the gross forms of Michelangelo's design have survived later remodellings. The bronze *Pigna*, set on an antique capital, was brought to the Belvedere from the atrium of St Peter's by Paul V shortly before 1615; the original peperino balustrade was replaced by Clement XI (1700–1721), who added his family insignia and the over-scaled spheres at the base of the steps, and probably the central fountain (Ackerman 1954, pp. 113, 116).

Probably Michelangelo shaped the whole programme of the two-story villa of Julius III, though he left the design to others, since it was merely a problem of extending Bramante's scheme into the second story. Documents of 1550–1551 indicate that Girolamo da Carpi was in charge of the construction, though Vignola may have been the architect (*ibid.*, pp. 76 f.) The partially completed villa and the staircase first appear in a view attributed to Ammanati which I have dated 1552–1553 (Cambridge, Mass., Fogg Museum; *ibid.*, pp. 216 f.; Fig. 25), and the finished structure in Dosio's view of 1558–1561 (Pl. 65c, Uffizi, *Arch.* 2559; *ibid.*, pp. 219 f.; Fig. 26) and in a drawing of the same date recently discovered and tentatively attributed to Sallustio Peruzzi by Lotz (*Kunstchronik*, XI, 1958, p. 99, Fig. 1; subsequently sold in New York. The drawing adds to the then existing portions of the Cortile proposals for the continuation of the unexecuted western galleries and for the completion of Bramante's lower court). Both views show a roof over the concave central portion of the villa, which implies that the great *Nicchione* created by Pirro Ligorio with the addition of a semidome and loggia above in 1562–1565 (Ackerman 1954, pp. 73 f.; 87 ff.) was not anticipated in the original programme. D. Frey (1920, pp. 29–36), who recognized Ligorio as the designer and builder, argued persuasively that a concept as dynamic as that of the *Nicchione* can only have been Michelangelo's. But a comparison of the earlier views with the finished structure (Pls. 65a and 65c) shows that no provision for the support of the *Nicchione* was made in Michelangelo's time; the great arch rests on piers which had to be erected from the ground up in the 1560's.

Aside from his contribution to Julius' villa, Michelangelo did no work in the court itself, but he designed for Clement VII (1523–1534) a niche for a statue of the Tigris in the sculpture garden behind Bramante's exedra (Vasari, I, p. 114; Ackerman, pp. 58 f.) The niche, as it appears in a drawing by Heemskerk, follows the pattern of those built by Bramante (Huelsen and Egger, I, 1913, Pl. 63). Michelangelo's project for a fountain with a figure of Moses to be placed at the head of the gallery leading from the Vatican palace to the sculpture garden was rejected by Julius III as too costly, and the commission went, at Michelangelo's suggestion, to Daniele da Volterra (Vasari, VII, p. 58).

Rome, San Giovanni dei Fiorentini, 1559–1560

I HISTORY

Construction of a new church to replace the small oratory of the Florentine colony in Rome situated on a triangular plot between the Via Giulia and the Tiber river (Pl. 70a) was decided upon in 1518. The building commissioners invited Baldassare Peruzzi, Raphael, Antonio da Sangallo the Younger, and Jacopo Sansovino to submit projects for the new church, and awarded the commission to Sansovino (Vasari, V, 454; VII, 497 f.) The support of the Medici Pope, Leo X, was assured by a Bull of January 1519, and by 1520 the model had been completed and the foundations started (for documents on the history of construction, see A. Nava 1935–1936; *idem.*, 1936. Nava's numerous errors in interpretation have been corrected in Siebenhüner 1956, which, however, does not deal with Michelangelo's project). At the outset, Sansovino was supplanted by Sangallo, either because he was injured on the job or because he lacked the technical skill to extend the substructure into the river. About ten Sangallo studies for the project, mostly plans, are preserved in the Uffizi, and show a gradual development from a circular scheme (Pl. 66a) to a broad basilical plan with a five-bay nave flanked by side aisles and an outer row of chapels (for bibliography, cf. Siebenhüner, *op. cit.* One of Sangallo's drawings, Uffizi 1055, an alternative plan study with a nave elevation and a perspective of the choir has escaped notice). The huge expense of laying the foundations exhausted the funds of the commissioners and construction was indefinitely postponed, probably during the 1520's, when the substructure reached only a height of "several ells over the water" (Vasari, V, 455). Siebenhüner's study of the present church revealed that Sangallo completed the foundations from the façade to the foremost transept piers but did not initiate the transept or choir (Pl. 70a). These foundations were used with minor changes in the final structure of 1582–1614. (On the Sangallo projects, see now Giovannoni 1959, pp. 214–223, Figs. 164, 167–175.)

To assess Michelangelo's role we must establish how much of the project Sangallo managed to complete. The appearance of a rectangular building with a pitched roof in the perspective view of Rome in 1577 by Dupérac (D. Frey 1920, Fig. 30) led most scholars before Siebenhüner to assume that Sangallo executed the entire nave. Siebenhüner himelf neglected to notice that this engraving shows the building to be a temporary and probably earlier one; the new church is being built around it, and apparently is finished only up to the height of the entrance portal of the façade. Further evidence of slow progress is provided by Pinardo's perspective plan of 1555 (Pl. 70a), which shows San Giovanni from the rear, revealing a foundation platform extending beyond the temporary chapel by almost half its width, while the London plan of 1562 attributed to Dosio shows the nave foundations to be roughly three times the length of the chapel (cf. A. Frutaz 1956, Pls. XXI, XXIV). The demonstration that the church was barely begun supports Vasari's evidence and saves us the embarrassment of proposing that

Michelangelo, in returning to a central-plan project, intended to waste the already in-sufficient funds of the commissioners by tearing down a newly completed nave.

Michelangelo first became involved in the history of the church in 1550, when the recently elected Pope Julius III briefly considered placing his family tombs, originally planned for San Pietro in Montorio, in San Giovanni dei Fiorentini. Julius asked Michel-angelo for his opinion and for designs, but the project was abandoned within two months (Vasari VII, 229 f.; Vasari, *Nachlass*, I, 289, 294). Popp published three plans which she believed to be studies for the project of 1550 (1927, pp. 389, 409 ff.) Although these drawings were executed by a minor architect, two from the Dresden Kupferstichkabinett (D.390, 391) bear an old attribution to Michelangelo, while the third, in the Uffizi (No. 1819; D.518; cf. Tolnay 1951, Pl. 366; identified in a sixteenth-century hand as a sketch for the Gesù, see below, pp. 142 f.), has important alterations rapidly sketched in red chalk by a different architect whom Popp identified as Michelangelo himself. The presence of tombs in one of the Dresden sheets and a scale roughly approximate to the San Giovanni projects is surely insufficient evidence for associating these studies with San Giovanni or for attributing them to Michelangelo. Only a fundamental misunder-standing of Michelangelo's architectural style can explain the attribution; the three plans betray an anti-plastic aesthetic employing weakly projecting pilasters and counting heavily on the planar effect of the wall. They are feeble reflections of Antonio Sangallo's early style by a conservative master of mid-century and, in fact, are closely related to plans published by Serlio (Bk. V) in 1547. If we allow that the corrections on the Uffizi study are by Michelangelo, which is possible, we must recognize that the suggested changes are so drastic that they reveal the master attempting to rescue the work of an incompetent contemporary from disaster.

By 1559 the Florentine colony, with the assistance of the Tuscan Grand Duke Cosimo I, was prepared to continue construction without papal support, and persuaded Michel-angelo, now 84 years of age, to submit designs. The master agreed, but insisted that his age and infirmity did not permit him either to prepare the final drawings and model or to supervise the final construction (Vasari, VII, 261 ff.; *Lettere*, pp. 551–553; for a complete chronology, cf. D. Frey 1920, pp. 79–81). He submitted five studies of which one was selected, and his young assistant, Tiberio Calcagni, was chosen to execute measured drawings and a clay model, and later to supervise the construction of a wooden model.

II THE DESIGN

Three major plan studies are preserved in the Casa Buonarroti (Nos. 120, 121, 124; Pls. 68, 67 and 66b). The wooden model was destroyed in the eighteenth century, but engravings were made from it by Jacques Le Mercier in 1607 (Pl. 71a; cf. Robert Dumes-nil, *Le peintre-graveur français*, VI, Paris, 1842, p. 152) and by Valerian Régnard (Pl. 71b from G. G. de' Rossi, *Insignium Romae templorum prospectus*, Rome, 1683, Pls. 18, 19; Frey 1920, Fig. 32). Another model appears in a contemporary drawing by Giovanni Antonio Dosio (Pl. 70b; Modena, Bibl. Estense, MS. 1775, fol. 140v, 141, publ. by Luporini 1957, pp. 459, 464, Fig. 13).

The plans in the Casa Buonarroti may be three of the five presented to the commissioners, although one, Pl. 66 b (D.143; F.296) is not sufficiently developed to be considered a presentation drawing. Pl. 67 (D.142; F.295) obviously was prepared for laymen, since several parts of the plan, the function of which would be obvious to a professional, are identified in the author's hand ("arches," "barrel vaults," etc.) Pl. 68 (D.145; F.294), or a further development of the same scheme, was selected by the commission. Dagobert Frey (1920, pp. 57–69) is responsible for definitively identifying these drawings, for isolating them from a number of central plan sketches with which they were previously associated, and for recognizing a fourth, Casa Buon. No. 36 (D.80; F.223) as being a preliminary study for the support system of Pl. 68 (Thode anticipated Frey, but only in his *corrigenda*: 1908, III, pp. 290, 293). He showed that the project developed chronologically from Pl. 66b to 68. But D. Frey made one error that misled some later writers, in assuming the focal platform at the centre of the church in Pls. 66b and 68 to be a wall ("Mauerkern") placed in a hypothetical lower church or crypt as support for the floor of the church itself. He apparently was misled by K. Frey's facsimile reproductions of the drawings that fail to show clearly that this is a podium – probably for the main altar – as indicated by the three steps that raise it from the main floor. His error was compounded by its supposed proof, that a similar form appears in a group of drawings by Antonio Sangallo, which he imagined to be for San Giovanni (Uffizi, *Arch.* 551, 865, 866). There the form, lacking steps, unquestionably belongs to a crypt; but when the Sangallo drawings were proven later to be intended for the church of San Tolomeo in Nepi (Giovannoni 1935, pp. 111 ff.), Frey's argument lost its principal prop. Not only is it unlikely that a crypt would have been planned for construction on fill over the river, but the absence in the final plans of access to, or ventilation and lighting for a crypt cannot be ignored. In fact, the central position of the altar appears to be a primary motivation for the axial scheme proposed in Pls. 66b and 68.

A few small tentative plan studies, faintly sketched in chalk, appear on Pl. 67. Probably the plan on the *recto* precedes the main drawing, while those on the *verso* (published by Tolnay 1932, p. 248, Fig. 12; 1951, Pl. 367) follow, providing a transition to Pl.68. The latter sheet has faint indications of piers, an arch, and a groin vault alongside the plan. A group of closely related drawings is discussed on pp. 123 f. below (see especially Oxford, Ashmolean, No. 344v).

Pl. 68 required major revision before reaching the definitive stage of the model plan as we know it from the engraving of Régnard and from a plan – apparently Calcagni's working drawing – in the Uffizi (*Arch.* 3185; Pl. 69a; published – upside down – in Venturi, *Storia*, XI, 2, Fig. 189. A valuable analysis of difference between the drawing and the model may be found in Panofsky 1920/1921, pp. 41 f.)

Two more drawings, discovered recently, document transitional designs between Michelangelo's sketches and the model. In 1950 I found in the sketchbook of Oreste Vannocci Biringucci (Siena, Bibl. Comunale, S. IV. 1, fol. 42; executed shortly before the author's death in 1585) a plan copied from one of Michelangelo's or Calcagni's (Pl. 69b). Inscribed "Da Michelang(el)o p(er) la chiesa de fior(enti)ni à Ro(ma)", it shows essentially the scheme of Pl. 68: the central position of the altar, the identity in span of

entrances to the porticos, chapels and apse, and the details of interior and exterior articulation. But it approaches the model plan in limiting the free-standing columns of the
central space to their final role as a plastic relief to the piers, thus eliminating the concept
of an ambulatory and escaping the insoluble problem of supporting a dome on such
slight supports. Only in Vannocci's plan are free-standing columns employed in the
corners of the four entrance porticos and the apse – they are inked out in Pl. 68 (cf. a
similar proposal for the Sforza chapel, Pl. 72c). But more important is the fact that this
drawing provides the only evidence we have of the intended measurements of Michelangelo's scheme: the central space is 12 *canne* (26·76 m.) and the depth of the entrance
ways 5 *canne* (11·5 m.), making the total length and breadth 22 *canne*, or 49·06 m. This
is precisely the size of the domed area in the central-plan project by Antonio Sangallo
(Pl. 66a – inscribed "palmi 120" – Uffizi, *Arch.* 199, 200. Cf. Siebenhüner, p. 183) and
within inches of the 220-odd *palmi* overall breadth of Sangallo's final scheme for a longitudinal plan (Uffizi 862; Siebenhüner, p. 181). Thus Vannocci's copy demonstrates that
Michelangelo's return to the central plan system did not necessitate a complete abandonment of Sangallo's expensive foundations, which could have been partly utilized
for at least the porticos and the apse.

A second drawing (Pl. 70b) appears in the rich record of Cinquecento architecture
left in a sketchbook by Giovanni Antonio Dosio identified by Ragghianti and Luporini
(1957, pp. 442 ff.) It is a perspective view of the interior of a model inscribed "ritratto
dal modello di Sa(n) Giovan(n)i de fiorentini in Roma inve(n)tione di Michelagniolo
buonaroti B.M. ia"), similar in form to the model preserved in later engravings (Pl. 71a),
yet different enough in detail to be identified as an alternative – probably preliminary –
scheme. The dome has an open, Pantheon-like oculus at its crown rather than a lantern;
but unlike the Pantheon and the model of the engravings, no steps at the base; it is a
pure hemisphere. Inside, the coffering contains only superimposed circular panels
between the intersecting ribs rather than alternating circles and ovals. The windows have
triangular, not segmental pediments, and the framing differs. The greatest disparities are
in the entrances: those on either side are suppressed; a window appears in place of the
portal, but we cannot see if the design here is otherwise altered. The principal entrance,
in turn, is more elaborate; the vestibule is transformed into a portico by removing the
outer wall and replacing its two inner pilasters by columns. Consequently, the portal
has to be shifted to the interior of the portico; it is placed in a new screen wall erected
across the passageway leading into the church.

Dosio's drawing forces us to account for two models. Since Vasari speaks of a study
in clay preparatory to the wooden model, this appears to be no problem. But Dosio's
model, with its free-standing columns, sharp profiles, and open windows, would have
been exceedingly difficult to execute in a soft material. There may have been two wooden
models.

The final model of the church appears in perspective in the engraving by Le Mercier
(Pl. 71a; first cited by Panofsky 1920/1921; published by Tolnay 1930, pp. 15 ff.) as a half-
model cut through the principal axis to enable one to see at once the plan, the section, and
the interior and exterior form. Possibly it was built in the full round with one side fixed

to the base and the other movable. As Tolnay pointed out, Le Mercier's engraving reveals far more of the plastic quality of the design than the academic tightness of the plan and elevation/section by Régnard (Pl. 71b). Indeed, Michelangelo's concept was so compromised in the latter, that D. Frey (1920, pp. 82–87) assumed the model to be one executed by Giacomo della Porta in 1600 (Panofsky disproves this on documentary grounds, *op. cit.*, p. 43).

In April 1560, Calcagni travelled to Pisa to show Michelangelo's drawings to Cosimo I, and on his return in May (*Briefe*, pp. 377–378), a conference was held on the site of the church to consider a new stretch of foundation wall along the river (Nava 1936, pp. 354 f.); but by June of 1562 Calcagni had been replaced by another official. This is the last surviving evidence for Michelangelo's project. Evidently the 5000 scudi spent on the programme to this point (Vasari, VII, p. 263) had again exhausted the funds of the Florentine colony.

Another project for San Giovanni survives in a drawing attributed to Giovannantonio Dosio (Uffizi 233. D. Frey 1920, p. 84; Nava 1935/1936, p. 107; Wachler 1940, p. 220, Fig. 155). It is an elevation/section of a central plan structure that represents a classicistic variation on Sangallo's circular scheme, and is fundamentally opposed to Michelangelo's concept (Venturi, *Storia*, XI, 2, p. 195, Fig. 190, attempted to make it fit Calcagni's model plan, to which it bears no relationship). The fact that Vannocci copied this drawing into his sketchbook (*op. cit.*, fol. 42v) on the reverse of the folio he used for the Michelangelo plan indicates that in the 1580's the two were kept together – probably in the church archives – and I conclude that Dosio was asked to prepare a scheme suitable to Sangallo's foundations sometime during the fifteen years between Michelangelo's death and Vannocci's visit to the church. In a second project of the period 1560–1580, an unknown architect proposed to add a four-bay nave to a central plan apse using the existing foundations (E. Rufini, *San Giovanni de' Fiorentini*, Rome, 1957, Fig. 6, p. 90. The plan was discovered by H. Siebenhüner, who kindly brought it to my attention).

In 1582 Giacomo della Porta was commissioned to proceed with a longitudinal nave based as nearly as possible on the existing foundations (Siebenhüner, pp. 186 ff.), and by 1592 it was completed up to the crossing. Lack of funds prevented the realization of Porta's model of 1600 for the apse, but after a delay of eight years, Porta having died in 1602, Carlo Maderno laid foundations for a domed crossing and an apse on new designs; the drum was completed in 1611 and the cupola by 1614 (documents in Rufini, *op. cit.*, pp. 87 ff.)

Rome, Santa Maria Maggiore, Cappella Sforza, *ca.* 1560

Vasari says (VII, p. 264) that Michelangelo "assigned to Tiberio (Calcagni) following his instructions, a chapel begun at Santa Maria Maggiore for the Cardinal di Santa Fiore (Guido Ascanio Sforza, d. 1564), which remained incomplete on account of the death of that Cardinal, and of Michelangelo and Tiberio . . ." At the entrance to the chapel, which was added to the left side aisle of the Early Christian basilica, alongside the later Presepe chapel of Sixtus V, are two tablets, the first of 1564, commemorating its foundation by Guido and the legacy for its completion by his heirs, and the second, of 1573, commemorating the decoration by his brother, Cardinal Alexander Sforza, and the consecration to SS. Flora and Lucilla. The Cardinals' tombs (Pls. 72b, 73a) are placed in the lateral niches of the chapel; Alexander's was put up in 1582, before his death (inscription); Guido's perhaps in the '70's; neither is related to Michelangelo's design. (On the history of the chapel, see Fasolo 1923/1924, pp. 433 ff.) The destruction in 1748 of the travertine chapel façade facing the aisle (Pl. 73b), by classicists who believed it disrupted the symmetry of the basilica, was mournfully recorded by Stefano Bottari, who hoped to prevent it (quoted by Thode 1908, II, p. 186; Fasolo 1923/1924, pp. 436 f. See also the remarks of the younger Vanvitelli: Schiavo 1954, p. 27n). It may be seen in an engraving from Paolo de Angelis, *Basilicae S. M. Majoris de urbe . . . descriptio et delineatio*, Rome, 1621 (Fasolo, Fig. 5), and to best advantage in a pen-and-wash elevation by an anonymous early-eighteenth-century draughtsman discovered by Tolnay in the Cabinet des Estampes of the Bibliothèque Nationale, Paris (Pl. 73b; *Urbanisme et Architecture*, 1954, pp. 361 f., Pl. XX; also 1951, Pl. 264). Since Michelangelo put Tiberio Calcagni in charge of the chapel after it had been started (Vasari), he must have designed at least the final plan and have selected the materials himself. But the principal features of the elevations were left to the assistant; the entire Corinthian Order is the work of a confirmed classicist, far removed from the designer of the Porta Pia. It is a slipshod job; the capitals (Pl. 73c) are composed of two drums, the lower of which was left unfinished so that the stems of the acanthus leaves in the upper one are awkwardly cut off at the joint and do not continue to the neck. The blind windows flanking the tombs (Pl. 73a) in the side chapels and the feeble strings that bind them to the pilaster capitals are dreary designs. Only the splayed windows in the vaults of all four arms suggest Michelangelo's participation. He had used the splayed form in the Medici chapel (Fig. 2) and the combination of segmental and triangular pediments at the Porta Pia, where we also find *guttae* used as consoles; but the windows are not so effectively designed or placed as to eliminate the possibility that they were added by Giacomo della Porta, Michelangelo's most sensitive disciple, if it was he who took charge after the master's death.

So far as we can judge from reproductions, the lost chapel façade (Pl. 73b) also may have been designed by Michelangelo's successors. It is a handsome solution, but one that fits better into della Porta's style than Michelangelo's. The arms and tablets, which are inscribed 1564 and 1573, were composed as pairs, and as an integral part of the façade, which must therefore have been built after Michelangelo's death. Furthermore, the Order differs in detail from that of the interior: there are no projections in the entablature over the pilasters; there are consoles in the cornice; and the capitals differ. The absence of pedestals is due to the fact that the façade Order was lower than that of the interior, a peculiarly inorganic relationship. The design is a conservative version of the façade project reputed to be by Michelangelo for Santa Maria degli Angeli, which appears on a medal of Pius IV (Siebenhüner 1955, Fig. 26).

The addition of polychrome tombs and modern furnishings to the interior conspires to deprive the visitor of the excitement he may have experienced in Michelangelo's earlier buildings. But the strange ingenuity of the plan, and the austere impact of the monochrome walls and travertine members – heretofore used only out-of-doors – dominates the interior details.

DRAWINGS

1. Casa Buonarroti, No. 104 (Pl. 72c, D.132; F.95; F. Burger 1908, pp. 103 ff.; D. Frey 1920, pp. 64 f.; Fasolo 1923/1924, p. 442. Burger, K. Frey and Thode 1908, III, No. 69, did not detect the connection with the chapel).

Chalk sketches of a chapel plan, plan details, and an elevation of three small niches framed by a composite pilaster or column order with an entablature. Only the small plan can be associated confidently with the chapel, which it resembles in having a short entrance vestibule, semicircular tomb-chapels to the right and left, a somewhat large semi-circular altar-chapel with three windows on the main axis, and a square crossing. Initially, columns were placed in the four corners of the crossing, but one corner was later cut back, forcing one of the columns into the tomb chapel, as in the final plan. The absence of windows in the side niches and the oblong block into which the plan is sketched both support an identification with the Sforza chapel. Wilde's claim (1953, p. 121) that the unpublished *verso* of this sheet has "similar sketches" is rejected by Dussler.

2. British Museum, No. 84 (D.181; Tolnay 1935, p. 100; Wilde. *loc. cit.*; Pl. CXXIX).

A plan roughly sketched over ruled lines, in which the square of the crossing in Pl. 72c, with its corner columns, is repeated in the altar chapel. The crossing and semi-circular side chapels here are faintly drawn, without details. The additional square bay ruled in before the entrance may indicate the proportions of the side aisle of Santa Maria Maggiore so that it could be used as a module for the chapel. This suggests that No. 2 was drawn before No. 1.

RELATED DRAWINGS

The plan studies in the upper right of Pl. 72c, which aim to integrate columns with niches and chapels of different sizes and shapes, are related to the chapel and to a number of unidentified sketches which have affinities to both the chapel and San Giovanni Fiorentini (see Fasolo 1923/1924, pp. 445 ff., Figs. 10, 17).

Casa Buon., No. 103r (D.131; F.233; Thode, III, No. 158; D. Frey 1920, pp. 65 f.) A plan detail with columns, niches, and semicircular chapels, and a tomb elevation, the latter probably by an assistant (a Calcagni study for the Sforza tombs?)

Casa Buon., No. 109 (D.135; F.284; Thode, III, No. 159, p. 290; D. Frey 1920, p. 62, Fig. 23). Plans and elevations for a central plan church or chapel, some with rectangular and some with semi-circular altar-chapels. As in other studies, columns are either set into recessions in the piers or pushed back into the chapel entrances. The style of draughts-manship and of the elevations suggests a date prior to the San Giovanni projects.

Oxford, Ashmolean, No. 333v (D.352; F.273; Thode, III, No. 453; Parker 1956, p. 173). Several quickly sketched semicircular chapels for a central-plan church with paired free-standing columns before the piers and single columns in the chapel entrances. The sheet also contains intriguing details of an oval-plan stairway, a palace(?) façade and entablatures; it is probably also prior to San Giovanni.

Oxford, Ashmolean, No. 344v (D.207; F.169; Thode, III, No. 454; Parker 1956, p. 181). Plans, interior elevations, and a section of a large central-plan church. A scheme for eight semi-circular radiating chapels in a circular plan is considered together with a Greek cross plan containing chapels in the angles, basically the final solution for San Giovanni. The section (not in the plans) shows the dome supported on free-standing columns which are separated from the ring of chapels by an ambulatory as in Pl. 68 for San Giovanni. The chapels in the elevations have low niches like those of San Giovanni (Pls. 70b–71b), but are semi-circular and have broad openings. The *recto* of the sheet contains a study for the dome of St Peter's and a *ricordo* of the late 1550's which misled K. Frey, Thode, and Parker into interpreting the sketches on the *verso* as studies for the Basilica.

Casa Buon., No. 123 (D.144; F.293a; Thode, III, No. 72). A half-plan in chalk and wash for a centralized church or chapel; the plan is square, with semi-circular chapels protrud-ing on three sides. A square crossing is marked off by four columns connected by arches to columns at the chapel entrances. Pairs of columns in each corner at the plan are in-tended to screen the angles rather than to serve a structural function. In a preliminary study on the same sheet, the church is circular, the chapels rectangular, and there are no crossing columns; this sketch has a central altar. The scale of the columns and of the chapel-windows in the later drawing indicates that the building is much smaller than San Giovanni, though the technique is close to Pls. 66b and 67.

Newbury, England, Gathorne-Hardy Coll. A sheet (D.593, Fig. 266; Thode, 908, III, No. 370) with plan-sketches for a chapel by an assistant or follower, with variations on the theme of the Sforza chapel.

Rome, Porta Pia, 1561–1565

I HISTORY

"January 18, 1561 . . . (Pius IV) then went to the gardens of Girolamo Bellai to see a street called Pia, after his name, which he is having built, razing houses and ruining vineyards. It starts at Monte Cavallo (the Quirinal) and will finish at the city walls between Porta Salaria and Porta St Agnese between which two gates they will build a new one called Porta Pia at the head of that street." This report from the Mantuan ambassador at the Vatican to his home court is supplemented six months later by a second (Pastor, *Geschichte*, VII, pp. 638, 644): 18 June 1561 . . . "He went out in the company of many cardinals along the . . . Via Pia, which is now a most beautiful street, since almost all those who live along it have made fine walls with the most handsome portals leading into the villas, and other ornaments, and this has been done all the way to the city walls, where he is building the Porta Pia, and there he performed the usual ceremony and laid the first stones with numerous medals inside . . ." From the eye-witness account we see the Porta Pia in the context of a major planning programme. Documents confirm the report; an act of August 1561 ceding the Baths of Diocletian to the Roman Carthusians opens with a reference to the reclamation of the neighbouring Via Pia (Schiavo 1953, p. 278).

The programme was more extensive than the reports indicate. The Porta Nomentana just to the south of the new gate (to the left of the Porta Pia in Pl. 81a) was closed off, and the ancient Via Nomentana was re-sited and straightened for a mile beyond the walls to a point just short of the church of Sant' Agnese (Zanghieri 1953, pp. 32 ff.; 68 ff., Fig. 33). This programme, directed by Battista del Morco (Lanciani 1902, III, p. 232), was under way in September 1561, when the architect Valperga was paid for surveying, and was still in progress in February 1564 (Bertolotti, *Bartolomeo Baronino*, Casale, 1876, pp. 75, 77).

On 24 March 1561, the monks of St Pietro in Vincoli were granted compensation for the loss of tolls occasioned by the construction of the gate. At this time Michelangelo had already submitted projects: a preliminary design appears on the foundation medals (Pl. 76b) commissioned from Giovanni Federigo da Parma, called Bonzagni, before April 1561 (Bertolotti, *Archivio storico artistico della città e provincia di Roma*, I, 1875, p. 77; K. Frey 1909, p. 166). In May, masons were employed to dismantle the ancient gate and to start the new foundations (Bertolotti, *Archivio*, p. 76). Pietro Gaeta, who had assisted Michelangelo at St Peter's, was the foreman, and Paolo dal Borgo the "sotto-architetto" (Gotti 1875, II, p. 162). The foundation ceremony of 18 June must have been a livelier affair than the Mantuan ambassador admitted: a wine bill was paid the following week for "allegrezze date a diversi" (Bertolotti, *Archivio*, p. 77). On 2 July an agreement was signed between the Maestri delle Strade – today we would say City Planning Commission – and a contracting firm, for the construction of the Porta (Gotti 1875, II, pp. 160 f.; Bertolotti, *Archivio*, pp. 74 ff.) It establishes the ultimate authority of the architect for the design and setting of prices; he is not named, but since the contract includes a clause that at the completion of the construction "maestro Michelangnilo" may authorize at his discretion a bonus of 40–50 scudi, there is no doubt of his identity. It is further confirmed by payments of 1563–1564, when Michelangelo received 50 scudi monthly "per conto di Pier Luigi Gaeta suo agiente" (Podestà 1875, p. 137).

A papal *motuproprio* of August 1561 conceded the new Porta and the adjoining towers in the enclosure behind it to Conte Raniero (Caraciotti?), requiring that he build a hostelry there, and ordered the sealing of the Salaria and Nomentana gates, between which the new Porta had been opened (Pastor, *Geschichte*, VII, p. 601; Schiavo 1953, p. 261). In May 1562, Jacomo siciliano (del Duca) and "Luca" were paid for carving the papal arms, and three years later Nardo de' Rossi added the travertine angels that flank the arms (Bertolotti, *Archivio*, p. 77). The last construction records are of July 1565 (*loc. cit.*)

In a view of the area painted about thirty years later (Pl. 76a), and in others of the seventeenth and eighteenth centuries (Zanghieri 1953, Figs. 9–17), the gate appears without the upper portion of the attic, which suggests that it remained unfinished. Zanghieri (*op. cit.*, pp. 15–39) first proposed that this condition was the result of a collapse of the crown not long after its construction. In the two earliest representations of the gate, the attic is intact; Mario Cartaro's large plan of Rome of 1576 (*ibid.*, Fig. 5; Rocchi 1902, Pl. 16) and Dupérac's plan of 1577 (Pl. 81a) both show the pediment in place. Renaissance cartographers did not always record such details accurately, as proven by the fact that Cartaro placed the gate in line with the old walls and eliminated the enclosure behind it (Zanghieri, p. 20, naïvely accepted this as evidence that the gate was entirely rebuilt in its present position in the period between the two surveys). But an inspection of the incomplete attic in later and more exact views also favours the hypothesis that it was first completed and later destroyed. In the Falda plan of 1676, the Bonanni engraving of 1699, and an aquatint from Nibby's Roman volume of 1826 (Zanghieri, Figs. 13, 16, 17), the breaks in the attic appear as uneven fractures in the blocks of masonry caused by some violent shock; the ragged silhouette is precisely what is found in ancient ruins. Had the masons been unexpectedly called off the job before its completion, the upper edge would have remained a level course of masonry composed of squared and unbroken blocks. The bulky masses seen lying at the foot of the gate in Tempesta's plan of 1593 may have fallen there in the collapse of the attic shortly before (Zanghieri, p. 24, Fig. 9).

The attic cannot have been finished under Michelangelo's supervision. When he died in 1564, the angels flanking the papal arms had not been carved, and the engraving of 1568 (Pl. 75, see below) still shows a project for the attic rather than the structure itself.

The damaged attic was restored and completed in 1853 by the architect Virginio Vespignani (1808–1882), after a stroke of lightning caused concern for the stability of the whole structure; in 1861–1868 Vespignani built barracks in the enclosure behind and raised the exterior portal (Schiavo 1949, Fig. 163; Zanghieri, pp. 42 ff.; Schiavo 1953, pp. 265 f.) The restoration is recorded in an inscription of Pius IX in the entablature beneath the second papal arms.

II THE DESIGN

According to Vasari's report (VII, p. 260), "Michelangelo, urged by the Pope at this time to provide a design for the Porta Pia, made three, all extravagant and beautiful, from which the Pope chose the least costly to execute, which may be seen today and is much praised: and since the Pope had in mind to restore the other gates of Rome as well, he made other drawings for him".

Several sketches by Michelangelo and his assistants, the foundation medal, and an engraving of 1568 support Vasari's account of the Porta Pia. But the process of design cannot be reconstructed fully since most of the drawings are for the central portal alone, and since some of them may have been for the other gates referred to by Vasari.

The drawings were cited by Thode (1908, II, pp. 207 ff.); but Tolnay (1930, pp. 42 ff.) published the first critical analysis in a valuable study that brought to light the medal and the engraving.

I am indebted to Elisabeth MacDougall for permitting me to benefit from her article on the Porta Pia before its publication in 1960.

A. THE FOUNDATION MEDAL AND THE ENGRAVING (Pls. 76b and 75)

1. The medal (Tolnay 1930, p. 42; Schiavo 1949, Figs. 164 f.), commissioned before April 1561, records a rejected design. The portal (I use "portal" to designate the central, pedi- mented structure around the opening and "gate" to designate the entire *Porta*) is com- posed of columns supporting a segmented pediment which encloses a central shell and volutes on either side; the jambs are not drafted. There is a heavy cornice between the main story and the low, oblong attic. Alongside the attic are two thin towers topped by spheres, which in the engraving are reduced to simple obelisks; to support these towers the substructure must have been considerably more massive than that illustrated in the engraved plan.

The gate shown in the medal evidently was designed for a different site than the present one; instead of being planned as the city-façade of the rectangular enclosure within the walls (Pl. 81a), it was to be set into the perimeter of the walls themselves, as indicated by the crenellated curtains appearing alongside it. The present site proved to be more economical, since it could be used without demolishing the old enclosure, which is shown as it appeared before Michelangelo's time in Cartaro's early map (published 1575 but based on a survey of before 1561. Zanghieri, p. 15, Fig. 4; Rocchi 1902, Pl. XIII).

2. Faleti's engraving of 1568 (Pl. 75; Tolnay 1930, p. 45, Fig. 35; Schiavo 1953, p. 266) represents the executed gate except for the upper portions where, beside changing the proportions of the attic, Faleti shows features that were not executed: the obelisks and the spheres on the pediment (compare Pls. 75 and 74). There are major differences in the papal insignia and their supporting angels, which Faleti shows without wings. Probably the gate was not finished in 1568, and the engraver found it necessary to turn to projects in the hands of Michelangelo's successors. The projects were probably not Michel- angelo's; the dull attic and its Corinthian Order – so much more conventional than the

medal design – is completely out of harmony with the portal below or with any other late work of Michelangelo, and is suspiciously close to the pedestrian model of Serlio (Pl. 80a). Furthermore, the surviving drawings give no evidence that a final attic design was produced before Michelangelo's death, though the general outline had been fixed, and the horizontality of the attic and heavy cornice in the medal had been abandoned. We know from Catalani, the sixteenth-century historian of Santa Maria degli Angeli, that when the Pope praised the design of the coat of arms, Michelangelo replied that Giacomo del Duca was wholly responsible (Schiavo 1953, p. 228). If the principal feature of the attic could be left to assistants, the architectural detailing probably was too, as suggested by Pl. 75. On stylistic grounds nothing in the upper story of the engraving except the row of spheres or volutes can be given with conviction to Michelangelo. (On 1 and 2, see now MacDougall 1960, pp. 99 f., Figs. 4, 5.)

B. SKETCH FOR THE WHOLE GATE

Casa Buonarroti, No. 99r. (Pl. 77a, D.129; Thode, 1908, II, p. 208; III, No. 154; Tolnay 1930, pp. 42 f., Fig. 31; *idem* 1951, Pl. 372; MacDougall 1960, pp. 101 ff., Fig. 9).

The portal is drawn in hard, ruled chalk lines, and the outline of the gate in light, freehand chalk strokes. The rectilinear arch of the opening anticipates the final solution, but the comparatively low portal with its orthodox entablature is quite different.

In proportion the gate is close to the medal: there is space only for paired pilasters on the wall beside the portal on the lower story, and the low attic has a horizontal axis; the horizontal is also emphasized by a cornice between the two stories. This is the only surviving drawing of the gate as a whole.

C. DRAWINGS FOR THE PORTAL

1. Casa Buon. No. 106r. (Pl. 77b; D.134; Thode, II, p. 209; III, No. 70; Fasolo 1926/1927, Fig. 2; Tolnay 1930, p. 44n, Fig. 33; Schiavo 1949, Fig. 166; MacDougall 1960, p. 100, Fig. 6).
2. Casa Buon., No. 102r. (Pl. 78a; D.476; F.237; Thode, II, p. 208; III, No. 157; Fasolo 1926/1927, Fig. 8; Tolnay 1930, p. 45n; Schiavo 1949, Fig. 165; MacDougall 1960, pp. 101 ff., Fig. 11).

Though finished in wash by an assistant, these drawings probably were begun by Michelangelo; they have his characteristic superimposing of successive ideas. Underlying construction lines in both indicate the alignment with the attic above, which in Pl. 78a has been supplied amateurishly by the assistant. Pl. 77b is like the medal in form (Tolnay), and in its volutes, shell and segmental pediment, though the latter is broken off over the shell and retired to a subordinate position. But the flat, drafted arch and the tablet in the pediment are closer to the final project. The Tuscan columns used in both studies are from the medal project. Pl. 78a abandons the volutes to place a segmental within a triangular pediment, but in so doing fixes the essential rhythms of the final design, which reintroduces volutes. The tympanum with two recessed "eyes", faintly sketched over a more prominent oblong panel, also approaches the actual portal. In introducing the tympanum, Michelangelo felt the need of an inverted semi-circle to echo its curve, and added to the pediment a patera with crescent-shaped horns. In the final design the horns became a garland and an anthropomorphic mask appeared in place of the bull's skull; the introduction of the garland justified a return to the volutes, which were now given a function not originally anticipated. A morphology of this kind reveals the pre-eminence of the form over the symbol in Michelangelo's mind. Geymüller (1904, p. 40), Frey and Thode dated Pl. 77b before the Porta Pia, but they were unaware of the medal.

3. Windsor Castle Library, No. 433; (Pl. 78b; D.240; F.207; Thode, III, No. 551; Tolnay 1930, p. 45n; Popham-Wilde 1949, p. 256; MacDougall 1960, pp. 101 ff., Fig. 10).

Among several chalk sketches by Michelangelo, that on the lower left approaches the final design in substituting fluted pilasters for Tuscan columns, but is more distant than No. 2 in the tympanum and pediment, where the few motifs that can still be distinguished are unresolved. A pediment on the right of the sheet, however, has the volutes of Pl. 77b supporting a garland and enclosed within a triangular pediment, and nearly reaches the definitive design, except for the uncertain position of the tablet. But apparently this pediment was drawn on a window, as indicated by the proportions, the simple moulding on all sides, and the absence of either an arch or a flanking Order. Possibly Michelangelo started to draw one of the side windows of the gate and in the process came upon a solution for the portal pediment. Another (window?) pediment appears below. The two plans at the top of the sheet do not appear to be related to the Porta Pia. Drawings No. 2 and 3 must be nearly contemporary, on the verge of the final solution.

4. Giovanantonio Dosio, Uffizi, *Arch.* 2148 (MacDougall 1960, p. 103, Fig. 13).

This sheet appears to be copied from a working drawing in Michelangelo's atelier. Corrections and measurements in chalk probably were made later from the building itself. The underlying pen drawing represents the final design except that (*a*) Tuscan columns are still indicated rather than pilasters – as in No. 2 – and there are six, not seven, *guttae* in the capitals; as in the engraving, the jambs are not drafted, and (*b*) the stems of the pediment volutes are not curved but flat against the triangular frame. The most important addition in chalk is the correction of point *b*; I doubt that the straightening of the volutes was intended by Michelangelo, since the opposition of the curve and triangle is a basic theme in the authentic drawings.

Nos. 1 to 4 must be in proper chronological order, but since the final solution is a combination of elements in 2 and 3, these two may be regarded as contemporary.

D. PORTAL SKETCHES, possibly for the Porta Pia.

The three following sketches are for free-standing portals, not set into a gate structure. All are by Michelangelo.

1. Haarlem, Teyler Museum, No. A29, bis. (Pl. 79b. D.296; F.326. Recently detached from a sheet of studies for St Peter's to which it had been pasted: Thode, II, p. 209; III, No. 264; Tolnay, p. 42, Fig. 28; MacDougall 1960, pp. 102 f., Fig. 12).

This super little sketch has been associated with the Porta Pia on the grounds of similarity of motifs: the flat drafted arch and the tympanum with recessed "eyes". But it is

more suitable to a villa than to a great urban project (Tolnay). It is much lower than the
Porta Pia, and the pilaster bases seem to be three steps below the level of the openings.
Finally, the arms are not papal, and the curving motifs at the head of the portal which
look like dolphins suggest that the patron may have been Zaccaria Delfino, Pope Pius'
Nuncio to the Imperial Court, who became a cardinal in 1565; dolphins are the family
impresa. The surety of hand and precise technique is not characteristic of Michelangelo's
late drawings, but the formal concept recommends a date not long before the Porta Pia.
2. Casa Buon. 97 (D.128, 473; Thode, II, p. 208; III, No. 152; Tolnay, *loc. cit.*, Fig. 30;
MacDougall 1960, p. 104, Fig. 15).

Aside from several quick sketches of portal or window frames including motifs
foreign to the Porta Pia, this sheet has a more elaborate portal study. The familiar
drafted arch appears again, though the haunches are angled directly from the keystone
to the jambs; as in the preceding sketch there is an eyed tympanum – which is placed
above a complete entablature so as to form the centre of an attic – and a small coat of
arms is set on top; the dolphin motif of No. 1 above is altered to a pair of volute-like
curves. The entablature is supported by heavy paired columns or pilasters which make
the portal substantially broader and more imposing than No. 1 above, though still not
on the scale of the major gates of Rome.
3. Casa Buon., No. 84 (D.118; F.211c; Thode, II, p. 209; III, No. 146; Tolnay 1930,
p. 45n; MacDougall 1960, pp. 101 f., Fig. 7).

Thode excluded this drawing from the Porta Pia group because it lacks the familiar
motifs. It has the paired columns of No. D2, but raised on pedestals and supporting a
segmental pediment, not an entablature. A triangular pediment appears over the round-
arched opening. A smaller fragmentary section of the two shells of St Peter's dome noted
by MacDougall suggests a connection with the Basilica. The harshly ruled chalk lines
certify a date after 1550 rather than in the 1530's as proposed by Frey.
4. Casa Buon., No. 73 bis. (D.470; Thode, II, p. 208; III, No. 68; Fasolo 1926/1927, Fig. 3;
Tolnay 1930, p. 45n; MacDougall 1960, p. 101, Fig. 8).

A portal drawn in the technique of Nos. C1 and 2, but more conventional in design.
Pure Tuscan columns support a triangular pediment with a broken base. The arch of
the opening is semicircular and its voussoirs are not indicated. The proportions and
underlying construction lines link the drawing with the Porta Pia, but it may have been
largely designed by an assistant. Michelangelo probably added indeterminate lines over
the columns suggesting a segmental(?) pediment.

E. DETAILS

1. Casa Buon., No. 106v (Pl. 79a; D.134; Tolnay, p. 45, Fig. 34).

Tolnay identified the two drawings at the centre of this sheet as studies for the
cartouches over the windows of the Porta Pia. The upper one is close to the final
solution; the lower, as MacDougall noted, revives a motif invented over thirty-five
years before for the ceiling of the Laurentian library (cf. Pl. 19a). A sketch to the far
right for a door frame and the harshly stroked frame in the centre are too rough to
identify.

F. REJECTED DRAWING

Casa Buon., No. 40 (D.83; F.285; Schiavo 1953, p. 266, Fig. 64).

Schiavo's association of this sketch with the attic of the Porta Pia is unlikely because (1) like an altarpiece, the structure stands on a socle that flares out at the base as if it were resting on the ground and (2) the central field is flanked by two pairs of columns on either side; no Renaissance architect would superimpose eight columns on a ground floor with only two pilasters. Frey called it an altarpiece: Tolnay (1948, p. 206, No. 60) dated the sheet around 1520 and suggested that it may have been drawn for the altar of San Silvestro in Capite, Rome (planned 1518). Wilde (1953, p. 40) followed by Dussler, suggests a date of *ca.* 1525.

The drawings account for only two features of the final design: the portal and the rectangular cartouches. Aside from these, the round discs with pendant tassels and the spheres and volutes perched on the crenellations are typical of Michelangelo in their fantasy, and were no doubt visible when Faleti made his engraving (Pl. 75). Other details of the upper story in the engraving – including the obelisks, which were never set up – could have been designed by an assistant. The windows at ground level are closer to Michelangelo and may reflect a lost sketch by him, but they are typical of his imitators in substituting ponderousness for monumentality. Giacomo del Duca, the architect of Porta San Giovanni, may have designed and executed them while working on the Porta Pia.

The gate was built as a two-dimensional façade onto the existing enclosure of low walls (Pl. 81a). In a letter of August 1561, Tiberio Calcagni reported to Leonardo Buonarroti that Michelangelo was occupied with "disegni per la Porta della parte di fuore che non li aveva fatti" (Papini, *Vita di Michelangelo*, 1949, p. 603). This probably did not refer to the rear of the present structure, but to another façade on the outside face of the enclosure – in line with the city walls. Possibly some of the surviving drawings were intended for this second façade. The rear of the present Porta appears in only one view prior to the nineteenth-century reconstruction, a print in Vasi's *Magnificenze di Roma* of 1747 (Zanghieri, Fig. 15); it is without decoration except for a balcony on corbels behind the crenellations, and there are two small apertures in the rear of the attic giving onto the balcony. The unfinished gateway in the outer walls has a simple frame with a segmental arch; it may have been started by Michelangelo.

An engraving of the main façade portal, executed from the building, appeared in Vignola's *Cinque Ordine, con le aggionte del Michel-Angelo Buonarroti* (Amsterdam, 1617, fol. 84 ff.) The other gates in the *aggionte* are interesting examples, though not by Michelangelo: the portal of the Conservators' palace on the Campidoglio (fol. 89; Giacomo della Porta); the Porta del Popolo (fols. 82–84; Nanni di Baccio Bigio; and the anonymous and lost gates to the villas of Cardinal Rodolfo Pio of Carpi (Pl. 80b), the Sforza, Grimani, and the Cardinal of Sermoneta (fols. 91–95). All of these were along the Via Pia (cf. MacDougall 1960, pp. 106 ff., and Fig. 1, a plan of the street), which explains the attribution to Michelangelo, although the style is closer to that of Vignola himself.

Rome, Santa Maria degli Angeli, 1561–

I HISTORY

The huge central hall of the Baths of Diocletian was preserved almost intact into the Renaissance, and the idea of converting it into a church was entertained during Michelangelo's early days in Rome: Giuliano da Sangallo and Baldassare Peruzzi both left drawings for the reconstruction, which may have been commissioned by the Holy See (identified by Tolnay 1930, p. 21; Siebenhüner 1955, pp. 191 ff.; Figs. 17, 18, misleadingly calls them Utopian schemes). The project lay dormant until 1541 when a Sicilian priest, Antonio del Duca, was inspired by a vision to demand from the papacy the establishment of a church in the Baths consecrated to the cult of the angels. Detailed knowledge of del Duca's campaign and of the construction of the church up to the 1580's is due to the chronicle of his friend Mattia Catalani (*Vat. lat.* 8735, cf. excerpts in A. Pasquinelli, *Roma*, 1925, pp. 349 ff.; Schiavo 1953, pp. 225 ff.) Rebuffed by Paul III, del Duca persuaded Julius III to issue a Bull of Consecration for the Holy Year, 1550 (Catalani, cf. Schiavo 1953, p. 226. Bonanni 1699, I, p. 253, says 1554); no construction was undertaken, but an entrance way was cleared at the NW end of the great hall, and fourteen temporary altars were installed and dedicated to the seven angels and principal martyrs, whose names were inscribed in red on the columns and pilasters alongside (Schiavo 1953, p. 226). The makeshift solution proved unsatisfactory because the Roman nobility, accustomed to use the Baths as a stadium for riding and other sports, refused to recognize the consecration; they were justified legally by the fact that the control of antique sites traditionally rested with the city government, not with the Vatican (Siebenhüner, p. 190), and del Duca was unable to gain papal protection for the consecration.

In 1561 del Duca's scheme won enthusiastic support from Pius IV, since it complemented the Pope's urbanistic programme along the nearby Via Pia (see Pls. 76a and 81a). According to Vasari (VII, pp. 260 f.), Michelangelo won a competition for the design of the church, but Catalani, an eye-witness, was probably more correct in reporting that the Pope called him directly to submit plans (Pasquinelli 1925, pp. 350 f.; Schiavo 1953, p. 228). Catalani recorded the visit of Michelangelo and Antonio del Duca to the Baths, where they drew the existing plan and discussed the orientation of the church. Del Duca favoured his temporary scheme, a longitudinal arrangement with the entrance on the NW and the altar on the SE (reconstructed by Siebenhüner 1955, Fig. 16), but Michelangelo proposed to "design it as a cross, restricting the size and removing the low chapels where the vaults had collapsed, so that the highest parts would constitute (the main portion of) the church, the vault of which is supported by eight columns on which the names of the martyrs and angels are inscribed; and he designed three portals, one to the (S-)W, another on the N(-W), and the third on the S(-E) as they may be seen now; and the main altar toward the (N-)E". (Fig. 14. Pasquinelli, p. 351; Schiavo 1953, p. 228; Marcel Reymond [*Gazette des Beaux-Arts*, LXIV, 2, 1922, pp. 195–217] properly reconstructed Michelangelo's plan on internal evidence before the discovery of

Catalani's account; previously it was thought to have been the same as the scheme now known to be del Duca's.)

In a Bull of 27 July 1561 the Pope assumed the responsibility for building the church and assigned the construction of the neighbouring monastery to the Carthusian Order (Lanciani 1902, II, p. 136; Pastor *Geschichte*, VII, p. 609), and on 5 August he laid the foundation stone under the altar in a ceremony attended by nineteen cardinals, magistrates of the city, and "a great part of the Roman nobility" (Pastor, p. 608; Schiavo 1953, pp. 230, 278). The Act of Concession to the Carthusians, of the same date, was followed on 14 August by a statement of concensus from the Conservatori (both transcribed by Schiavo 1953, pp. 277 ff., 282 f.) In letters of 20 August and 11 October 1561, an ambassador to the Vatican wrote "si edifica la chiesa di Santa Maria degli Angeli ..." (Pastor, *op. cit.*, pp. 645 f.), which suggests that construction began immediately, though it is not conclusive evidence (the translation by Meliù – 1950, pp. 20 f. – of a papal Breve dated 10 March 1560 with the phrase "abbiamo già cominciato ad edificare la chiesa", is too much in conflict with other documents to accept without returning to the source, which the author did not indicate; Siebenhüner 1955, p. 188, increased the confusion by reading Meliù's date as 1562). The first documents of construction date from April 1563, less than a year before Michelangelo's death; progress was hampered by lack of funds, and in July 1564 the Pope unsuccessfully attempted to force the Cardinals to assume the cost of completing at least the chapels (Siebenhüner, *loc. cit.*)

In January 1565 a bronze ciborium for the main altar based on Michelangelo's design was ordered from Giacomo del Duca and Jacopo Rocchetto (Schiavo 1949, Fig. 142; 1953, p. 241, and contract, pp. 287 ff.; Lavagnino, *Rivista del Istituto di Archaeol. e Storia dell' Arte*, II, 1930, pp. 104 ff.; the ciborium, now in the Naples Museum, shows little dependence on Michelangelo except in its shape, which Venturi compared to a sketch in Haarlem: *Storia*, XI, 2, Fig. 172). The first Mass was said in May, and in the same month Pius, ignoring his contract with the Carthusians, made Santa Maria degli Angeli a titular church (Pastor, VII, 609). The only indications of construction in the course of 1565 were payments for columns to be used on the altar of one of the chapels – probably the main altar – and for replacing one of the ancient capitals of the colossal columns in the great hall (Pl. 83b; Siebenhüner, pp. 188 f., with bibliography). An inscription of 1565 records the foundation of the cloister (Pl. 81a), which made slow progress in the ensuing years.

The costs of the programme were totalled in June 1566 at 17,492 scudi (Lanciani 1902, II, p. 137). This surprisingly modest sum – only twice what was spent on partially completing the Porta Pia – indicates how little Michelangelo could have altered the original appearance of the baths.

II THE DESIGN

According to Catalani's summary of the programme of Pius IV: "he first covered the main vaults in tile, built the main chapel with the apse from the foundation up, opened the (S-)W portal, and reduced the body of the church by two walls, in one of which he made the N(-W) portal, and in the other the S(-E) portal, and began to stucco the inside of the vaults" (Pasquinelli, p. 352; Schiavo 1953, p. 231, cf. Fig. 14). Siebenhüner's analysis of drawings and prints of the Baths before the remodelling (1955, pp. 180–184; my identification of the original functions of the several halls in the Baths, based on Platner and Ashby, *A Topographical Dictionary of Ancient Rome*, Oxford, 1929, differs from that of Schiavo and Siebenhüner) shows that the portions used by Michelangelo were excellently preserved: the vaults of the great hall and their supporting columns were intact, as were those of the two chambers between the great hall and the palaestrae on the NW and SE. Michelangelo had only to insert curtain walls into the arches of the two innermost chambers, to make vestibules at the ends of the long axis (Fig. 14, E, F). On the short axis he decided to use the central rotonda (tepidarium), between the ruined calidarium and the great hall, as the principal vestibule (Fig. 14, G, H). Only the altar chapel at the opposite end of the short axis had to be especially designed and raised on new foundations; the shallow hall which led through a colonnade to the open frigidarium of the Baths provided insufficient space for a presbytery large enough to accommodate the monks, whose rule discouraged contact with lay worshippers. And the main altar had to be given a setting that would not be overwhelmed by the vastness of the high transverse axis.

There is little in Michelangelo's scheme that actually required designs on paper; verbal instructions to the masons would have sufficed for the construction of all but the entrance portals. Thus the church did not attract many student draughtsmen and *vedutisti*, and a few prints by artists unconcerned with the architecture are the only bases for reconstructing the pre-eighteenth-century church.

The main hall, where the vaults and columns were nearly intact, was virtually unchanged. Michelangelo walled in the vestibules at either end, placing portals at the exterior vestibule entrances (Fig. 14, E, F); and in each of the windows of the main hall he placed two simple mullions, dividing them vertically into three bays (Pl. 82a).

The vestibule portal on the SE appears in several views before its removal in the eighteenth century: 1, a sketch (Pl. 82b) done by or for G. Dosio (Uffizi, *Arch.* 2576; Schiavo 1949, Fig. 135); 2, an engraving after the sketch published by Cavalieri in 1569 (Siebenhüner, Fig. 9; Ricci 1909, Fig. 10); 3, an engraving with the same view by Alò Giovannoli of 1615–1619 (Siebenhüner, Fig. 22; Ricci 1909, Fig. 11); 4, a wash sketch by an anonymous Poussinesque artist of the late seventeenth century (Rome, Gab. delle Stampe, Ricci 1909, Fig. 12; though Ricci dated the drawing in the eighteenth century, it must have been made before the print of 1703 discussed below). All four show a conventional Renaissance portal with a triangular pediment supported on volutes of the type of the later SW portal, which is preserved. It lacks the inventiveness of Michelangelo's earlier frames and probably was not designed by him.

The portal was decorated only on the exterior, as shown by an interior view of 1703 which illustrates a solar clock installed by Clement XI (Pl. 83). This engraving (published by Tolnay 1930, pp. 18 ff., Fig. 10) also shows the windows with an elaborate frame in the centre bay and extraordinary volutes embracing the outer bays. Tolnay (*loc. cit.*) first attributed the windows to Michelangelo, but later changed his mind (1951, p. 196); the earlier views prove that Michelangelo supplied only two simple mullions. The windows appear without the frame and volutes in Pl. 82a (1588); and the anonymous sketch (No. 4 above), where we see the interior of another of the windows of the great hall in the background, shows that they stayed this way for a century or more. The same may be seen in Giovannoli's exterior views (in addition to No. 3 above, see Ricci 1909, Fig. 8; Venturi *Storia*, XI, 2, Fig. 170). Michelangelo's simple system is still visible today on the exterior (Siebenhüner, Fig. 23), where we see that the later insertion of the frames and volutes awkwardly screened off about one-fourth of his aperture at the top. The voluted windows were added in the short span between the visit of the anonymous draughtsmen and 1703, by an architect who also changed the windows over the entrance portal by suppressing the side bays and leaving only one rectangular central opening (compare Pls. 82b and 83a); only Dosio showed mullions in this window; the later draughtsmen represented the apertures without them.

The marble bases of the columns in the main hall (Pl. 83b) are probably Renaissance, but not necessarily after Michelangelo's design. They may be contemporary to the paving of the church under Gregory XIII in the 1570's. The fact that the pavement is 1·15 m. above the level of neighbouring ancient structures (Siebenhüner, p. 285n) led to the misapprehension that it was raised this distance in the sixteenth century, but modern excavations disclosed remains of ancient column bases behind the present ones and at the same level (Schiavo 1954, pp. 19 ff., Fig. 6).

The Chancel, which Michelangelo built on new foundations, first appears in an exterior view of 1577 (Pl. 81a), where the round apse abuts a refectory at the edge of the cloister. Since the apse was demolished and extended by Vanvitelli (see his plan, Schiavo 1954, Fig. 10), we know its interior form only from a woodcut in Martinelli's guidebook (Pl. 81b, *Roma ricercata . . .*, 1644, discovered but incorrectly identified by Schiavo 1954, p. 21, Fig. 7) and in the 1703 engraving (Pl. 83a). In both, the ancient chamber leading from the great hall to the frigidarium was used as the first bay, and beyond a long barrel-vaulted choir terminates in the apse, where the altar is placed. We know from inscriptions and Catalani's account that the two chapels with ornamental portals in the chamber (Fig. 14, a, b) were planned after Michelangelo's death: one in 1574 and the other, perhaps at the same time, but certainly before 1608 (Meliù 1950, pp. 86, 116). But even these views distort Michelangelo's intention (as noted by Siebenhüner, p. 200, Figs. 13, 29); still earlier woodcuts in the guidebooks of Gamucci (1565; the altar is shown but none of the new construction) and Franzini (Pl. 82a; 1588) place the altar in the chamber, with two ancient columns supporting an entablature and blind arch behind it. When Pius IV consecrated the altar in 1561, it must have been placed here, and when Michelangelo built the chancel he probably had no intention of moving it into the apse, because the traditional position of the monks' choir was behind the altar to insure privacy. Thus Pl. 82a, for all its crudity, is the best indication of the original design. In 1596, the original wooden altar was replaced by one in stone (Schiavo 1954, p. 19n); probably the new altar was then put in the apse, thereby forcing the destruction of the ancient screen of columns.

The entrance rotunda, called by Vasari (VII, p. 261) "una entrata fuor della openione di tutti gli architetti", served as the principal vestibule of the church (Catalani refers to the SW portal as "principale": Schiavo 1953, p. 234). The interior decoration was done by Vanvitelli after 1749, except for the pilasters of the Ionic tomb tabernacles between the four axial openings, which were believed by his nephew and biographer to have been designed by Michelangelo (Schiavo 1954, pp. 18, 27n). They probably were done, however, when the side chambers of the rotunda (Fig. 14; G, H) were transformed into chapels in 1575 and 1579 (Siebenhüner, pp. 204 f.), since they are close in style to those of the portals of that date in the first bay of the chancel, and since the earliest of their tombs was inserted in 1580 (Meliù 1950, p. 55). Since Vanvitelli rebuilt the original lantern of the rotunda (Schiavo 1954, p. 33) we cannot tell whether it was designed originally by Michelangelo or by an immediate follower; it was completed before 1577 (Pl. 81a). In short, there is no evidence that Michelangelo planned anything beyond the repair of the ancient calidarium.

The concave entrance façade (Fig. 14; J) in Michelangelo's time was a niche within the poorly-preserved hall of the tepidarium at the SW limit of the building, the remains of which were removed by Sixtus V in 1587–1589 (Lanciani 1902, II, pp. 145 f.; for a view before the removal, see Grassi's engraving, Ricci 1909, Fig. 9). Long after the demolitions, it remained undecorated except for a portal, probably modelled on the two built during Michelangelo's time. Sometime between Maggi's plan of Rome in 1625 and Falda's plan of 1676 the walls were embellished with an order of pilaster strips (Siebenhüner, pp. 196 f., Fig. 25).

The model of a church façade reproduced on a medal of Pius IV inscribed VIRGINI MATRI has been identified as a project of Michelangelo for Santa Maria degli Angeli (*loc. cit.*, Fig. 26; reviving Bonanni 1699, I, p. 284). The identification should be correct; the design is Michelangelesque, and it would be strange if no medal were cast to celebrate the building of a titular church. But the inscription does not specify the Angeli and the model is not suited either to the proportions or to the concave shape of the façade. The papal arms over the portal are larger than the portal itself, which in the actual church is over twenty feet high; and the entrance bay is flanked by two windows, behind which there would have been only a mass of masonry (Fig. 14). Judging from the scale of the arms, this façade should be no larger than the similar one for the Sforza chapel (Pl. 73b). Finally, there is the question whether Michelangelo would have designed, and Pius have immortalized in a medal, the decoration of a façade which for twenty years after their deaths remained buried in the rubble of the tepidarium. The identification must remain in question.

A drawing of a Michelangelesque portal from a collection of drawings misattributed to Giorgio Vasari the Younger (Uffizi *Arch.* 4628, unpublished), inscribed "nella faciata del Chiesino(?) degli Angioli" should be mentioned, though it may be a study for the Florentine church of the same name. It appears on a sheet with a project for the cornice of the Farnese palace, which suggests a Roman provenance, but the design is in any case too mannered for Michelangelo.

The cloister, begun in 1565 (Pl. 81a), was greatly expanded before the time of Falda's map of 1676, at which time the original design was fundamentally altered. There are no documents indicating whether Michelangelo was involved in the initial project.

III SUBSEQUENT HISTORY

In the course of the seventeenth century the only major alterations to the church were the addition of interior window frames and the decoration of the façade. The transformations which ultimately buried all traces of the original interior began in 1700 with closing off the NW vestibule to transform it into a chapel of S. Bruno (Schiavo 1954, p. 23; the following information is excerpted from pp. 23–38). Beginning in 1727 the choir was remodelled to receive a group of monumental Baroque paintings from St Peter's, and in 1746 the SE vestibule was closed for the construction of a chapel corresponding to that of San Bruno. At this time, the architect Clemente Orlandi closed off three of the four chambers on the sides of the main hall, which had proven to be too large to attract prospective chapel donors; when Luigi Vanvitelli was appointed as architect for the Carthusians in 1749 he wanted to reopen these bays, but his clients demanded that he close the fourth. Vanvitelli undertook a major redecorating programme (Pl. 82b) covering with stucco and veneer all parts of the church except the vaults of the main hall, adding six columns along the entrance axis, and replacing the rotunda lantern and possibly the main altar. These alterations, particularly the extension of the huge entablature throughout the church, had the effect of breaking the continuity between the walls and the ancient vaulting – an effect exaggerated by abrupt transition from gaudy marble veneer to neutral stucco – and confused the structural logic of the ancient remains. After Titi's description of the church in 1763 and before Cancellieri's in 1794 the chancel was extended, redecorated, and terminated with a polygonal apse (Pasquinelli 1925, pp. 403 f.; Schiavo 1954, p. 35), as had been suggested in the earlier plan of Vanvitelli (Schiavo 1954, Fig. 10). By the close of the eighteenth century the church was completed substantially in its present form; the façade has been altered by a restoration of 1911 which also removed Vanvitelli's lantern.

Recorded Commissions
for which no projects survive

Rome, Palace of the Cardinal Santiquattro, 1525

On 28 January and 8 February 1525, Giovanfrancesco Fattucci wrote from Rome to Michelangelo in behalf of Cardinal Santiquattro (the Florentine, Lorenzo Pucci), who requested "un poco di disegnio" for a palace façade, with a rusticated ground floor and a central portal flanked by two windows with grilles (*Briefe*, pp. 245 ff.) On 4 February Michelangelo received a letter (Arch. Buon., discovered by Tolnay 1947, p. 255) from his friend Pietro Roselli, a foreman at St Peter's, reporting that Giuliano Leno, chief foreman there, had shown to the Cardinal a drawing for a façade (presumably of the proposed palace) in the style of Bramante's Raphael house, which he had made and which he claimed to be by Michelangelo. Roselli, because he was familiar with Michelangelo's hand, offered to expertise the drawing, but was refused. Nothing more was heard of the commission. Thode (II, pp. 203, 205; III, No. 273) proposed that an unpublished façade drawing in the Musée des Beaux-Arts, Lille (No. 90; D.540) might be a sketch for the palace; there are no grounds for the suggestion, and the drawing, of doubtful authenticity, is rejected by Dussler.

Venice, Bridge of the Rialto, 1529?

Condivi (Ch. XLVII) reports a design for "un ponte, che andavo sopra del Canal grande di Vinegia, di forma e maniera non più vista". In Vasari's version (VII, p. 199), the bridge, identified as that of the Rialto, was drawn for Doge Gritti during the period of Michelangelo's flight to Venice in 1529. Thode (1908, II, pp. 149 f.) pointed out that Andrea Gritti died in 1528, and that Vasari probably combined Condivi's report with Varchi's statement that Gritti was a friend of Michelangelo.

Florence, House of Baccio Valori, 1532?

In a letter dated 1532 by Frey (*Briefe*, pp. 323 f.; Thode 1908, II, pp. 141 f.), Baccio Valori, the first governor of Florence after the siege, requests certain changes in the plan of a house designed for him by Michelangelo, and offers any assistance the architect may require to speed construction. It is not known if or when the house was built.

Rome, Ponte Sta Maria, 1548–1551

Michelangelo was commissioned by Paul III to strengthen the Ponte Sta Maria, the stability of which was menaced by the current of the Tiber; after he had constructed caissons and started buttressing the piers, he was dismissed by the administrators of Julius III (1550–1555) in favour of Nanni di Baccio Bigio, who promised to complete the work at less expense. This summary of Vasari's account (VII, pp. 234 f.) is confirmed by documents (published by Podestà 1875, pp. 130 ff. and Lanciani 1902, II, p. 22) starting in October 1548. Michelangelo's name appears on payments up to January 1549, the year of Paul III's death. In July 1551 Nanni was commissioned to refound a "pontoon" attached to one of the piers which had been repaired insufficiently the year before. By September this work was completed (*ibid.*, p. 135; cf. Nanni's account in Thode 1908, II, p. 213). Vasari tells of crossing the bridge later with Michelangelo, who claimed that it trembled and cautioned him to walk carefully, lest it collapse while they were on it. This proved to be a prediction, not a joke. In the flood of September 1557 the bridge collapsed; after its restoration in 1574–1575 it fell a second time in 1598 (Fulvio-Ferrucci 1588, fol. 74; Bonanni 1699, I, pp. 344 ff.) and has since been called the Ponte Rotto. The original failure was attributed to Nanni and was a factor in his dismissal from the *Fabbrica* of St Peter's in 1563 (Vasari, VII, p. 266).

The bridge is illustrated before and after its destruction in two sketches by Dosio (Uffizi, *Arch.* 2582; Bartoli, *I Monumenti Antichi* ... Rome, 1914–1922, p. 135, Fig. 788). The earlier, inscribed "Ponte S. Maria con la parte restaurata" shows a large reinforced pontoon on one of the piers. Its rather ponderous design suggests Nanni's authorship, but it may have been initiated by Michelangelo.

Rome, Villa Giulia, 1550

Although actual designs for the Villa Giulia were made by Vignola, Ammanati, and Vasari (E. Vodoz, *Mitt. des Kunsthist. Inst. in Florenz*, VII, 1942, pp. 5 ff.; J. Coolidge, *Art Bulletin*, XXV, 1943, pp. 177 ff.), Michelangelo was active from the start as an adviser. Vasari speaks (VII, p. 228) of the Pope's unwillingness to make decisions concerning the villa without Michelangelo's help, and tells of a visit to the site "where we had many discussions together, which brought that work almost to its present beauty, nor was any aspect of the design made or considered without his opinion and judgment" (*ibid.*, p. 233). In his autobiography, Vasari again refers to Michelangelo's assistance in correcting his work (*ibid.*, p. 694). Since the account comes from this source alone, it must be taken cautiously; Vasari, in seeking to magnify his own contribution to the building, probably found it useful to imply that only he had the benefit of Michelangelo's confidence.

Rome, Façade for the Palace of Julius III, 1551

We know from Condivi (Ch. LI) that "Michelangelo made, at His Holiness' request, a drawing of a façade for a palace, which he wanted to build in Rome; and everyone who saw it (held it to be) an extraordinary and new thing, not bound to any style or law whatever, whether ancient or modern". Vasari probably used this passage as the basis for his account (VII, p. 233): "He had him make a model of a façade for a palace, which His Holiness wanted to build alongside San Rocco, intending to use the mausoleum of Augustus for the remainder of the walls. One could not find a façade design more varied, more ornate, or newer in style and order, since, as may be seen in all his work, he never felt bound to ancient or modern law in architectural matters, and is one of those who have had the ingenuity always to find new and varied things, and not in the least less beautiful (than those of the past). This model now belongs to Duke Cosimo de' Medici, to whom Pope Pius IV gave it when he went to Rome, and he regards it as one of his most cherished possessions." Payments for the construction of the "modello che M.ro Michelangelo pittore ha cominciato per fare una facciata di un Palazzo di ordine di S. B.ne" were allotted to Bastiano Malenotti from October 1551 to February 1552 (Podestà 1875, p. 136; Frey 1909, pp. 162 f.)

The project does not appear to have been carried further. Julius III was an unusually fickle patron, and immediately shifted his attention to the construction of the Villa Giulia. None of the modern accounts has mentioned the most peculiar aspect of the project as described by Vasari: the palace itself was to be built in the mausoleum of Augustus, a huge circular structure on the Via Ripetta which connected the Piazza del Popolo to the principal boat landing on the Tiber. The scheme was proven to be practical in the nineteenth century, when the tomb was remodelled into a concert hall. This explains why Michelangelo was called upon to design only a façade.

A painting by Fabrizio Boschi (1570–1642) in the Casa Buonarroti (Pl. 65b) shows a façade model – of which we see only one bay at the side – being presented to the Pope. Although done about half a century later, the painting may represent the original model, which presumably stayed in the Medici collection. But it poses a difficult problem, because what can be seen of the model never would have inspired Condivi and Vasari to describe it as revolutionary. It is a pedestrian three-story elevation with quoins at the corner and a heavy cornice, which varies the design of the Farnese palace chiefly in the window pediments and in the oval oculi inserted in the frieze. The only original features are the recessed window bays and the uncommonly high proportions of the lower story. If Boschi accurately reproduced the side of Michelangelo's model, there must have been some features of the invisible front façade that more adventurously departed from tradition. The painting is inscribed "Romanae Curiae formam Julio III ostendit . . .", which may be explained in two ways: either the model is Michelangelo's and the inscription is incorrect; or the inscription is accurate, and the model is another architect's project for a palace of the Curia which had come to be ascribed to Michelangelo. The former alternative is more likely, though the latter would explain the conventional design.

Rome, Il Gesù, 1554

In June 1554 Michelangelo agreed to produce drawings and a model for the mother church of the new Jesuit Order. The agreement was referred to in three letters written by P. Polanco, *procuratore* of the Order, on 10, 14, and 21 June and a fourth by St Ignatius of 21 July, all referring to Michelangelo as the most celebrated artist of the time (reproduced by Pirri 1941, p. 201; first cited by P. Tacchi-Venturi, *Studi e documenti di storia e di diritto*, XX, 1899, pp. 326 f.; these extensive studies of the prehistory of the church are best summarized by Tacchi-Venturi, *Storia della Compagnia di Gesu in Italia*, 2nd ed., Rome, II, 1951, pp. 545 ff.)

At this time the planning of the church already had been in progress for four years; St Francesco Borgia assumed the initiative for its construction in 1550, and gained permission to use the present site. Nanni di Baccio Bigio was chosen as chief architect, and Vignola, who began the existing building in 1568, served as adviser. Nanni's preliminary site plan, preserved in the Bibliothèque Nationale in Paris (Pirri 1941, pp. 177 ff., Fig. on p. 179), shows the existing buildings on the site and a proposal for the church and cloister. The church plan has superficial similarities to Vignola's (large semi-circular apse, broad nave, dwarf transepts) but it is awkwardly disposed, and would have to have been covered in wood; its façade has corner towers (later considered by Vignola, cf. Lotz, *Römische Jahrbuch* VII, 1955, Fig. 26) and a single central portal. It was probably on the basis of this design that the first cornerstone was laid in December 1550 (Pirri, 1941, p. 181). Shortly problems arose over the acquisition of private property in the area, chiefly from the Altieri and Muti families, which were responsible for delaying construction for eighteen months. In May 1553 an attempt made by the city planners to evade the difficulties by bending the axis of the church was rejected by members of the Order, who responded, probably early in 1554, with an alternative plan presumably by Nanni in which the axis could be retained by drawing the façade back several meters (Pirri, p. 200).

At this point the direction and financing of the project was assumed by Cardinal de la Cueva, who called Michelangelo to make a plan on the basis of a counter-proposal by the city officials. On 6 October 1554 the Cardinal and St Ignatius laid a second cornerstone, and "the architect descended into the foundations to lay the stone" (Pirri, p. 202). The unnamed architect was probably Nanni; Michelangelo's name does not appear in the documents of this time or later, nor in the account of the ceremony, and the laying of masonry was an activity no more congenial to his convictions than to his advanced age. The ceremony was followed by a renewed attack from the neighbours, both in the courts and in the streets, and no further progress was made until 1568.

The only concrete evidence of Michelangelo's intervention in the design of the Gesù appears in the form of some corrections lightly sketched in chalk on to a presentation plan in pen and wash published by Popp (1927, pp. 413 ff., Fig. 18; Uffizi, *Arch.* 1819; D.518; it is inscribed in an eighteenth-century [?] hand "Il Jesu Alli Altieri"). Popp identified the drawing as Michelangelo's plan of 1550 for San Giovanni de' Fiorentini (see page 118) which she claimed was offered subsequently by him to the Jesuits; she took the traditional ascription of the drawing to Bartolommeo de' Rocchi as evidence that that architect was employed by Michelangelo as a draughtsman. Except for the discovery of Michelangelo's jottings the whole argument is pure fantasy. The plan is a variant of Nanni's design of 1550; the chapels are reduced in number, the towers suppressed, and the transepts widened; it is still incapable of being vaulted or domed. The probability of Nanni's authorship is strengthened by the similarity in detailing to the work of his master, Antonio da Sangallo the Younger.

Apparently Michelangelo's first action on receiving the commission was to explain with a few rapid strokes the deficiencies of his predecessor's plan. He reduced the length of the transept and the width of the apse, but as he did not carry his suggestions into the corresponding portions of the nave, his intentions cannot be ascertained. Perhaps this was the full extent of his contribution to the design of the Gesù.

Rome, Systematization of Trajan's Column, 1558

The base of the Column of Trajan was excavated under Paul III, who left an unsightly ditch around it. Michelangelo, whose house on the Macello de' Corvi was alongside Trajan's forum, produced on his own initiative a plan for the systematization of the area which was accepted in a meeting of the Communal Council on 27 August 1558 but was not put into effect (Gnoli, *Nuova Antologia*, XC, 1886, pp. 542 ff.; Lanciani 1902, II, p. 125).

Rome, Triple Stairway from the Piazza Venezia to the Quirinal, 1558

On 28 September 1558, the Florentine Ambassador Gianfigliazzi wrote from Rome: "[Francesco] Bandini came to see me Sunday evening and told me that he had been in the Minerva that morning with Michelangelo Bonarotti who told him how His Holiness [Paul IV] wanted him to be there [at the Vatican] every day and how he conversed at length with the Pope, but most of the time merely listened and protested that now he was old, and that His Holiness had around him able architects who knew more than he and that he could get a design from them. And he said that His Holiness put before him so much material that he was amazed and did not believe that his life could possibly continue long enough even to begin, much less to carry out such projects. And when asked what these projects might be, Michelangelo replied – 'it is enough to say that they are great, extremely great' – and, pressed to say something more, he replied 'matters of . . .' and stopped, saying 'it is not proper that I should speak of a Pope'. And then, though he [Bandini] was curious and though they spoke in privacy, he got no more out of him, except that he said 'His Holiness has the extraordinary idea that, beginning at San Silvestro [al Quirinale] three stairways should be built, one behind the other, and that the first and last should be covered and the middle one open, and that then one of them should actually extend as far as San Marco, and designs of this sort that tickle the . . .' and from here he would go no farther" (R. Ancel, "Le Vatican sous Paul IV", *Rev. Bénédictine*, XXV, 1908, p. 70n).

The triple stairway project was quite as grandiose as Michelangelo claimed; it would have joined the plateau at the summit of the Quirinal hill (Pl. 76a) to the Piazza Venezia, a distance of several hundred yards over an extremely steep and irregular slope that was far less congenial to architectural treatment than the access to the Campidoglio.

Two years later a similar project was considered by Paul's successor, Pius IV, who began to cut a street, rather than steps, up the slopes of the Quirinal, with the intention of extending the new Via Pia from the city walls right to the entrance portal of the Palazzo Venezia. We know from Ferrucci (see Vol. I, p. 114) that the construction proved to be so difficult that it was decided to start the Via Pia at the summit rather than at the base of the Quirinal; even today the approach to the hill is by a winding street that follows its natural contours.

Perhaps Michelangelo's project for the Via and Porta Pia represents a flowering of the seed planted by Paul IV during the discussions of the summer of 1558.

Florence, Ponte Santa Trinita (1560?), 1567–1572

The Ponte Santa Trinita, begun in 1567, was nearly completed in 1569, though construction continued slowly for another three years. Contemporary sources confirm the tradition that Bartolomeo Ammanati was the architect (Kriegbaum 1941, pp. 136 ff.) In September 1557 the medieval bridges on the site collapsed in a flood of the Arno river (*Nachlass*, I, pp. 487 ff., 543), and in March of 1560, Giorgio Vasari was commissioned by Cosimo I Medici to consult Michelangelo in Rome; "d'alcune cose attenenti al nostro servizio" (Gaye, III, p. 29; *Nachlass*, I, p. 549) – the most urgent of them being the construction of San Giovanni dei Fiorentini. On 8 April 1560 Vasari wrote to the Duke (Gaye, *loc. cit.*; *Nachlass*, I, p. 559) that on one of his visits to Michelangelo "Aviano atteso a i disegni del ponte Sta Trinita, che ci a rasgionato su assai, che ne porterò memoria di scritti et disegni secondo l'animo suo, con le misure ch gli ò portate secondo il sito . . ." The notes and drawings, which probably would have been in Vasari's hand, have not survived; conceivably they established a rough scheme for the bridge upon which Ammanati based his design (Kriegbaum 1941, pp. 143 ff.) Ammanati's bridge, destroyed by the German army in 1945, was both more distinguished and less mannered than his other buildings. Its beautiful elliptical arches appear previously only in Michelangelo's galleries of the Farnese palace. Ammanati, who had just executed for Michelangelo the steps of the Laurentian library, would have accepted willingly prompting from the old master; but we do not know how specific the prompting was, or even whether it reached Ammanati.

Rejected Attributions

Rome, Sapienza, 1514–1520

According to an old tradition, Michelangelo made for Leo X a design for the University of Rome, but construction was halted at the Pope's death (Callari, *Le Ville di Roma*, Rome, 1943, p. 244). Leo X is known to have built a chapel at the Sapienza and to have planned to complete the university building begun under Alexander VI (Thode 1908, II, pp. 204 f.), but no record remains of Michelangelo's participation. In April 1562 a competition for the design of the "Studio" was announced by the *Conservatori* of Rome; the participating architects were Vignola, Nanni di Baccio Bigio, and Guidetto Guidetti (see p. 53). Nothing further was heard of this project, and no drawings have been identified with it. The present building was not begun until *ca.* 1575 by Giacomo della Porta in his capacity of *Architetto del popolo romano* (W. Arslan, *Boll. d'Arte*, VI, 1927, p. 508).

Marmirolo, Gonzaga Villa, 1523

Felice di Sora, in a letter from Mantua of 16 June 1523 to Duke Francesco Maria of Urbino says: "M. Baldasarre da Castiglione has brought from Rome a model of a garden with a habitation in it, designed by Michelangelo. And those who saw it when it was shown to her Ladyship told me it was a most beautiful thing and a building of the greatest ingenuity and most delightful. The Marchese says he wants to build it at Marmirolo [a place] not generally praised, where he wants to have a beautiful *Theatro da representare* costing about 20,000 ducats, for which reason it is believed that it will have to be thought about for some time" (Gaye 1840, II, p. 154). The only major error in the report is the attribution; the model was by Giulio Romano, who was paid for it on 20 March 1523 and who followed it to Mantua in 1524. In May 1525 the construction was nearing completion under his supervision (F. Hartt, *Giulio Romano*, New Haven, 1958, pp. 67, 73, 259 ff.)

Civitavecchia, Upper Portion of the Fortress Keep, 1535

The central keep of the fortress of Civitavecchia was left incomplete by Bramante in 1508; according to the inscription of Paul III, it was finished in 1535 with the addition of a second story of the same octagonal shape. Guglielmotti's attribution of the upper portion to Michelangelo (V, 1887, pp. 218 ff.), based only on a local tradition, has been repeated by later writers (Rocchi 1908, p. 147; Schiavo 1953, p. 253), but it is difficult to believe that any architect was needed to design the simple walls and rather medieval cornice.

Florence, St Apollonia, Portal

The portal of St Apollonia (Tolnay 1951, Pl. 208) was believed to be by Michelangelo in the early seventeenth century when a French architect made a sketch from it ("Destailleur", codex in the Staatliche Kunstbibliothek, Berlin-Charlottenburg, reported by Geymüller 1904, p. 34n), and the old guides of Florence repeat the attribution, which may be based on the fact that Michelangelo donated sketches for the lost altar of the church (Vasari, V, p. 344; Thode 1908, II, p. 137). Wachler (1940, pp. 183 f.) discovered drawings (Uffizi, *Arch.* 3018, 3019; *ibid.*, Fig. 118) that prove Giovannantonio Dosio to have been the designer, a conclusion reached independently by Paatz (1952, pp. 211, 219) on stylistic grounds.

Rome, Porta del Popolo, 1561–1564. Porta San Giovanni, *ca.* 1580

The new Porta del Popolo was built at the same time as the Porta Pia. Begun in the autumn of 1561, the construction continued for three years; the architect, Nanni di Baccio Bigio, appears in the documents of the Maestri di Strada (Bertolotti, *Bartolomeo Baronino*, Casale, 1876, p. 82; Lanciani 1902, III, p. 234; Pastor, *Geschichte*, VII, pp. 601 f., 646). The misattribution to Michelangelo is based on Vasari's postscript to the description of the Porta Pia (VII, p. 260), "since it was the Pope's whim that he (Michelangelo) should restore the other gates of Rome, he made many other drawings for him". The Sangallesque style of the Porta del Popolo excludes the possibility that Nanni could have been the executor of a design by Michelangelo.

The Porta San Giovanni was executed for Gregory XIII by Giacomo del Duca (E. Lavagnino, *Capitolium*, 1931, p. 207). Venturi (*Storia*, XI, 2, pp. 154–162) suggested that it probably was based on designs by Michelangelo. No doubt del Duca learned from sketches made by Michelangelo when both were working on the Porta Pia, but his solution appears to be independent.

Fortress of San Michele at the Tiber Mouth, 1560–1570

The compact octagonal fortress of San Michele at the mouth of the Tiber was planned by Pius IV in 1560 and built under Pius V in 1567–1570 by Nanni di Baccio Bigio (Guglielmotti 1887, V, pp. 387–420; Rocchi 1908, pp. 294 f.; Schiavo 1953, pp. 257 ff.) Its bold and handsome design (see Schiavo, Figs. 57–62), and the imaginative innovation of a cylindrical interior well for lighting and ventilation suggest a more inspired designer than Nanni. Guglielmotti found confirmation of the traditional attribution to Michelangelo in a drawing of a closely related plan (in the Uffizi? Facsimile in Guglielmotti, X, Pl. LXXIX; Rocchi, Fig. on p. 296; Schiavo 1948, Fig. 162; the original has not been rediscovered since Guglielmotti's time). But the authenticity of the drawing is uncertain; though Michelangelesque in style, the draughtsmanship is not that of his late years. Lacking other documentation, we are justified only in assuming that the building was designed by an able follower, possibly under the Master's direction.

Rome, Sant' Andrea della Valle, Strozzi Chapel, before 1616

This chapel – the second from the entrance on the right side of the nave – is ascribed to Michelangelo in Baroque topographical literature (notably G. G. de' Rossi, *Disegni di vari altari e cappelle* . . ., Rome [1713?], Pls. 6, 7). However, the church itself was not started until 1591, and statues for the chapel – copies of Michelangelo's early *Pietà* and the *Rachel* and *Lea* – were not cast until 1616 (S. Ortolani, *S. Andrea della Valle*, Rome [*ca.* 1924], p. 5, Figs. 20, 21). The architecture, like the sculpture, is an academic imitation of Michelangelo, adapted to Late Renaissance taste by veneers of highly coloured marble. A full documentation of the history of the church is being published by Prof. Howard Hibbard.

Obsolete Attributions

The following attributions from Baroque guidebooks and collections of engravings have disappeared justifiably from the modern literature on Michelangelo. Sources for them are cited in the indices of Steinmann-Wittkower 1927 and Steinmann 1932.

FLORENCE:
Il Gesù Pellegrino, side portal
Palazzo Uguccioni
San Giuseppe
Santa Maria della Neve
(environs) Villas Alvisi, dei Collazzi, Mazzei, Liccioli

ROME:
Palatine Hill, Farnese Gardens
Sant' Anna dei Palafrenieri
SS. Faustino e Giovita
San Giovanni in Laterano, nave ceiling
Santa Maria della Pace, Cesi Chapel
Santa Maria dell' Orto
San Pietro in Vincoli, cloister well
Santa Susanna, well

OTHER CITIES:
Capranica, parish church
Genoa, Palazzo Giustiniani

INDEX

Authorities are cited when they appear in the text but not in the parenthetical notes. The museum-catalogue numbers of drawings are cited in *italics* to distinguish them from page numbers.